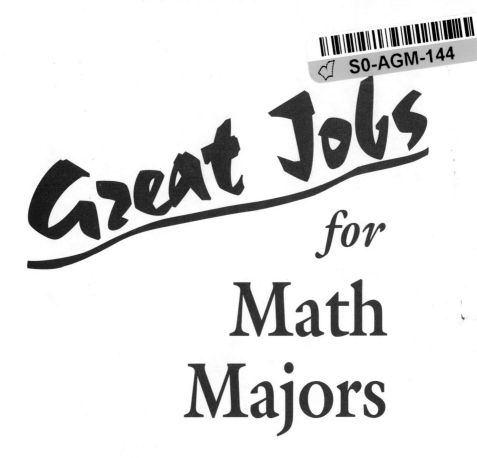

Great Jobs *for* Math Majors

Stephen E. Lambert
Ruth J. DeCotis

SERIES DEVELOPERS AND CONTRIBUTING AUTHORS
Stephen E. Lambert
Julie Ann DeGalan

VGM Career Horizons
NTC/Contemporary Publishing Group

Library of Congress Cataloging-in-Publication Data

Lambert, Stephen E.
     Great jobs for math majors / Stephen E. Lambert, Ruth J.
DeCotis.
          p.   cm.
     Includes bibliographical references (p. –) and index.
     ISBN 0-8442-6422-9 (Great Jobs for . . .)
     1. Mathematics—Vocational guidance.   I. DeCotis,
Ruth J.   II. Title.
QA10.5.L36   1998
510′.23—dc21   98-7868
                                                   CIP

Published by VGM Career Horizons
A division of NTC/Contemporary Publishing Group, Inc.
4255 West Touhy Avenue, Lincolnwood (Chicago), Illinois 60646-1975 U.S.A.
Printed in the United States of America
International Standard Book Number: 0-8442-6422-9
          01   02   03   LB   6   5   4   3   2

This book is dedicated with great affection to my CAGS colleagues: Jack Barry, Gail Carr, Alan Davis, Maria Dreyer, Daniel Ferrera, Kathleen Norris, and Marianne True. During the writing of this book, I was uplifted and supported by their humor and intelligence and by their remarkable individual gifts. I cannot believe my good fortune in knowing each of you.

—Stephen E. Lambert

This book is joyously dedicated to my husband, Terry, for loving me through thick and thin, no matter what I was trying to balance in my life. To my wonderful children, Greg, Curtis, and Erin, and their families; to my father, David, and my mother, Olive; to my seven sisters; to my friends Lee and Nancy. All of them were with me in spirit, listening to my joys and concerns. All of you supported me as I balanced my commitments on an overbooked calendar of my life's events, which included taking time out to coauthor my first book with Stephen.

—Ruth J. DeCotis

CONTENTS

Acknowledgments

The authors want to acknowledge the superb contributions of Ms. Kendra Cantin, our Undergraduate Fellow in Career Services for 1996–98. Her research efforts, telephone skills, and computer facility added immeasurably to *Great Jobs for Math Majors*. Beyond those stellar efforts, she has been a wonderful colleague, and we will miss her tremendously. Thank you, Kendra, from both of us.

INTRODUCTION

MATHEMATICS: THE PERFECT FORMULA FOR A CAREER

athematics is like the Roman god Janus, it has two faces. One face is the abstract world of numbers and the intellectual challenges that hold mathematicians spellbound. Separated from human values and mundane concerns, abstract mathematical reasoning can lead mathematicians to deep and powerful conclusions that ultimately influence other branches of thinking. A good example of this trickle-down effect is the current fascination with a new school of management theory based on a rejection of Newtonian physics and embracing a quantum perspective on how organizations shape and reshape themselves.

One of the most profound questions philosophy asks us is "What is truth and how can we know it?" Though we are still wrestling with this question, the science of mathematics has been one of the primary sources of what truths man *has* discovered. Certainly math has its place in history as the most challenging example of the powers of the human mind. It is not too difficult for even the average educated person among us to truly appreciate the work of the chemist dealing with molecules, the biologist with DNA, or the physicist with the black holes of space. But to approach some of the arcane heights of mathematics, not even analogies or metaphors can help us to appreciate, much less understand, the world of abstract mathematics.

In art, too, math has its place and not just in architecture or music but in the search for beauty itself. The study of fractals, for example, has given us some insight into why we are attracted to and utilize certain motifs over and over again in art—the scroll, for example. Designs such as this and others have pronounced similarities to some fractal patterns.

This book, however, deals with the practical face of mathematics. Though most of us are not familiar with abstract math, practical mathematics are seldom called into question by anyone, including those with no mathematical ability. Most of us know the value of math skills in everyday life and often wish we had better skills in math than we do. In spite of the general math envy of the public, however, math majors are seldom aware of the value of their own degree—and this becomes very pronounced as they approach college graduation. We hope, as you read this book, you'll be surprised at how valuable your education has been and, most importantly, how you can combine who you are and what you want with your education to find a spot in the employment market that's just right for you!

As career counselors, it's no surprise to us that graduating math majors may be unaware of the wonderful possibilities for employment with their degree. After all, you've been involved in a very demanding curriculum. There is seldom time in any advanced math course to cover all the material *and* look at real-world applications for career potential as well. The demands of delivering the content of the courses are not the only reasons why careers are not a big topic of discussion in math classes. Another reason is that many math faculty have had a fairly direct, linear progression through college and graduate work to their current positions. Though they may have had some employment using their math skills and many are involved in research on math topics, their knowledge of the breadth and depth of career possibilities may be quite limited. Still, mathematics is not an isolated body of knowledge and to be most useful, it really ought to be taught in contexts that are meaningful and relevant to learners. If, after taking a math course, you couldn't answer the question, "Now, what am I going to do with this?", your course was lacking in making those "connections" to real life.

It's pretty depressing to be about to graduate from college, no matter what your major, and find a big gap between what you know and the plans you've made and the reality of an actual job search. Add to that the fact that most people know only a few of the employment possibilities that exist for their educational preparation. The advice you've had from your parents, your friends, or college teachers is helpful, but it will never take the place of your own personally designed, structured exploration of the various career pathways available to you with your degree. That's what we hope to do in this book.

Here's a familiar scene. Mention you are a math major to most people and they respond by saying, "Oh, I'm terrible at math," or "I wish I was smart enough to be able to do math." Many people are very insecure about their math skills. You know this to be true because you've had these conversations and experienced these reactions. It is a frequent disappointment and a continual puzzle to math graduates like yourself that so many people are put off by a subject because of a bad experience in school or by the scary look of written math. But now, as you approach the job search, you may find you're suddenly grateful for the public's admiration of people who can "do" math. It may help you get a job!

A math major is a wonderful degree to bring away from college because there are so many opportunities—almost unlimited opportunities—for graduates who have superior math skills and some openness and curiosity about a variety of possible occupational settings. And, as Chapter 10 of this book makes clear, women and minorities are currently not well represented in math careers, so employers are making a special effort to encourage those groups to apply and be considered. Jobs requiring significant educational preparation in mathematics are always among the top fifty jobs listed in the *Jobs Rated Almanac* published each year.

So, public esteem is high for your degree and there is sufficient demand for employment of math majors. This is good news. To have the most flexibility in your job search, your academic record in your major should be superior. Not just your academic record as a paper document, but your acquisition of the skills, reasoning ability, and problem-solving techniques those high grades should accurately represent.

Now, in addition to this positive information, you'll notice right away in this book that the authors put a lot of emphasis on your communication skills as well. The reason we do this is because the ability of the math major to communicate effectively is a unifying element for all the jobs we discuss. In job after job, you're called upon to work on teams, in groups, to explain and teach, to clarify and to listen. The application of mathematical models, the use of math techniques to analyze and solve problems comes only *after* problems have been discussed and understood. All of this interaction and interpersonal work demands excellent, if not superior, oral and written communication skills.

You know that mathematics is, at its heart, a linguistic activity whose ultimate aim is a precise communication of meaning. This is the great difference between the science of mathematics and the natural and biological sciences. In the natural sciences, things are considered proven to be true until we have information to the contrary. We can never be quite sure. In math, we have the certainty of the proof. When Pythagorus discovered the

Pythagorean theorem, he knew with certainty that this proof would be true forever. Mathematics communicates precisely and absolutely.

The clarity of communication afforded by mathematics is made dramatically clear in a number of movies about outer space. In *Close Encounters of the Third Kind*, and a more recent movie, *Contact*, math is the language of choice between us and our visitors! In *Contact*, Jodie Foster, the American actress, plays an astronomer who is searching the heavens for extraterrestrial life signs. When contact is made, it is made through a pattern of binary numbers. The language of numbers is certainly a brilliant conception of man and, as this fictional movie demonstrates, math holds the possibility of being a more effective bridge of meaning than vernacular language. What a great cultural lineage you help to perpetuate when you bring your math skills into the workplace.

Of course, we know that math is more than a skill. Math is an entire world of ideas, and its history reflects some of the most brilliant minds ever encountered including Pythagoras, Euclid, Descartes, and Srinivasa Ramanujan, the genius Indian mathematician who came to Cambridge University in England from a very humble village in India. In Chapter 11, we talk a bit about the current interest in Pierre de Fermat and Andrew Wiles, the Princeton mathematician who solved Fermat's theorem.

But this book is not a history of math, it is a guide for college math graduates who want an answer to the question "How can I use my math degree to forge a productive and happy life for myself?" To answer that question, we have written a self-contained guide that will not only prepare you for the job search in general, but will direct your thinking about mathematics into a number of possible pathways. This is not generalized "how-to" advice, but very specific, concrete information on different industries and job fields within those industries. For each functional area we discuss, we look at duties, career advancement, training and qualifications, related job skills, and how to locate these jobs. Let's take a quick look at each of the chapters that follow and what you'll find there.

JOB SEARCH PREPARATION

In Chapter 1, "The Self-Assessment," perhaps the most important aspect of the job search is addressed. We ask you to take an inventory of who you are, how you like to work, and how you want to be in the workplace. Reflecting on your personality, your work experience, and your educational background will prepare you to both write and talk about your plans to others.

If you want to act on the suggestions put forth in this book, you need both a resume and the ability to write a good cover letter. You're not really ready to job hunt until you have both these documents ready to go. Chapter 2, "The Resume and Cover Letter," teaches you what you need and provides some examples particularly designed for math majors.

No matter what direction your job search is headed in, there's good advice in Chapter 3, "Researching Careers," about where to learn more about the career you've chosen. We discuss the value of researching the job setting, the best job directories, and various sources of job information. When you add the information in this chapter to the specific professional associations and websites listed at the close of each of the career path chapters, you'll have your own personal job search library.

Every successful job seeker knows that you shouldn't keep your job search a secret! Tell your friends, your teachers, your past employers and have your parents tell their friends. The more people you talk to, the greater the possibility you'll connect with someone who may have some interesting information or a contact who may prove helpful. Chapter 4, "Networking," gives you solid techniques for networking successfully.

The best resume, the sharpest cover letter, and all the networking in the world won't overcome a bad interview. The reason interviews sometimes don't work is because we don't understand the concept behind them and what our role is. Chapter 5, "Interviewing," gives you a good understanding of what the employer hopes to accomplish during an interview and how you can make the interview work for you. It's an important chapter.

Chapter 6, "Networking or Interviewing Follow-Up," is a brief chapter that addresses some details job seekers often forget. We teach you how to leave the network you've established once you've been hired, in case you ever need to "reactivate" it at some point in the future. We also discuss what job search activities take place *after* the interview and how your post-interview behavior can enhance or detract from your chances for success.

You've been offered a job! Congratulations! Before you sign on the dotted line, we ask you to consider a few points in Chapter 7, "Job Offer Considerations." We also give you some tips on negotiation strategies and how to compare offers.

For some math graduates, the post-college decision is not a job, but additional education through a graduate program. Chapter 8, "The Graduate School Choice," offers some of the important pointers that we suggest in working with our clients who are contemplating a master's degree or doctoral program.

THE CAREER PATHS

Before you read Chapters 10 through 13, in Chapter 9, "Introduction to the Mathematics Career Paths," we give you a broad overview of each of the career path chapters and some advice on how to approach comparing and contrasting the various jobs.

Teaching any subject is an art, and Chapter 10, "The Math Job You Know Best: Teaching," attempts to convey some of the special demands of the teaching profession. Whether it's elementary school or college-level work, teaching at any level will draw on far more than your mastery of mathematics. We give you a very realistic overview of the profession at every grade level.

The "classic" math graduate jobs are discussed in Chapter 11, "Math as a Primary Skill," but with a twist. Actuarial, mathematician, statistician, and operations research analyst positions are discussed with special attention paid to those job factors (training, salary, and career outlook) that will be important in your decision making.

Chapter 12, "Working Toward an Advanced Degree," looks at market and financial analyst, and research analyst and associate positions that are available to both math and other quantitatively skilled graduates. This chapter addresses these jobs both as destination career positions or as possible shorter-stay jobs if you are contemplating a return to graduate school.

Chapter 13, "Math in the Marketplace: Buyer, Sales Representative, and Purchasing Agent," focuses on jobs where your math skill is an invaluable aptitude: buyers and merchandisers, sales service representatives, and purchasing agent positions. Each of these career paths welcomes a variety of majors, but especially values the math major. Since math is not a primary skill for these positions, we address the other important qualifications to help you see if your career may be a job buying and/or selling in the workplace.

The career paths are all different, but there are some unifying themes. Applications, problem solving, and reasoning are some of the elements that bind most math jobs. All the jobs in this book share a connection with these three skills. Of course, problem solving and reasoning have been the mainstays of mathematics instruction since the beginning of teaching, and applications have recently been through a major revival of interest. Data analysis projects or opportunities for modeling occur in settings as diverse as the popular music industry, fashion design houses, major medical facilities, and the automobile industry. There's simply no reason why you can't take your interests and apply math methodologies and concepts in the job setting of your choice.

I hope you sense, as you read these chapters, not only our emphasis on communication, but our general strong feeling that one of your principal roles in the workplace will be to communicate the duality of mathematics—its usefulness and its beauty. Computers, in many ways, have, with their software applications and speed of performance, unfortunately only served to further distance some people from approaching and understanding mathematics. You can help in this by utilizing all the skills in your repertoire, including models, pictures, diagrams, and graphs to suggest the possibilities of math in business situations. This will help those you work with who are math phobic to deal with abstract ideas by having a visual realization of them. Of course, none of your tools needs to be static, because you can use the same technology that has alienated some people to bring others closer to math. These tools don't have to create distance, because when used by the skilled mathematician, they become powerful tools for communication. Mathematics is changing, and your role is changing as a mathematician.

For example, we have now recognized the disservice visited on young women during their preadolescent and adolescent years in school when interest and achievement in math accelerates in young men but not in women. That's now being addressed across the country and the growth we'll see of women in math professions will be remarkable and far-reaching. Hopefully, regardless of your own gender, in your math career you will provide encouragement and positive role modeling for all young people.

The four career paths we outline display the virtuosity of math and the fact that math is present and has penetrated every aspect of business and industry. Math takes on issues and problems of quantity, space, pattern, arrangement, structure, and logic that help us define, understand, and build our world. The career paths we outline each contain suggestions for countless other possibilities where your math degree will add an essential ingredient to the success of an organization.

Another exciting aspect about the variety of jobs available to the math major will be of personal importance to you. The fact that math majors can be employed in a variety of settings increases your chances of finding a job that satisfies both your educational preparation and your own personal demands. Do you want the fast-paced life of a major city or would you prefer to work in a rural environment? With many analyst jobs and consulting positions, the city will be your home. However, as a math teacher, you could settle almost anywhere. Do you prefer a highly socially interactive workplace, or do you like to work uninterrupted for long stretches of time? You can work in international banking or in the machine tool industry. You could travel year-round or have a desk job. There are jobs that pay very well for math majors and the opportunity to earn very high incomes. You'll find we address these issues in the career paths that follow. This should give you another reason to turn to Chapter 1 and make a list of work values—those things you consider important or essential in a job. It may be a combination of financial reward, stability or risk, potential for growth or a chance to learn new skills, or any combination of these. Whatever your list, our feeling is there is a job that uses your math background that can satisfy most of your demands.

USE AN INTERNSHIP TO TEST THE WATERS

If you're feeling unsure about the kind of job that might be best for you and your degree, by all means, consider an internship. Now, there's no question that an internship is easier said than done. Most are unpaid, and that presents real challenges with the high cost of college today. Many students simply feel they cannot afford to not work during the summer or other breaks from school. But think about this. Giving up some income now can pay real dividends at graduation time. Many, many internships turn into real jobs for graduates. For others, the internship gives them deeper, more concrete insights into their own skills and an appreciation of the roles they can play in an organization. It will accomplish your basic need to learn more about the workplace and where you might fit. But other great things take place, too. You'll find it easier to "connect" to people when you're interviewing, you'll have more to say, and, as a result, of your internship, more to offer. You'll get hired!

Internships often require relocation. If you live or go to college in a non-metropolitan area, nearby internships will be scarce. The greatest concentration of internships tend to be in and around metropolitan areas where there are more organizations that can afford to train temporary, nonpaid additions to their staff and provide meaningful work for them. You may have to seek the hospitality of a relative or one of your parent's friends or even seek inexpensive temporary housing in order to put yourself where the internships are located. The payoff still applies.

Finding and applying for internships is a monumental task, though not as difficult as finding your first job. In fact, every activity you'll do in searching for and obtaining your internship is identical to your actual career job search. Just as with full-time jobs, not all good internships are published in directories. Information on some arrives in your math department or career office on flyers or in brochures. Check directories and bulletin boards in both places as well as at your college library. In our career services office, we use the Internet for up-to-date internship listings. Some good starting points are Rising Star Internships at *http://www.rsinternships.com* and Career Mosaic at *http://www.careermosaic.com*. The University of Virginia's career services office also has a page that will lead you to a number of internship search engines. Check them out at *http://www.uva.edu/~career/intern.html*.

Expect to write many, many cover letters. Mail them out with your resume, and be sure to do it early. Many summer internships have January or February application deadlines. Each year in our career office, we assist scores of students with their internship materials. Invariably those students who did their major mailings around Thanksgiving vacation seem to do the best in securing the sites they want.

Expect to receive requests for transcripts (both official and unofficial), essays of intent or goals, or requests to complete formal applications that may include essay writing. All of this correspondence must be perfect, because in most cases, interns are chosen on the basis of the written materials submitted as well as phone interviews. Your written work is your first impression.

The competitiveness of the internships today is good practice and mirrors the competitiveness of the job market in general. Books such as *Internships '99* and *America's Top Internships: 1999* detail the previous year's competition. Some internships receive 500 applicants for three or four available internship spots.

Expect a well-chosen internship experience to stay with you for the rest of your life. That summer or term in a government agency, actuarial office, corporate research and analysis department, or with an employer in industry will become part of your experiential base as long as you are in the workforce. Internships represent a smart move for your future.

You understand the responsibility you have to make the most of the rest of your college years, and you have some specific techniques by which you can do that. You've heard some people say college isn't the real world and you can kind of float along, "treading water." We guarantee if you get out and meet some recent alumni of your school, they will assure you that college has the potential for being as real a world as you want to make it and that it can be an important aspect of your preparation for a career in mathematics.

Perhaps you are reading this as a junior or even a senior approaching graduation. Your most important goal right now is probably determining a strategy for finding that job. How do you go about that, considering all you've learned about the changing climate in the employment market?

REALIZE YOU'LL HAVE MANY CAREERS AND PLAN FOR THAT

You've seen all the warning signs that, regardless of how talented you are, shifts in employers and employee bases do occur and some people must move on. Those that have the least trouble moving do the following:

Watch trends. If you're in a statistician job and you see an increasing use of certain new software programs, it's a clear sign not only that you need to be acquiring those new skills for the future, but that the employer who produces such software may also be a new employment site. Stay abreast of changes in your field by reading professional journals and association newsletters so you have some ready reference points if you do need to jump-start your career at some point. At the end of each career path chapter, we give you names, addresses, electronic mail, and websites for many of the top professional associations in those fields. It's not too early to join, and many have attractive membership prices for students.

Understand your needs. Every time we make a job change, we have to address issues such as geographic location, housing options, pay levels, our consumption patterns, the duties and responsibilities of the new position, our interest and belief in the nature of the work, and a thousand other issues that profoundly impact who we are and how we live and work. Begin to appreciate and understand what you need and what is important to you. That will make job choices and job shifts easier. We pay a lot of attention to these issues in discussing the career paths in this book. Hopefully, our focus on the "fit" between you and your work will influence your thinking.

As college career counselors who see many adult alumni clients, we are too familiar with the economic realities of the job search. The most common laments we hear are "I haven't saved enough money to make a job change," and "I have so much debt I can't afford to take any less salary with a new job, no matter how great that new job is." These are sad comments on a situation that is easily remedied by reducing your consumption and increasing your savings to give you the needed flexibility to change jobs when you want to or have to.

Stay alert to the difference between contextual and portable skills. Contextual skills are those understandings, techniques, vocabularies, relationships, and factors directly related to your business but of little value outside your field of work. For example, if you are working as an operations research analyst in the airline industry, your knowledge of aircraft loading weight will not be very helpful if you find your next job with a child's clothing manufacturer. But in both jobs, your ability to analyze a delivery system and isolate potential problems and correct them does go with you from job to job. The "portable skills" are those talents, knowledge, and techniques that you carry from job to job. You need both contextual and portable skills to succeed in any position, but you want to pay attention to the balance. If your employer offers training and that training is portable, take advantage of it.

All of our suggestions and advice is simply based on the precept that you both enjoy and utilize your college degree to the maximum without sacrificing your own individuality or personal agenda. And it is possible! However, it doesn't just "happen." It takes the kind of planning, researching, and exploration suggested by this book. Most importantly, it begins with you knowing who you are and what you want—at least for the next few years after graduation. Things will change as you gain experience in that first job after college and build a life for yourself. That's as it should be. But take the time right now to explore this guide and begin to make a plan for right now!

PART ONE

THE JOB SEARCH

CHAPTER ONE

THE SELF-ASSESSMENT

Self-assessment is the process by which you begin to acknowledge your own particular blend of education, experiences, values, needs, and goals. It provides the foundation for career planning and the entire job search process. Self-assessment involves looking inward and asking yourself what can sometimes prove to be difficult questions. This self-examination should lead to an intimate understanding of your personal traits, your personal values, your consumption patterns and economic needs, your longer-term goals, your skill base, your preferred skills, and your under-developed skills.

You come to the self-assessment process knowing yourself well in some of these areas, but you may still be uncertain about other aspects. You may be well aware of your consumption patterns, but have you spent much time specifically identifying your longer-term goals, or your personal values as they relate to work? No matter what level of self-assessment you have undertaken to date, it is now time to clarify all of these issues and questions as they relate to the job search.

The knowledge you gain in the self-assessment process will guide the rest of your job search. In this book, you will learn about all of the following tasks:

- Writing resumes
- Exploring possible job titles
- Identifying employment sites
- Networking
- Interviewing
- Following up
- Evaluating job offers

In each of these steps, you will rely on and return often to the understanding gained through your self-assessment. Any individual seeking employment must be able and willing to express to recruiters and interviewers throughout the job search these facets of his or her personality. This communication allows you to show the world who you are so that together with employers you can determine whether there will be a workable match with a given job or career path.

HOW TO CONDUCT A SELF-ASSESSMENT

The self-assessment process goes on naturally all the time. People ask you to clarify what you mean, or you make a purchasing decision, or you begin a new relationship. You react to the world and the world reacts to you. How you understand these interactions and any changes you might make because of them are part of the natural process of self-discovery. There is, however, a more comprehensive and efficient way to approach self-assessment with regard to employment.

Because self-assessment can become a complex exercise, we have distilled it into a seven-step process that provides an effective basis for undertaking a job search. The seven steps include the following:

1. Understanding your personal traits

2. Identifying your personal values

3. Calculating your economic needs

4. Exploring your longer-term goals

5. Enumerating your skill base

6. Recognizing your preferred skills

7. Assessing skills needing further development

As you work through your self-assessment, you might want to create a worksheet similar to the one shown in Exhibit 1.1. Or you might want to keep a journal of the thoughts you have as you undergo this process. There will be many opportunities to revise your self-assessment as you start down the path of seeking a career.

STEP 1 Understanding Your Personal Traits

Each person has a unique personality that he or she brings to the job search process. Gaining a better understanding of your personal traits can help you

Exhibit 1.1

Self-Assessment Worksheet

STEP 1. **Understand Your Personal Traits**
The personal traits that describe me are:
(Include all of the words that describe you.)

The ten personal traits that most accurately describe me are: *(List these ten traits.)*

STEP 2. **Identify Your Personal Values**
Working conditions that are important to me include:
(List working conditions that would have to exist for you to accept a position.)

The values that go along with my working conditions are:
(Write down the values that correspond to each working condition.)

Some additional values I've decided to include are:
(List those values you identify as you conduct this job search.)

STEP 3. **Calculate Your Economic Needs**
My estimated minimum annual salary requirement is:
(Write the salary you have calculated based on your budget.)

Starting salaries for the positions I'm considering are:
(List the name of each job you are considering and the associated starting salary.)

STEP 4. **Explore Your Longer-Term Goals**
My thoughts on longer-term goals right now are:
(Jot down some of your longer-term goals as you know them right now.)

continued

continued

STEP 5. Enumerate Your Skill Base

The general skills I possess are: (List the skills that underlie tasks you are able to complete.)

The specific skills I possess are:
(List more technical or specific skills that you possess and indicate your level of expertise.)

General and specific skills that I want to promote to employers for the jobs I'm considering are:
(List general and specific skills for each type of job you are considering.)

STEP 6. Recognize Your Preferred Skills

Skills that I would like to use on the job include:
(List skills that you hope to use on the job, and indicate how often you'd like to use them.)

STEP 7. Assess Skills Needing Further Development

Some skills that I'll need to acquire for the jobs I'm considering include:
(Write down skills listed in job advertisements or job descriptions that you don't currently possess.)

I believe I can build these skills by:
(Describe how you plan to acquire these skills.)

evaluate job and career choices. Identifying these traits, then finding employment that allows you to draw on at least some of them can create a rewarding and fulfilling work experience. If potential employment doesn't allow you to use these preferred traits, it is important to decide whether you can find other ways to express them or whether you would be better off not considering this type of job. Interests and hobbies pursued outside of work hours can be one way to use personal traits you don't have an opportunity to draw on in your work. For example, if you consider yourself an outgoing person and the kinds of jobs you are examining allow little contact with other people, you may be able to achieve the level of interaction that is comfortable for you outside of your work setting. If such a compromise seems impractical or otherwise unsatisfactory, you probably should explore only jobs that provide the interaction you want and need on the job.

Many young adults who are not very confident about their attractiveness to employers will downplay their need for income. They will say, "Money is not all that important if I love my work." But if you begin to document exactly what you need for housing, transportation, insurance, clothing, food, and utilities, you will begin to understand that some jobs cannot meet your financial needs and it doesn't matter how wonderful the job is. If you have to worry each payday about bills and other financial obligations, you won't be very effective on the job. Begin now to be honest with yourself about your needs.

Inventorying Your Personal Traits. Begin the self-assessment process by creating an inventory of your personal traits. Using the list in Exhibit 1.2, decide which of these personal traits describe you.

Exhibit 1.2

Accurate	Cooperative	Flexible
Active	Courageous	Formal
Adaptable	Critical	Friendly
Adventurous	Curious	Future-oriented
Affectionate	Daring	Generous
Aggressive	Decisive	Gentle
Ambitious	Deliberate	Good-natured
Analytical	Detail-oriented	Helpful
Appreciative	Determined	Honest
Artistic	Discreet	Humorous
Brave	Dominant	Idealistic
Businesslike	Eager	Imaginative
Calm	Easygoing	Impersonal
Capable	Efficient	Independent
Caring	Emotional	Individualistic
Cautious	Empathetic	Industrious
Cheerful	Energetic	Informal
Clean	Excitable	Innovative
Competent	Expressive	Intellectual
Confident	Extroverted	Intelligent
Conscientious	Fair-minded	Introverted
Conservative	Farsighted	Intuitive
Considerate	Feeling	Inventive
Cool	Firm	

continued

continued

Jovial	Pleasant	Sensible
Just	Poised	Sensitive
Kind	Polite	Serious
Liberal	Practical	Sincere
Likable	Precise	Sociable
Logical	Principled	Spontaneous
Loyal	Private	Strong
Mature	Productive	Strong-minded
Methodical	Progressive	Structured
Meticulous	Quick	Subjective
Modest	Quiet	Tactful
Motivated	Rational	Thorough
Objective	Realistic	Thoughtful
Observant	Receptive	Tolerant
Open-minded	Reflective	Trusting
Opportunistic	Relaxed	Trustworthy
Optimistic	Reliable	Truthful
Organized	Reserved	Understanding
Original	Resourceful	Unexcitable
Outgoing	Responsible	Uninhibited
Patient	Reverent	Verbal
Peaceable	Self-confident	Versatile
Personable	Self-controlled	Wholesome
Persuasive	Self-disciplined	Wise

Focusing on Selected Personal Traits. Of all the traits you identified from the list in Exhibit 1.2, select the ten you believe most accurately describe you. If you are having a difficult time deciding, think about which words people who know you well would use to describe you. Keep track of these ten traits.

Considering Your Personal Traits in the Job Search Process. As you begin exploring jobs and careers, watch for matches between your personal traits and the job descriptions you read. Some jobs will require many personal traits you know you possess, and others will not seem to match those traits.

....

Working in statistics, for example, will draw upon your skills of data manipulation, analytical thinking, and research. Statistics is essentially problem solving, not number crunching. Your abilities to work in a team, analyze problems, and apply innovative solutions will be far more important personal traits for success than merely having a purely technical background. Statisticians must also possess self-discipline and time-management skills since many projects are independent. Statistics positions for graduates often require the mastery of quantitative analysis. Attention to detail and excellent communication skills are also important attributes for this work.

∙∙∙

Your ability to respond to changing conditions, decision-making ability, productivity, creativity, and verbal skills all have a bearing on your success in and enjoyment of your work life. To better guarantee success, be sure to take the time needed to understand these traits in yourself.

STEP 2   Identifying Your Personal Values

Your personal values affect every aspect of your life, including employment, and they develop and change as you move through life. Values can be defined as principles that we hold in high regard, qualities that are important and desirable to us. Some values aren't ordinarily connected to work (love, beauty, marriage, family, or religion), and others are (autonomy, cooperation, effectiveness, achievement, knowledge, and security). Our values determine, in part, the level of satisfaction we feel in a particular job.

Defining Acceptable Working Conditions. One facet of employment is the set of working conditions that must exist for someone to consider taking a job.

Each of us would probably create a unique list of acceptable working conditions, but items that might be included on many people's lists are the amount of money you would need to be paid, how far you are willing to drive or travel, the amount of freedom you want in determining your own schedule, whether you would be working with people or data or things, and the types of tasks you would be willing to do. Your conditions might include statements of working conditions you will *not* accept; for example, you might not be willing to work at night or on weekends or holidays.

If you were offered a job tomorrow, what conditions would have to exist for you to realistically consider accepting the position? Take some time and make a list of these conditions.

Realizing Associated Values. Your list of working conditions can be used to create an inventory of your values relating to jobs and careers you are exploring. For example, if one of your conditions stated that you wanted to earn

---

Exhibit 1.3

Work Values

Achievement	Development	Physical activity
Advancement	Effectiveness	Power
Adventure	Excitement	Precision
Attainment	Fast pace	Prestige
Authority	Financial gain	Privacy
Autonomy	Helping	Profit
Belonging	Humor	Recognition
Challenge	Improvisation	Risk
Change	Independence	Security
Communication	Influencing others	Self-expression
Community	Intellectual stimulation	Solitude
Competition	Interaction	Stability
Completion	Knowledge	Status
Contribution	Leading	Structure
Control	Mastery	Supervision
Cooperation	Mobility	Surroundings
Creativity	Moral fulfillment	Time freedom
Decision-making	Organization	Variety

---

at least $25,000 per year, the associated value would be financial gain. If another condition was that you wanted to work with a friendly group of people, the value that goes along with that might be belonging or interaction with people. Exhibit 1.3 provides a list of commonly held values that relate to the work environment; use it to create your own list of personal values.

Relating Your Values to the World of Work. As you read the job descriptions in this book and in other suggested resources, think about the values associated with that position.

· ·

For example, as a statistician your duties may include designing, collecting, analyzing, and interpreting data for the planning of service provisions in government agencies or, in a more specific example, investigating the effect of a new drug for AIDS.

· ·

If you were thinking about a career in this field, or any other field you're exploring, at least some of the associated values should match those you extracted from your list of working conditions. Take a second look at any values that don't match up. How important are they to you? What will happen if they are not satisfied on the job? Can you incorporate those personal values elsewhere? Your answers need to be brutally honest. As you continue your exploration, be sure to add to your list any additional values that occur to you.

STEP 3   Calculating Your Economic Needs

Each of us grew up in an environment that provided for certain basic needs, such as food and shelter, and, to varying degrees, other needs that we now consider basic, such as cable TV, reading materials, or an automobile. Needs such as privacy, space, and quiet, which at first glance may not appear to be monetary needs, may add to housing expenses and so should be considered as you examine your economic needs. For example, if you place a high value on a large, open living space for yourself, it would be difficult to satisfy that need without an associated high housing cost, especially in a densely popu-lated city environment.

As you prepare to move into the world of work and become responsible for meeting your own basic needs, it is important to consider the salary you will need to be able to afford a satisfying standard of living. The three-step process outlined here will help you plan a budget, which in turn will allow you to evaluate the various career choices and geographic locations you are considering. The steps include (1) developing a realistic budget, (2) exam-ining starting salaries, and (3) using a cost-of-living index.

Developing a Realistic Budget. Each of us has certain expectations for the kind of lifestyle we want to maintain. In order to begin the process of defining your economic needs, it will be helpful to determine what you expect to spend on routine monthly expenses. These expenses include housing, food, trans-portation, entertainment, utilities, loan repayments, and revolving charge accounts. A worksheet that details many of these expenses is shown in Exhibit 1.4. You may not currently spend for certain items, but you probably

---

Exhibit 1.4

Estimated Monthly Expenses Worksheet

		Could Reduce Spending? (Yes/No)
Cable	$ _____	_____
Child care	_____	_____

continued

continued

		Could Reduce Spending? (Yes/No)
Clothing	_____	_____
Educational loan repayment	_____	_____
Entertainment	_____	_____
Food	_____	_____
At home	_____	_____
Meals out	_____	_____
Gifts	_____	_____
Housing		
Rent/mortgage	_____	_____
Insurance	_____	_____
Property taxes	_____	_____
Medical insurance	_____	_____
Reading materials		
Newspapers	_____	_____
Magazines	_____	_____
Books	_____	_____
Revolving loans/charges	_____	_____
Savings	_____	_____
Telephone	_____	_____
Transportation		
Auto payment	_____	_____
Insurance	_____	_____
Parking	_____	_____
or		
Cab/train/bus fare	_____	_____
Utilities		
Electric	_____	_____
Gas	_____	_____
Water/sewer	_____	_____
Vacations	_____	_____
Miscellaneous expense 1	_____	_____
Expense: _____		
Miscellaneous expense 2	_____	_____
Expense: _____		
Miscellaneous expense 3	_____	_____
Expense: _____		

TOTAL MONTHLY EXPENSES:_____

YEARLY EXPENSES (Monthly expenses x 12): _____

INCREASE TO INCLUDE TAXES (Yearly expenses x 1.35): ___ =

MINIMUM ANNUAL SALARY REQUIREMENT _____

will have to once you begin supporting yourself. As you develop this budget, be generous in your estimates, but keep in mind any items that could be reduced or eliminated. If you are not sure about the cost of a certain item, talk with family or friends who would be able to give you a realistic estimate.

If this is new or difficult for you, start to keep a log of expenses right now. You may be surprised at how much you actually spend each month for food or stamps or magazines. Household expenses and personal grooming items can often loom very large in a budget, as can auto repairs or home maintenance.

Income taxes must also be taken into consideration when examining salary requirements. State and local taxes vary by location, so it is difficult to calculate exactly the effect of taxes on the amount of income you need to generate. To roughly estimate the gross income necessary to generate your minimum annual salary requirement, multiply the minimum salary you have calculated (see Exhibit 1.4) by a factor of 1.35. The resulting figure will be an approximation of what your gross income would need to be, given your estimated expenses.

Examining Starting Salaries. Starting salaries for each of the career tracks are provided throughout this book. These salary figures can be used in conjunction with the cost-of-living index (discussed in the next section) to determine whether you would be able to meet your basic economic needs in a given geographic location.

Using a Cost-of-Living Index. If you are thinking about trying to get a job in a geographic region other than the one where you now live, understanding differences in the cost of living will help you come to a more informed decision about making a move. By using a cost-of-living index, you can compare salaries offered and the cost of living in different locations with what you know about the salaries offered and the cost of living in your present location.

Many variables are used to calculate the cost-of-living index, including housing expenses, groceries, utilities, transportation, health care, clothing, entertainment, local income taxes, and local sales taxes. Cost-of-living indices can be found in many resources, such as *Equal Employment Opportunity Bimonthly*, *Places Rated Almanac*, or *The Best Towns in America*. They are constantly being recalculated based on changes in costs.

· ·

If you lived in Des Moines, Iowa, for example, and you were interested in working as an actuary in the insurance industry, you would earn, on average, $36,000 annually. But let's say you're also thinking about moving to either Boston, Denver, or Houston. You know you can live on $36,000 in Des Moines, but you want to be able to equal that salary in the other locations you're considering. How much will you need to earn in those locations to do this? Figuring the cost of living for each city will show you.

Let's walk through this example. In any cost-of-living index, the number 100 represents the national average cost of living, and each city is assigned an index number based on current prices in that city for the items included in the index (housing, food, etc.). In the index we used, Boston was assigned the number 138.5, Denver's index was 106.4, Houston's was 94.3, and Des Moines's index was 99.1. In other words, it costs almost 50 percent more to live in Boston as it does in Des Moines. We can set up a table to determine exactly how much you would have to earn in each of these cities to have the same buying power that you have in Des Moines.

Job: Actuary

CITY	INDEX	EQUIVALENT SALARY
$\frac{\text{Boston}}{\text{Des Moines}}$	$\frac{138.5}{99.1}$	$\times\ \$36,000\ =\ \$50,313$ in Boston
$\frac{\text{Denver}}{\text{Des Moines}}$	$\frac{106.4}{99.1}$	$\times\ \$36,000\ =\ \$38,652$ in Denver
$\frac{\text{Houston}}{\text{Des Moines}}$	$\frac{94.3}{99.1}$	$\times\ \$36,000\ =\ \$34,256$ in Houston

You would have to earn $50,313 in Boston, $38,652 in Denver, and $34,256 in Houston to match the buying power of $36,000 in Des Moines.

If you would like to determine whether it's financially worthwhile to make any of these moves, one more piece of information is needed: the salaries of actuaries in these other cities. The *American Salaries and Wages Survey* (4th edition) reports the following average salary information for actuaries in their 1997 edition:

State	Annual Salary	Salary Equivalent to Iowa	Change in Buying Power
Massachusetts (Boston)	$66,102	$50,313	+$15,789
Colorado (Denver)	$46,995	$38,652	+$ 8,343
Texas (Houston)	$33,989	$34,256	-$ 267
Iowa (Des Moines)	$50,291	—	—

If you moved to Houston and secured employment as an actuary at an insurance company, you would not be able to maintain a lifestyle similar to the one you led in Des Moines. The same would not be true for a move to Boston or Denver. You would increase your buying power given the rate of pay and cost of living in these cities; in fact, you would have almost 25 percent more buying power in Boston.

• •

You can work through a similar exercise for any type of job you are considering and for many locations when current salary information is available. It will be worth your time to undertake this analysis if you are seriously considering a relocation. By doing so you will be able to make an informed choice.

STEP 4 Exploring Your Longer-Term Goals

There is no question that when we first begin working, our goals are to use our skills and education in a job that will reward us with employment, income, and status relative to the preparation we brought with us to this position. If we are not being paid as much as we feel we should for our level of education, or if job demands don't provide the intellectual stimulation we had hoped for, we experience unhappiness and, as a result, often seek other employment.

Most jobs we consider "good" are those that fulfill our basic "lower-level" needs of security, food, clothing, shelter, income, and productive work. But even when our basic needs are met and our jobs are secure and productive, we as individuals are constantly changing. As we change, the demands and expectations we place on our jobs may change. Fortunately, some jobs grow and change with us, and this explains why some people are happy throughout many years in a job.

But more often people are bigger than the jobs they fill. We have more goals and needs than any job could fulfill. These are "higher-level" needs of self-esteem, companionship, affection, and an increasing desire to feel we are employing ourselves in the most effective way possible. Not all of these higher-level needs can be fulfilled through employment, but for as long as we are employed, we increasingly demand that our jobs play their part in moving us along the path to fulfillment.

Another obvious but important fact is that we change as we mature. Although our jobs also have the potential for change, they may not change as frequently or as markedly as we do. There are increasingly fewer one-job, one-employer careers; we must think about a work future that may involve voluntary or forced moves from employer to employer. Because of that very real possibility, we need to take advantage of the opportunities in each position we hold to acquire skills and competencies that will keep us viable and attractive as employees in a job market that is not only increasingly technology/computer dependent, but also is populated with more and more small, self-transforming organizations rather than the large, seemingly stable organizations of the past.

It may be difficult in the early stages of the job search to determine whether the path you are considering can meet these longer-term goals. Reading about career paths and individual career histories in your field can be very helpful in this regard. Meeting and talking with individuals further along in their careers can be enlightening as well. Older workers can provide valuable guidance on "self-managing" your career, which will become an increasingly valuable skill in the future. Some of these ideas may seem remote as you read this now, but you should be able to appreciate the need to ensure that you are growing, developing valuable new skills, and researching other employers who might be interested in your particular skills package.

···

If you are considering a position as a retail buyer, you would gain a better perspective on this career if you could talk to an entry-level associate buyer, a more senior and experienced department head, and finally, a vice president for sales merchandising or store operations who has had a considerable work history in the retail sector. Each will have a different perspective, unique concerns, and an individual set of value priorities.

···

STEP 5 Enumerating Your Skill Base

In terms of the job search, skills can be thought of as capabilities that can be developed in school, at work, or by volunteering and then used in specific job settings. Many studies have documented the kinds of skills that employers seek in entry-level applicants. For example, some of the most desired skills for individuals interested in the teaching profession include the ability to interact effectively with students one on one, to manage a classroom, to adapt to varying situations as necessary, and to get involved in school activities. Business employers have also identified important qualities, including enthusiasm for the employer's product or service, a businesslike mind, the ability to follow written or verbal instructions, the ability to demonstrate self-control, the confidence to suggest new ideas, the ability to communicate with all members of a group, awareness of cultural differences, and loyalty, to name just a few. You will find that many of these skills are also in the repertoire of qualities demanded in your college major.

In order to be successful in obtaining any given job, you must be able to demonstrate that you possess a certain mix of skills that will allow you to carry out the duties required by that job. This skill mix will vary a great deal from job to job; to determine the skills necessary for the jobs you are seeking, you can read job advertisements or more generic job descriptions, such as those found later in this book. If you want to be effective in the job search, you must directly show employers that you possess the skills needed to be successful in filling the position. These skills will initially be described on your resume and then discussed again during the interview process.

Skills are either general or specific. General skills are those that are developed throughout the college years by taking classes, being employed, and getting involved in other related activities such as volunteer work or campus organizations. General skills include the ability to read and write, to perform computations, to think critically, and to communicate effectively. Specific skills are also acquired on the job and in the classroom, but they allow you to complete tasks that require specialized knowledge. Computer programming, drafting, language translating, and copy editing are just a few examples of specific skills that may relate to a given job.

In order to develop a list of skills relevant to employers, you must first identify the general skills you possess, then list specific skills you have to offer, and, finally, examine which of these skills employers are seeking.

Identifying Your General Skills. Because you possess or will possess a college degree, employers will assume that you can read and write, perform certain basic computations, think critically, and communicate effectively. Employers will want to see that you have acquired these skills, and they will want to know which additional general skills you possess.

One way to begin identifying skills is to write an experiential diary. An experiential diary lists all the tasks you were responsible for completing for each job you've held and then outlines the skills required to do those tasks.

You may list several skills for any given task. This diary allows you to distinguish between the tasks you performed and the underlying skills required to complete those tasks. Here's an example:

Tasks	Skills
Answering telephone	Effective use of language, clear diction, ability to direct inquiries, ability to solve problems
Waiting on tables	Poise under conditions of time and pressure, speed, accuracy, good memory, simultaneous completion of tasks, sales skills

For each job or experience you have participated in, develop a worksheet based on the example shown here. On a resume, you may want to describe these skills rather than simply listing tasks. Skills are easier for the employer to appreciate, especially when your experience is very different from the employment you are seeking. In addition to helping you identify general skills, this experiential diary will prepare you to speak more effectively in an interview about the qualifications you possess.

Identifying Your Specific Skills. It may be easier to identify your specific skills, because you can definitely say whether you can speak other languages, program a computer, draft a map or diagram, or edit a document using appropriate symbols and terminology.

Using your experiential diary, identify the points in your history where you learned how to do something very specific, and decide whether you have a beginning, intermediate, or advanced knowledge of how to use that particular skill. Right now, be sure to list *every* specific skill you have, and don't consider whether you like using the skill. Write down a list of specific skills you have acquired and the level of competence you possess—beginning, intermediate, or advanced.

Relating Your Skills to Employers. You probably have thought about a couple of different jobs you might be interested in obtaining, and one way to begin relating the general and specific skills you possess to potential employer needs is to read actual advertisements for these types of positions (see Part II for resources listing actual job openings).

....

For example, you might be interested in working as an actuary for a large insurance company, prior to returning to graduate school for your M.S. (master of science). A typical job listing might read, "Requires a B.A./B.S.

in statistics, math, or the equivalent, along with a superior knowledge of statistical methods. Some expertise performing statistical and actuarial analysis on personal line insurance, or completion of one or two actuarial exams, would be preferred. Strong PC skills and basic knowledge of insurance accounting concepts required." If you then used any one of a number of general sources of information that described the job of an actuary, you would find additional information.

Begin building a comprehensive list of required skills with the first job description you read. Exploring advertisements for and descriptions of several types of related positions will reveal an important core of skills that are necessary for obtaining the type of work you're interested in. In building this list, include both general and specific skills.

Following is a sample list of skills needed to be successful as an actuary in insurance. These items were extracted from general resources and actual job listings.

Job: Actuary/Insurance Company

General Skills	Specific Skills
PC skills	Analyze insurance rates and loss reserves
Gathering information	
Decision making	Test system changes
Meeting deadlines	Prepare rate and statistical filings for submission to regulatory agencies
Reading	
Writing	
Collaborating on projects	Develop market share and CPI studies
Attending meetings	
	Evaluate alternatives
	Master various software packages
	Mathematical computation
	Generate ratios

On separate sheets of paper, try to generate a comprehensive list of required skills for at least one job you are considering.

The list of general skills that you develop for a given career path would be valuable for any number of jobs you might apply for. Many of the specific skills would also be transferable to other types of positions. For example, evaluating alternatives is a required skill for actuaries, mathematicians, operations researchers, and would be helpful for statisticians, as well.

....

Now review the list of skills you developed and check off those skills that *you know you possess* and that are required for jobs you are considering. You should refer to these specific skills on the resume that you write for this type of job. See Chapter 2 for details on resume writing.

STEP 6 Recognizing Your Preferred Skills

In the previous section, you developed a comprehensive list of skills that relate to particular career paths that are of interest to you. You can now relate these to skills that you prefer to use. We all use a wide range of skills (some researchers say individuals have a repertoire of about 500 skills), but we may not be particularly interested in using all of them in our work. There may be some skills that come to us more naturally or that we use successfully time and time again and that we want to continue to use; these are best described as our preferred skills. For this exercise, use the list of skills that you developed for the previous section and decide which of them you are *most interested in using* in future work and how often you would like to use them. You might be interested in using some skills only occasionally, while others you would like to use more regularly. You probably also have skills that you hope you can use constantly.

As you examine job announcements, look for matches between this list of preferred skills and the qualifications described in the advertisements. These skills should be highlighted on your resume and discussed in job interviews.

STEP 7 Assessing Skills Needing Further Development

Previously you developed a list of general and specific skills required for given positions. You already possess some of these skills; those that remain to be developed are your underdeveloped skills.

If you are just beginning the job search, there may be gaps between the qualifications required for some of the jobs being considered and skills you possess. These are your underdeveloped skills. The thought of having to admit to and talk about these underdeveloped skills, especially in a job interview, is a frightening one. One way to put a healthy perspective on this subject is to target and relate your exploration of underdeveloped skills to the types of positions you are seeking. Recognizing these shortcomings and planning to overcome them with either on-the-job training or additional formal education can be a positive way to address the concept of underdeveloped skills.

On your worksheet or in your journal, make a list of up to five general or specific skills required for the positions you're interested in that you *don't currently possess.* For each item, list an idea you have for specific action you could take to acquire that skill. Do some brainstorming to come up with possible actions. If you have a hard time generating ideas, talk to people currently working in this type of position, professionals in your college career services office, trusted friends, family members, or members of related professional associations.

If, for example, you are interested in a job for which you don't have some specific required experience, you could locate training opportunities such as classes or workshops offered through a local college or university, community college, or club or association that would help you build the level of expertise you need for the job.

Many excellent jobs in today's economy demand computer skills you probably already have. Most graduates are not so lucky, and have to acquire these skills—often before an employer will give their application serious consideration. So, what can you do if you find there are certain skills you're missing? If you're still in school, try to fill the gaps in your knowledge before you graduate. If you've already graduated, look at evening programs, continuing education courses, or tutorial programs that may be available commercially. Developing a modest level of expertise will encourage you to be more confident in suggesting to potential employers that you can continue to add to your skill base on the job.

In Chapter 5 on interviewing, we will discuss in detail how to effectively address questions about underdeveloped skills. Generally speaking, though, employers want genuine answers to these types of questions. They want you to reveal "the real you," and they also want to see how you answer difficult questions. In taking the positive, targeted approach discussed above, you show the employer that you are willing to continue to learn and that you have a plan for strengthening your job qualifications.

USING YOUR SELF-ASSESSMENT

Exploring entry-level career options can be an exciting experience if you have good resources available and will take the time to use them. Can you effectively complete the following tasks?

1. Understand and relate your personality traits to career choices

2. Define your personal values

3. Determine your economic needs

4. Explore longer-term goals

5. Understand your skill base

6. Recognize your preferred skills

7. Express a willingness to improve on your underdeveloped skills

If so, then you can more meaningfully participate in the job search process by writing a more effective resume, finding job titles that represent work you are interested in doing, locating job sites that will provide the opportunity for you to use your strengths and skills, networking in an informed way, participating in focused interviews, getting the most out of follow-up contacts, and evaluating job offers to find those that create a good match between you and the employer. The remaining chapters guide you through these next steps in the job search process. For many job seekers, this process can take anywhere from three months to a year to implement. The time you will need to put into your job search will depend on the type of job you want and the geographic location where you'd like to work. Think of your effort as a job in itself, requiring you to set aside time each week to complete the needed work. Carefully undertaken efforts may reduce the time you need for your job search.

CHAPTER TWO

THE RESUME AND COVER LETTER

*T*he task of writing a resume may seem overwhelming if you are unfamiliar with this type of document, but there are some easily understood techniques that can and should be used. This section was written to help you understand the purpose of the resume, the different types of resume formats available, and how to write the sections of information traditionally found on a resume. We will present examples and explanations that address questions frequently posed by people writing their first resume or updating an old resume.

Even within the formats and suggestions given below, however, there are infinite variations. True, most resumes follow one of the outlines suggested below, but you should feel free to adjust the resume to suit your needs and make it expressive of your life and experience.

WHY WRITE A RESUME?

The purpose of a resume is to convince an employer that you should be interviewed. You'll want to present enough information to show that you can make an immediate and valuable contribution to an organization. A resume is not an in-depth historical or legal document; later in the job search process you'll be asked to document your entire work history on an application form and attest to its validity. The resume should, instead, highlight relevant information pertaining directly to the organization that will receive the document or the type of position you are seeking.

We will discuss four types of resumes in this chapter: chronological resume, functional resume, targeted resume, and the broadcast letter. The reasons for using one type of resume over another and the typical format for each are addressed in the following sections.

THE CHRONOLOGICAL RESUME

The chronological resume is the most common of the various resume formats and therefore the format that employers are most used to receiving. This type of resume is easy to read and understand because it details the chronological progression of jobs you have held. (See Exhibit 2.1.) It begins with your most recent employment and works back in time. If you have a solid work history, or experience that provided growth and development in your duties and responsibilities, a chronological resume will highlight these achievements. The typical elements of a chronological resume include the heading, a career objective, educational background, employment experience, activities, and references.

The Heading

The heading consists of your name, address, and telephone number. Recently it has come to include fax numbers and electronic mail addresses as well. We suggest that you spell out your full name and type it in all capital letters in bold type. After all, *you* are the focus of the resume! If you have a current as well as a permanent address and you include both in the heading, be sure to indicate until what date your current address will be valid. Don't forget to include the zip code with your address and the area code with your telephone number.

The Objective

As you formulate the wording for this part of your resume, keep the following points in mind.

The Objective Focuses the Resume. Without a doubt, this is the most challenging part of the resume for most resume writers. Even for individuals who have quite firmly decided on a career path, it can be difficult to encapsulate all they want to say in one or two brief sentences. For job seekers who are unfocused or unclear about their intentions, trying to write this section can inhibit the entire resume writing process.

Recruiters tell us, time and again, that the objective creates a frame of reference for them. It helps them see how you express your goals and career

Exhibit 2.1

Chronological Resume

ASHLEE CARTER

Boyd Hall #401
Lyndon State College
Lyndonville, VT 01234
(802) 555-4567
(until May 1998)

43 River Road
Littleton, NH 04523
(603) 555-1111

OBJECTIVE

High School Mathematics teaching position where I can motivate students to overcome the challenge and difficulties with all levels of mathematics.

EDUCATION

Bachelor of Science Degree in Mathematics Education
Lyndon State College, Lyndonville, VT, May 1998

HONORS

President's List, Dean's List, Lyndon State Scholar, Kappa Delta Phi Education Honor Society, Outstanding Student of Education

EXPERIENCES

Student Teacher, Lyndon Institute, Spring 1998
Class size ranged from fifteen to thirty students, grades nine through twelve. Administrative responsibilities included: constructed lesson plans, recorded grades, sent progress reports, and maintained the attendance report. Instructed daily lessons in Algebra, Geometry, and Advanced Math (Pre-Calculus). Attended all faculty and department meetings, workshops, and served as junior class advisor.

Help Session Instructor, Lyndon State College, 1995–97
Employed by the math department to assist students who had difficulties in Fundamental Mathematics (Pre-Algebra) and in Algebra. Held group sessions to aid students in preparing for exams.

continued

---

continued

Mathematics Tutor, Lyndon State College, 1994–96
Tutored individuals and groups of students in various
mathematics courses such as: Fundamental Math (Pre-Algebra),
Algebra, Statistics I, Discrete Math, Elementary Functions (Pre-
Calculus), Calculus and math lab activities.

Sales Associate, Price Chopper, St. Johnsbury, VT, 1994–97
Organized stock in produce department and submitted accurate,
daily paperwork in a timely manner. Interacted with customers all
day, every day. Selected twice as Sales Associate of the Month.

ACTIVITIES
National Council of Teachers of Mathematics
Future Teachers of America

---

focus. In addition, the statement may indicate in what ways you can immediately benefit an organization. Given the importance of the objective, every
point covered in the resume should relate to it. If information doesn't relate,
it should be omitted. With the word processing technology available today,
each resume can and should be tailored for individual employers or specific
positions that are available.

Choose an Appropriate Length. Because of the brevity necessary for a resume,
you should keep the objective as short as possible. Although objectives of only
four or five words often don't show much direction, objectives that take three
full lines would be viewed as too wordy and might be ignored.

Consider Which Type of Objective Statement You Will Use. There are many ways
to state an objective, but generally there are four forms this statement can
take: (1) a very general statement; (2) a statement focused on a specific position; (3) a statement focused on a specific industry; or (4) a summary of your
qualifications. In our contacts with employers, we often hear that many
resumes don't exhibit any direction or career goals, so we suggest avoiding
general statements when possible.

1. General Objective Statement. General objective statements look like the
following:

      ❑ An entry-level educational programming coordinator position

      ❑ An entry-level marketing position

This type of objective would be useful if you know what type of job you want but you're not sure which industries interest you.

2. Position-Focused Objective. Following are examples of objectives focusing on a specific position:

      ❑ To obtain the position of director of public information at the State Council for Environmental Quality

      ❑ To obtain a position as assistant town manager

When a student applies for an advertised job opening, this type of focus can be very effective. The employer knows that the applicant has taken the time to tailor the resume specifically for this position.

3. Industry-Focused Objective. Focusing on a particular industry in an objective could be stated as follows:

      ❑ To begin a career as a sales representative in the cruise line industry

4. Summary of Qualifications Statement. The summary of qualifications can be used instead of an objective or in conjunction with an objective. The purpose of this type of statement is to highlight relevant qualifications gained through a variety of experiences. This type of statement is often used by individuals with extensive and diversified work experience. An example of a qualifications statement follows:

••

A degree in mathematics and four years of progressively increasing job responsibility as a statistical analyst for a large company has prepared me to begin a career as a mathematical statistician for a company that values analytical and design skills.

••

Support Your Objective. A resume that contains any one of these types of objective statements should then go on to demonstrate why you are qualified to get the position. Listing academic degrees can be one way to indicate qualifications. Another demonstration would be in the way previous experiences, both volunteer and paid, are described. Without this kind of documentation in the body of the resume, the objective looks unsupported. Think of the resume as telling a connected story about you. All the elements should work together to form a coherent picture that ideally should relate to your statement of objective.

Education

This section of your resume should indicate the exact name of the degree you will receive or have received, spelled out completely with no abbreviations. The degree is generally listed after the objective, followed by the institution name and address, and then the month and year of graduation. This section could also include your academic minor, grade point average (GPA), and appearance on the Dean's List or President's List.

If you have enough space, you might want to include a section listing courses related to the field in which you are seeking work. The best use of a "related courses" section would be to list some course work that is not traditionally associated with the major. Perhaps you took several computer courses outside your degree that will be helpful and related to the job prospects you are entertaining. Several education section examples are shown here:

• •

❑ **Bachelor of Science Degree in Mathematics**
State University, Des Moines, Iowa, May 1998
Concentration: Actuarial Math

❑ **Bachelor of Science Degree in Mathematics Education**
State College, Keene, New Hampshire, May 1998
Option: Middle/Junior High School

❑ **Bachelor of Science Degree in Mathematics**
Community College, Baltimore, Maryland, May 1998
Minor: Operations Research
An example of a format for a related course section follows:

RELATED COURSES	
Statistics I and II	Numerical Methods Using
Calculus I and II	the Computer
Elements of Linear Algebra	Quantitative Methods with
Discrete Mathematics	Business Applications
Probability Theory	Time and Money

• •

Experience

The experience section of your resume should be the most substantial part and should take up most of the space on the page. Employers want to see what kind of work history you have. They will look at your range of experiences, longevity in jobs, and specific tasks you are able to complete. This section may also be called "work experience," "related experience," "employment history," or "employment." No matter what you call this section, some important points to remember are the following:

1. **Describe your duties** as they relate to the position you are seeking.

2. **Emphasize major responsibilities** and indicate increases in responsibility. Include all relevant employment experiences: summer, part-time, internships, cooperative education, or self-employment.

3. **Emphasize skills,** especially those that transfer from one situation to another. The fact that you coordinated a student organization, chaired meetings, supervised others, and managed a budget leads one to suspect that you could coordinate other things as well.

4. **Use descriptive job titles** that provide information about what you did. A "Student Intern" should be more specifically stated as, for example, "Magazine Operations Intern." "Volunteer" is also too general; a title like "Peer Writing Tutor" would be more appropriate.

5. **Create word pictures** by using active verbs to start sentences. Describe *results* you have produced in the work you have done.

A limp description would say something like the following: "My duties included helping with production, proofreading, and editing. I used a word processing package to alter text." An action statement would be stated as follows: "Coordinated and assisted in the creative marketing of brochures and seminar promotions, becoming proficient in WordPerfect."

Remember, an accomplishment is simply a result, a final measurable product that people can relate to. A duty is not a result, it is an obligation—every job holder has duties. For an effective resume, list as many results as you can. To make the most of the limited space you have and to give your description impact, carefully select appropriate and accurate descriptors from the list of action words in Exhibit 2.2.

Here are some traits that employers tell us they like to see:

▫ Teamwork

▫ Energy and motivation

▫ Learning and using new skills

▫ Demonstrated versatility

Exhibit 2.2

Resume Action Verbs

Achieved	Established	Operated
Acted	Estimated	Organized
Administered	Evaluated	Participated
Advised	Examined	Performed
Analyzed	Explained	Planned
Assessed	Facilitated	Predicted
Assisted	Finalized	Prepared
Attained	Generated	Presented
Balanced	Handled	Processed
Budgeted	Headed	Produced
Calculated	Helped	Projected
Collected	Identified	Proposed
Communicated	Illustrated	Provided
Compiled	Implemented	Qualified
Completed	Improved	Quantified
Composed	Increased	Questioned
Conceptualized	Influenced	Realized
Condensed	Informed	Received
Conducted	Initiated	Recommended
Consolidated	Innovated	Recorded
Constructed	Instituted	Reduced
Controlled	Instructed	Reinforced
Converted	Integrated	Reported
Coordinated	Interpreted	Represented
Corrected	Introduced	Researched
Created	Learned	Resolved
Decreased	Lectured	Reviewed
Defined	Led	Scheduled
Demonstrated	Maintained	Selected
Designed	Managed	Served
Determined	Mapped	Showed
Developed	Marketed	Simplified
Directed	Met	Sketched
Documented	Modified	Sold
Drafted	Monitored	Solved
Edited	Negotiated	Staffed
Eliminated	Observed	Streamlined
Ensured	Obtained	Studied

continued

continued		
Submitted	Tabulated	Updated
Summarized	Tested	Verified
Systematized	Transacted	

- ❏ Critical thinking

- ❏ Understanding how profits are created

- ❏ Displaying organizational acumen

- ❏ Communicating directly and clearly, in both writing and speaking

- ❏ Risk taking

- ❏ Willingness to admit mistakes

- ❏ Manifesting high personal standards

SOLUTIONS TO FREQUENTLY ENCOUNTERED PROBLEMS

Repetitive Employment with the Same Employer
EMPLOYMENT: **The Foot Locker,** Portland, Oregon. Summer 1995, 1996, 1997. Initially employed in high school as salesclerk. Due to successful performance, asked to return next two summers at higher pay with added responsibility. Ranked as the #2 salesperson the first summer and #1 the next two summers. Assisted in arranging eye-catching retail displays; served as manager of other summer workers during owner's absence.

A Large Number of Jobs
EMPLOYMENT: Recent Hospitality Industry Experience: Affiliated with four upscale hotel/restaurant complexes (September 1996–February 1998), where I worked part- and full-time as a waiter, bartender, disc jockey, and bookkeeper to produce income for college.

Several Positions with the Same Employer
EMPLOYMENT: Coca-Cola Bottling Co., Burlington, VT, 1995–98. In four years, I received three promotions, each with increased pay and responsibility.

Summer Sales Coordinator: Promoted to hire, train, and direct efforts of add-on staff of 15 college-age route salespeople hired to meet summer peak demand for product.

Sales Administrator: Promoted to run home office sales desk, managing accounts and associated delivery schedules for professional sales force of ten people. Intensive phone work, daily interaction with all personnel, and strong knowledge of product line required.

Route Salesperson: Summer employment to travel and tourism industry sites using Coke products. Met specific schedule demands, used good communication skills with wide variety of customers, and demonstrated strong selling skills. Named salesperson of the month for July and August of that year.

QUESTIONS RESUME WRITERS OFTEN ASK

How Far Back Should I Go in Terms of Listing Past Jobs?

Usually, listing three or four jobs should suffice. If you did something back in high school that has a bearing on your future aspirations for employment, by all means list the job. As you progress through your college career, high school jobs may be replaced on the resume by college employment.

Should I Differentiate Between Paid and Nonpaid Employment?

Most employers are not initially as concerned about how much you were paid. They are anxious to know how much responsibility you held in your past employment. There is no need to specify that your work was volunteer if you had significant responsibilities.

How Should I Represent My Accomplishments or Work-Related Responsibilities?

Succinctly, but fully. In other words, give the employer enough information to arouse curiosity, but not so much detail that you leave nothing to the imagination. Besides, some jobs merit more lengthy explanations than others. Be sure to convey any information that can give an employer a better understanding of the depth of your involvement at work. Did you supervise others? How many? Did your efforts result in a more efficient operation? How much did you increase efficiency? Did you handle a budget? How much? Were you promoted in a short time? Did you work two jobs at once or 15 hours per week after high school? Where appropriate, quantify.

Should the Work Section Always Follow the Education Section on the Resume?

Always lead with your strengths. If your education closely relates to the employment you now seek, put this section after the objective. Or, if you are weak on the academic side but have a surplus of good work experiences, consider reversing the order of your sections to lead with employment, followed by education.

How Should I Present My Activities, Honors, Awards, Professional Societies, and Affiliations?

This section of the resume can add valuable information for an employer to consider if used correctly. The rule of thumb for information in this section is to include only those activities that are in some way relevant to the objective stated on your resume. If you can draw a valid connection between your activities and your objective, include them; if not, leave them out.

Granted, this is hard to do. Center on the championship basketball team or coordinator of the biggest homecoming parade ever held are roles that have meaning for you and represent personal accomplishments you'd like to share. But the resume is a brief document, and the information you provide on it should help the employer make a decision about your job eligibility. Including personal details can be confusing and could hurt your candidacy. Limiting your activity list to a few very significant experiences can be very effective.

If you are applying for a position as a safety officer, your certificate in Red Cross lifesaving skills or CPR would be related and valuable. You would want to include it. If, however, you are applying for a job as a junior account executive in an advertising agency, that information would be unrelated and superfluous. Leave it out.

Professional affiliations and honors should *all* be listed; especially important are those related to your job objective. Social clubs and activities need not be a part of your resume unless you hold a significant office or you are looking for a position related to your membership. Be aware that most prospective employers' principle concerns are related to your employability, not your social life. If you have any, publications can be included as an addendum to your resume.

The focus of the resume is your experience and education. It is not necessary to describe your involvement in activities. However, if your resume needs to be lengthened, this section provides the freedom either to expand on or mention only briefly the contributions you have made. If you have made significant contributions (e.g., an officer of an organization or a particularly long tenure with a group), you may choose to describe them in more detail.

It is not always necessary to include the dates of your memberships with your activities the way you would include job dates.

There are a number of different ways in which to present additional information. You may give this section a number of different titles. Assess what you want to list, and then use an appropriate title. Do not use extracurricular activities. This terminology is scholastic, not professional, and therefore not appropriate. The following are two examples:

- ❑ ACTIVITIES: Society for Technical Communication, Student Senate, Student Admissions Representative, Senior Class Officer

- ❑ ACTIVITIES:
  - Society for Technical Communication Member
  - Student Senator
  - Student Admissions Representative
  - Senior Class Officer

The position you are looking for will determine what you should or should not include. *Always* look for a correlation between the activity and the prospective job.

How Should I Handle References?

The use of references is considered a part of the interview process, and they should never be listed on a resume. You would always provide references to a potential employer if requested to, so it is not even necessary to include this section on the resume if room does not permit. If space is available, it is acceptable to include one of the following statements:

- ❑ REFERENCES: Furnished upon request.

- ❑ REFERENCES: Available upon request.

Individuals used as references must be protected from unnecessary contacts. By including names on your resume, you leave your references unprotected. Overuse and abuse of your references will lead to less-than-supportive comments. Protect your references by giving out their names only when you are being considered seriously as a candidate for a given position.

THE FUNCTIONAL RESUME

The functional resume departs from a chronological resume in that it organizes information by specific accomplishments in various settings: previous

Exhibit 2.3

Functional Resume

PAUL HARRINGTON

Smith Hall, Room 412	25 Commercial Avenue
Boston College	Albany, NY 55212
Boston, MA 03456	(478) 555-6635
(615) 555-2246	
(until May 1998)	

OBJECTIVE
A position as an entry-level buyer for a major department or specialty goods store that will build upon my past retail experience and mathematics education.

CAPABILITIES
- Merchandising
- Excellent quantitative and analytical skills
- Effective communicator

SELECTED ACCOMPLISHMENTS
MERCHANDISING: Three years of retail experience with extensive exposure in display, signage, vendor relations, inventory, and customer contact. Participated in special merchandising events. Work assignments dealt mostly with store operations.
ANALYTICAL SKILLS: Developed, processed, classified, and analyzed the results of 200 computerized mail questionnaires. As a tutor, clarified problems, monitored student progress, and evaluated course work.
COMMUNICATION: Department honors in Mathematics for my senior presentation justifying concepts and explaining alternative approaches to creative problem solving. As a tutor, motivated others and assisted them in improving their performance.

AWARDS AND ACCOMPLISHMENTS
Graduated with honors in Mathematics
Dean's List (five semesters)
Employee of the month (six times over three years)

continued

---

continued

EMPLOYMENT HISTORY
Shaw's Supermarkets, Pine St., Albany, NY, 1992–94
Mathematics Office (student worker), Boston College, 1994–97
The Jeantique, Bridge St., Albany, NY, 1994–97

EDUCATION
Bachelor of Science in Mathematics
Boston College, Boston, MA, December 1997

REFERENCES
Provided on request.

---

jobs, volunteer work, associations, etc. This type of resume permits you to stress the substance of your experiences rather than the position titles you have held. (See Exhibit 2.3.) You should consider using a functional resume if you have held a series of similar jobs that relied on the same skills or abilities.

The Objective

A functional resume begins with an objective that can be used to focus the contents of the resume.

Specific Accomplishments

Specific accomplishments are listed on this type of resume. Examples of the types of headings used to describe these capabilities might include sales, counseling, teaching, communication, production, management, marketing, or writing. The headings you choose will directly relate to your experience and the tasks that you carried out. Each accomplishment section contains statements related to your experience in that category, regardless of when or where it occurred. Organize the accomplishments and the related tasks you describe in their order of importance as related to the position you seek.

Experience or Employment History

Your actual work experience is condensed and placed after the specific accomplishments section. It simply lists dates of employment, position titles, and employer names.

Education

The education section of a functional resume is identical to that of the chronological resume, but it does not carry the same visual importance because it is placed near the bottom of the page.

References

Because actual reference names are never listed on a resume, this section is optional if space does not permit.

THE TARGETED RESUME

The targeted resume focuses on specific work-related capabilities you can bring to a given position within an organization. (See Exhibit 2.4.) It should be sent to an individual within the organization who makes hiring decisions about the position you are seeking.

The Objective

The objective on this type of resume should be targeted to a specific career or position. It should be supported by the capabilities, accomplishments, and achievements documented in the resume.

Exhibit 2.4

Targeted Resume

DIANA GAGNON

Fleming Hall #324   2117 Piedmont Avenue
Arizona State University   San Diego, CA 05264
Tempe, AZ 85287   (514) 555-6798
(414) 555-1357

JOB TARGET
Operations Research position in the airline industry

CAPABILITIES
- Familiar with a variety of computer software
- Strong quantitative skills/practiced in research techniques
- Proven team skills

continued

---

continued

- Excellent communicator

ACHIEVEMENTS
- Winter Carnival Coordinator for College Union, 1997–98
- Worked with area travel agents to provide spring break vacation packages for students
- Assisted a committee of mathematics professors in researching employment patterns for operations research specialists

WORK HISTORY

1997   Intern, American Airlines, New York, NY
- Rotating internship that involved assisting research teams on designing and evaluating systems for booking flights
- Used various software programs

1995–96   Staff, Horizon Travel Agency, San Diego, CA
- Increasing responsibility in this busy travel agency assisting agents with booking flights and travel plans
- Extensive computer experience

1993–94   Head Waitress, Barbara's Restaurant, San Diego, CA
- Daily customer interaction
- Responsible for overseeing dining room activities

EDUCATION
Bachelor of Science in Mathematics
Arizona State University, Tempe, AZ, May 1998
Concentration: Operations Research

REFERENCES ON REQUEST

Capabilities

Capabilities should be statements that illustrate tasks you believe you are capable of based on your accomplishments, achievements, and work history. Each should relate to your targeted career or position. You can stress your qualifications rather than your employment history. This approach may require research to obtain an understanding of the nature of the work involved and the capabilities necessary to carry out that work.

Accomplishments/Achievements

This section relates the various activities you have been involved in to the job market. These experiences may include previous jobs, extracurricular activities at school, internships, and part-time summer work.

Experience

Your work history should be listed in abbreviated form and may include position title, employer name, and employment dates.

Education

Because this type of resume is directed toward a specific job target and an individual's related experience, the education section is not prominently located at the top of the resume as is done on the chronological resume.

THE BROADCAST LETTER

The broadcast letter is used by some job seekers in place of a resume and cover letter. (See Exhibit 2.5.) The purpose of this type of document is to

---

Exhibit 2.5

Broadcast Letter

RICHARD S. BROWN
80 Summer Street
Richmond, VA 62872
(714) 555-1723

Mr. Scott Raymond, President   June 8, 1997
Paints Unlimited, Inc.
Box 460, Route 101
Malvern, PA 23211

Dear Mr. Raymond:

I am writing to you because your organization may be in need of an entry-level analyst with my experience, education, and training. My long-term goal is to work in operations management in the area of wholesale marketing distribution systems,

continued

continued

especially those that both develop and deliver quality service to a wide range of customers. Today's marketplace challenges us to continue to attempt to provide the highest level of service within the competitive nature of an increasingly successful wholesale business sector. I feel well prepared to contribute to your excellent management team as they work hard to keep Paints Unlimited ahead of tomorrow's challenges. Some highlights of my experience that might particularly interest you include:

- My internship with a Fortune 500 Company involved participation in a structured, formal Management Training Program.

- I have developed practiced analytical skills through the experience of managing a business unit, including experience in: profit and loss responsibility, accounts receivable management, commercial/industrial and retail sales, human resource, and inventory management.

- As a member of the Student Senate here on campus, I have developed excellent communication and listening skills. These qualities I feel are crucial to today's management team.

- I have solid research, analytical, and computer software skills, including database and spreadsheet experience. My writing has been consistently recognized throughout college for its clarity and style.

I received my Bachelor of Science Degree in Mathematics with a concentration in Business Management from Green Mountain College in May of 1998.

It would be a pleasure to review my qualifications with you in a personal interview at some mutually convenient time. I will call your office at the end of next week to make arrangements. I look forward to discussing career opportunities with Paints Unlimited, Inc.

Sincerely,

Richard S. Brown

make a number of potential employers aware of the availability and expertise of the job seeker. Because the broadcast letter is mass-mailed (500 to 600 employers), the amount of work required may not be worth the return for many people. If you choose to mail out a broadcast letter, you can expect to receive a response from 2 to 5 percent, at best, of the organizations that receive your letter.

This type of document is most often used by individuals who have an extensive and quantifiable work history. College students often do not have the credentials and work experience to support using a broadcast letter, and most will find it difficult to effectively quantify a slim work history.

A broadcast letter is generally four paragraphs (one page) long. The first paragraph should immediately gain the attention of the reader and state some unusual accomplishment or skill that would be of benefit to the organization. It also states the reason for the letter. These can appear in paragraph form or as a bulleted list. Details of the sender's work history are revealed in the third paragraph. Education and other qualifications or credentials are then described. Finally, the job seeker indicates what he or she will do to follow up on the letter, which usually is a follow-up call one to two weeks after the letter is sent.

RESUME PRODUCTION AND OTHER TIPS

If you have the option and convenience of using a laser printer, you may want to initially produce a limited number of copies in case you want or need to make changes on your resume.

Resume paper color should be carefully chosen. You should consider the types of employers who will receive your resume and the types of positions for which you are applying. Use white or ivory paper for traditional or conservative employers, or for higher-level positions.

Black ink on sharply white paper can be harsh on the reader's eyes. Think about an ivory or cream paper that will provide less contrast and be easier to read. Pink, green, and blue tints should generally be avoided.

Many resume writers buy packages of matching envelopes and cover sheet stationery that, although not absolutely necessary, does convey a professional impression.

If you'll be producing many cover letters at home, be sure you have high-quality printing equipment, whether it be computerized or standard typewriter equipment. Learn standard envelope formats for business and retain a copy of every cover letter you send out. You can use it to take notes of any telephone conversations that may occur.

If attending a job fair, women generally can fold their resume in thirds lengthwise and find it fits into a clutch bag or envelope-style purse. Both men and women will have no trouble if they carry a briefcase. For men without a briefcase, carry the resume in a nicely covered legal-size pad holder or fold it in half lengthwise and place it inside your suitcoat pocket, taking care it doesn't "float" outside your collar.

THE COVER LETTER

The cover letter provides you with the opportunity to tailor your resume by telling the prospective employer how you can be a benefit to the organization. It will allow you to highlight aspects of your background that are not already discussed in your resume and that might be especially relevant to the organization you are contacting or to the position you are seeking. Every resume should have a cover letter enclosed when you send it out. Unlike the resume, which may be mass-produced, a cover letter is most effective when it is individually typed and focused on the particular requirements of the organization in question.

A good cover letter should supplement the resume and motivate the reader to review the resume. The format shown in Exhibit 2.6 is only a suggestion to help you decide what information to include in writing a cover letter.

Exhibit 2.6

Cover Letter Format

Your Street Address
Your Town, State, Zip
Phone Number
Date
Name
Title
Organization
Address

Dear _____:

First Paragraph. In this paragraph, state the reason for the letter, name the specific position or type of work you are applying for,

continued

---

continued

and indicate from which resource (career development office, newspaper, contact, employment service) you learned of the opening. The first paragraph can also be used to inquire about future openings.

Second Paragraph. Indicate why you are interested in the position, the company, its products or services, and what you can do for the employer. If you are a recent graduate, explain how your academic background makes you a qualified candidate. Try not to repeat the same information found in the resume.

Third Paragraph. Refer the reader to the enclosed resume for more detailed information.

Fourth Paragraph. In this paragraph, say what you will do to follow up on your letter. For example, state that you will call by a certain date to set up an interview or to find out if the company will be recruiting in your area. Finish by indicating your willingness to answer any questions they may have. Be sure you have provided your phone number.

Sincerely,

Type your name

Enclosure

Begin the cover letter with your street address twelve lines down from the top. Leave three to five lines between the date and the name of the person to whom you are addressing the cover letter. Make sure you leave one blank line between the salutation and the body of the letter and between each paragraph.

After typing "Sincerely," leave four blank lines and type your name. This should leave plenty of room for your signature. A sample cover letter is shown in Exhibit 2.7.

The following are guidelines that will help you write good cover letters:

1. Be sure to type your letter; ensure there are no misspellings.

2. Avoid unusual typefaces, such as script.

Exhibit 2.7

Sample Cover Letter

15 Canal Street
Lockport, CA 98772
(312) 555-2236
March 5, 1998

Ms. Candace Kincaid
Director of Employment Services
California State Automobile Association
150 Vancouver Avenue
San Francisco, CA 94102

Dear Ms. Kincaid:

In December of 1998, I graduated from the Lockport campus of University College with a bachelor's degree in mathematics. I read of your opening for an actuarial analyst on The Monster Board—Job Details web page, and I am very interested in the possibilities it offers. I am writing to explore the opportunity for employment with the California State Automobile Association.

The advertisement indicated that you were looking for someone with knowledge of statistical methods, strong PC skills, and knowledge of insurance accounting concepts. I believe my resume outlines a work and education history that you will find interesting and relevant. My work with local businesses on evaluating advertising strategies has allowed me to gain analytical knowledge, and my communication skills were enhanced by presenting my findings to the local merchants. Courses in computer skills and accounting have added to my major course work, and I had some excellent relevant experience working with the psychology department on statistical evaluation of various experiments. These experiences will help me to represent the California State Automobile Association in a professional manner.

As you will see by my enclosed resume, I have had exposure to considerable technology at college and am thoroughly familiar with the personal line insurance you mention in your ad. In addition, I have completed one actuarial exam successfully.

continued

continued

I would like to meet with you to discuss how my education and experience would be consistent with your needs. I will contact your office next week to discuss the possibility of an interview. In the meantime, if you have any questions or require additional information, please contact me at my home, (312) 555-2236.

Sincerely,

Adam Cormier
Enclosure

3. Address the letter to an individual, using the person's name and title. To obtain this information, call the company. If answering a blind newspaper advertisement, address the letter "To Whom It May Concern" or omit the salutation.

4. Be sure your cover letter directly indicates the position you are applying for and tells why you are qualified to fill it.

5. Send the original letter, not a photocopy, with your resume. Keep a copy for your records.

6. Make your cover letter no more than one page.

7. Include a phone number where you can be reached.

8. Avoid trite language and have someone read it over to react to its tone, content, and mechanics.

9. For your own information, record the date you send out each letter and resume.

CHAPTER THREE

RESEARCHING CAREERS

Many math majors made their degree choice with the expectation that their degree would be the ticket to employment after graduation. But "mathematics" is a vast field, populated with thousands of job titles you have never heard before. You know that as a mathematics major you have been given an overview of algebraic structures, statistics, quantitative methods, probability, and discrete mathematics. However, you still may be confused as to exactly what kinds of jobs you can do with your degree and what kinds of organizations will hire you. Are management positions only reserved for business majors? Where does a mathematics major fit into a retail store or an insurance company, the airline industry, or the U.S. government?

WHAT DO THEY CALL THE JOB YOU WANT?

There is every reason to be unaware. One reason for confusion is perhaps a mistaken assumption that a college education provides job training. In most cases, it does not. Of course, applied fields such as engineering, management, or education provide specific skills for the workplace, whereas most liberal arts degrees simply provide an education. A liberal arts education exposes you to numerous fields of study and teaches you quantitative reasoning, critical thinking, writing, and speaking, all of which can be successfully applied to a number of different job fields. But it still remains up to you to choose a job field and to learn how to articulate the benefits of your education in a way the employer will appreciate.

As indicated in Chapter 1 on self-assessment, your first task is to understand and value what parts of that education you enjoyed and were good at and would continue to enjoy in your life's work. Did your writing courses encourage you in your ability to express yourself in writing? Did you enjoy the research process, and did you find your work was well received? Did you enjoy any of your required quantitative subjects like algebra or calculus?

The answers to questions such as these provide clues to skills and interests you bring to the employment market over and above the credential of your degree. In fact, it is not an overstatement to suggest that most employers who demand a college degree immediately look beyond that degree to you as a person and your own individual expression of what you like to do and think you can do for them, regardless of your major.

COLLECTING JOB TITLES

The world of employment is a big place, and even seasoned veterans of the job hunt can be surprised about what jobs are to be found in what organizations. You need to become a bit of an explorer and adventurer and be willing to try a variety of techniques to begin a list of possible occupations that might use your talents and education. Once you have a list of possibilities that you are interested in and qualified for, you can move on to find out what kinds of organizations have these job titles.

Not every employer seeking to hire someone with a mathematics degree may be equally desirable to you. Some employment environments may be more attractive to you than others. A mathematics major considering a career as a statistician could do that as a marketing/sales data analyst, a biostatistician with a leading research organization, or a statistician with the Department of Commerce or the U.S. Bureau of the Census. Though income production might be exactly the same for each job, each environment presents a different "culture" with associated norms in the pace of work, interaction with other people, and the background and training of those you'll work with or encounter on the job. Your job title might be the same in each situation, but not all situations present the same "fit" for you.

If you majored in mathematics and enjoyed the analytical projects you did as part of your degree and have developed some strong analytical skills, you might naturally think statistics. But mathematics majors with these same skills and interests go on to work as retail buyers, actuaries, operations research analysts, city administrators, mortgage officers, and teachers. Each job title in this list can be found in a variety of settings.

••

Take training, for example. Trainers write policy and procedural manuals and actively teach to assist all levels of employees in mastering various tasks and work-related systems. Trainers exist in all large corporations, banks, consumer goods manufacturers, medical diagnostic equipment firms, sales organizations, and any organization that has processes or materials that need to be presented to and learned by the staff.

In reading job descriptions or want ads for any of these positions, you would find your four-year degree a "must." However, the academic major might be less important than your own individual skills in critical thinking, analysis, report writing, public presentations, and interpersonal communication. Even more important than thinking or knowing you have certain skills is your ability to express those skills concretely and the examples you use to illustrate them to an employer.

The best beginning to a job search is to create a list of job titles you might want to pursue, learn more about the nature of the jobs behind those titles, and then discover what kinds of employers hire for those positions. In the following section, we'll teach you how to build a job title directory to use in your job search.

Developing a Job Title Directory That Works for You

A job title directory is simply a complete list of all the job titles you are interested in, are intrigued by, or think you are qualified for. Combining the understanding gained through self-assessment with your own individual interests and the skills and talents you've acquired with your degree, you'll soon start to read and recognize a number of occupational titles that seem right for you. There are several resources you can use to develop your list, including computer searches, books, and want ads.

Computerized Interest Inventories. One way to begin your search is to identify a number of jobs that call for your degree and the particular skills and interests you identified as part of the self-assessment process. There are excellent interactive computer career guidance programs on the market to help you produce such selected lists of possible job titles. Most of these are available at high schools and colleges and at some larger town and city libraries. Two of the industry leaders are SIGI and DISCOVER. Both allow you to enter interests, values, educational background, and other information to produce lists of possible occupations and industries. Each of the resources listed here will produce different job title lists. Some job titles will appear again and again, while others will be unique to a particular source. Investigate them all!

Reference Books. Books on the market that may be available through your local library, bookstore, or career counseling office also suggest various occupations related to a number of majors. The following are only two of the many good books on the market: *What Can I Do with a Major In . . . ? How to Choose and Use Your College Major,* by Lawrence R. Malnig with Anita Malnig, and *The Occupational Thesaurus. What Can I Do with a Major In . . . ?* lists job titles by academic major and identifies those jobs by their *Dictionary of Occupational Titles* (*DOT*) code. (See following discussion.)

· ·

For mathematics majors, approximately forty-eight job titles are listed. Some are familiar ones, such as mathematician or actuary, statistician and stockbroker. Others are interestingly different, such as environmental planner, efficiency expert, or cryptanalyst.

The *Occupational Thesaurus* is another good resource, which essentially lists job title possibilities under general categories. So, if as a mathematics major you discovered actuary as a job title in the book *What Can I Do with a Major in . . . ?,* you can then go to the *Occupational Thesaurus,* which lists scores of jobs under that title.

> Under "Insurance" there is a list of over ten associated job titles, including accountant, contract administrator, investment analyst, operations research analyst, and market researcher. If actuary was a suggested job title for you, this source adds some depth by suggesting a number of different occupational settings.

••

Each job title deserves your consideration. Like the layers of an onion, the search for job titles can go on and on! As you spend time doing this activity, you are actually learning more about the value of your degree. What's important in your search at this point is not to become critical or selective, but rather to develop as long a list of possibilities as you can. Every source used will help you add new and potentially exciting jobs to your growing list.

Want Ads. It has been well publicized that newspaper want ads represent only about 10 to 15 percent of the current job market. Nevertheless, the Sunday want ads can be a great help to you in your search. Although they may not be the best place to look for a job, they can teach the job seeker much about the job market and provide a good education in job descriptions, duties and responsibilities, active industries, and some indication of the volume of job traffic. For our purposes, they are a good source for job titles to add to your list.

Read the Sunday want ads in a major market newspaper for several Sundays in a row. Circle and cut out any and all ads that interest you and seem to call for something close to your education and experience. Remember, because want ads are written for what an organization *hopes* to find, you don't have to meet absolutely every criterion. However, if certain requirements are stated as absolute minimums and you cannot meet them, it's best not to waste your time.

A recent examination of *The Boston Sunday Globe* reveals the following possible occupations for a liberal arts major with some computer skills and limited prior work experience. (This is only a partial list of what was available.)

❏ Admissions representative	❏ Technical writer
❏ Salesperson	❏ Personnel trainee
❏ Compliance director	❏ GED examiner
❏ Assistant principal gifts writer	❏ Direct mail researcher
❏ Public relations officer	❏ Associate publicist

After performing this exercise for a few Sundays, you'll find you have collected a new library of job titles.

The Sunday want ad exercise is important because these jobs are out in the marketplace. They truly exist, and people with your qualifications are being sought to apply. What's more, many of these advertisements describe the duties and responsibilities of the job advertised and give you a beginning sense of the challenges and opportunities such a position presents. Some will indicate salary, and that will be helpful as well. This information will better define the jobs for you and provide some good material for possible interviews in that field.

Exploring Job Descriptions

Once you've arrived at a solid list of possible job titles that interest you and for which you believe you are somewhat qualified, it's a good idea to do some research on each of these jobs. The preeminent source for such job information is the *Dictionary of Occupational Titles,* or *DOT.* This directory lists every conceivable job and provides excellent up-to-date information on duties and responsibilities, interactions with associates, and day-to-day assignments and tasks. These descriptions provide a thorough job analysis, but they do not consider the possible employers or the environments in which this job may be performed. So, although a position as public relations officer may be well defined in terms of duties and responsibilities, it does not explain the differences in doing public relations work in a college or a hospital or a factory or a bank. You will need to look somewhere else for work settings.

Learning More about Possible Work Settings

After reading some job descriptions, you may choose to edit and revise your list of job titles once again, discarding those you feel are not suitable and keeping those that continue to hold your interest. Or you may wish to keep your list intact and see where these jobs may be located. For example, if you are interested in public relations and you appear to have those skills and the requisite education, you'll want to know what organizations do public relations. How can you find that out? How much income does someone in public relations make a year and what is the employment potential for the field of public relations?

To answer these and many other good questions about your list of job titles, we will direct you to any of the following resources: *Careers Encyclopedia, Career Information Center, College to Career: The Guide to Job Opportunities,* and the *Occupational Outlook Handbook.* Each of these books, in a different way, will help to put the job titles you have selected into an employer context. *VGM's Handbook of Business and Management Careers* shows detailed career descriptions for over fifty fields. Entries include complete information on duties and responsibilities for individual careers and detailed entry-level requirements. There is information on working conditions and promotional opportunities as well. Salary ranges and career outlook projections are also provided. Perhaps the most extensive discussion is found in the *Occupational Outlook Handbook,* which gives a thorough presentation of the nature of the work, the working conditions, employment statistics, training, other qualifications, and advancement possibilities as well as job outlook and earnings. Related occupations are also detailed, and a select bibliography is provided to help you find additional information.

Continuing with our public relations example, your search through these reference materials would teach you that the public relations jobs you find attractive are available in larger hospitals, financial institutions, most corporations (both consumer goods and industrial goods), media organizations, and colleges and universities.

Networking to Get the Complete Story

You now have not only a list of job titles but also, for each of these job titles, a description of the work involved and a general list of possible employment settings in which to work. You'll want to do some reading and keep talking to friends, colleagues, teachers, and others about the possibilities. Don't neglect to ask if the career office at your college maintains some kind of alumni network. Often such alumni networks will connect you with another graduate from the college who is working in the job title or industry you are seeking information about. These career networkers offer what assistance they can. For some, it is a full day "shadowing" the alumnus as he or she goes about the job. Others offer partial day visits, tours, informational interviews, resume reviews, job postings, or, if distance prevents a visit, telephone interviews. As fellow graduates, they'll be frank and informative about their own jobs and prospects in their field.

Take them up on their offer and continue to learn all you can about your own personal list of job titles, descriptions, and employment settings. You'll probably continue to edit and refine this list as you learn more about the realities of the job, the possible salary, advancement opportunities, and supply and demand statistics.

In the next section, we'll describe how to find the specific organizations that represent these industries and employers, so that you can begin to make contact.

WHERE ARE THESE JOBS, ANYWAY?

Having a list of job titles that you've designed around your own career interests and skills is an excellent beginning. It means you've really thought about who you are and what you are presenting to the employment market. It has caused you to think seriously about the most appealing environments to work in, and you have identified some employer types that represent these environments.

The research and the thinking that you've done this far will be used again and again. It will be helpful in writing your resume and cover letters, in talking about yourself on the telephone to prospective employers, and in answering interview questions.

Now is a good time to begin to narrow the field of job titles and employment sites down to some specific employers to initiate the employment contact.

Finding Out Which Employers Hire People Like You

This section will provide tips, techniques, and specific resources for developing an actual list of specific employers that can be used to make contacts. It is only an outline that you must be prepared to tailor to your own particular needs and according to what you bring to the job search. Once again, it is important to stress the need to communicate with others along the way exactly what you're looking for and what your goals are for the research you're doing. Librarians, employers, career counselors, friends, friends of friends, business contacts, and bookstore staff will all have helpful information on geographically specific and new resources to aid you in locating employers who'll hire you.

Identifying Information Resources

Your interview wardrobe and your new resume may have put a dent in your wallet, but the resources you'll need to pursue your job search are available for free (although you might choose to copy materials on a machine instead of taking notes by hand). The categories of information detailed here are not hard to find and are yours for the browsing.

Numerous resources described in this section will help you identify actual employers. Use all of them or any others that you identify as available in your geographic area. As you become experienced in this process, you'll quickly figure out which information sources are helpful and which are not. If you live in a rural area, a well-planned day trip to a major city that includes a college career office, a large college or city library, state and federal employment centers, a chamber of commerce office, and a well-stocked bookstore can produce valuable results.

There are many excellent resources available to help you identify actual job sites. They are categorized into employer directories (usually indexed by product lines and geographic location), geographically based directories (designed to highlight particular cities, regions, or states), career-specific directories (e.g., *Sports Market Place,* which lists tens of thousands of firms involved with sports), periodicals and newspapers, targeted job posting publications, and videos. This is by no means meant to be a complete list of resources, but rather a starting point for identifying useful resources.

Working from the more general references to highly specific resources, we will provide a basic list to help you begin your search. Many of these you'll find easily available. In some cases, reference librarians and others will suggest even better materials for your particular situation. Start to create your own customized bibliography of job search references. Use copying services to save time and to allow you to carry away information about organization mission, location, company officers, phone numbers, and addresses.

Employer Directories. There are many employer directories available to give you the kind of information you need for your job search. Some of our favorites are listed here, but be sure to ask the professionals you are working with to make additional suggestions.

❑ *America's Corporate Families* identifies many major U.S. ultimate parent companies and displays corporate family linkage of subsidiaries and divisions. Businesses can be identified by their industrial code.

❑ *Million Dollar Directory: America's Leading Public and Private Companies* lists about 160,000 companies.

❑ *Moody's* various manuals are intended as guides for investors, so they contain a history of each company. Each manual contains a classification of companies by industries and products.

❑ *Standard and Poor's Register of Corporations* contains listings for 45,000 businesses, some of which are not listed in the *Million Dollar Directory.*

❑ *Job Seeker's Guide to Private and Public Companies* profiles 15,000 employers in four volumes, each covering a different geographic region. Company entries include contact information, business descriptions, and application procedures.

❑ *The Career Guide: Dun's Employment Opportunities Directory* lists more than 5,000 large organizations, including hospitals and local governments. Profiles include an overview and history of the employer as well as opportunities, benefits, and contact names. It contains geographic and industrial indexes and indexes by discipline or internship availability. This guide also includes a state-by-state list of professional personnel consultants and their specialties.

❑ *Professional's Job Finder/Government Job Finder/Non-Profits Job Finder* are specific directories of job services, salary surveys, and periodical listings in which advertisements for jobs in the professional, government, or not-for-profit sector are found.

❑ *Opportunities in Nonprofit Organizations* is a VGM career series edition that opens up the world of not-for-profit by helping you match your interest profile to the aims and objectives of scores of nonprofit employers in business, education, health and medicine, social welfare, science and technology, and many others. There is also a special section on fund-raising and development career paths.

❑ *The 100 Best Companies to Sell For* lists companies by industry and provides contact information and describes benefits and corporate culture.

❑ *The 100 Best Companies to Work for in America* rates organizations on several factors including opportunities, job security, and pay.

❑ *Companies That Care* lists organizations that the authors believe are family-friendly. One index organizes information by state.

❑ *Infotrac CD-ROM Business Index* covers business journals and magazines as well as news magazines and can provide information on public and private companies.

❑ *ABI/Inform On Disc* (CD-ROM) indexes articles in over 800 journals.

Geographically Based Directories. The Job Bank series published by Bob Adams, Inc., contains detailed entries on each area's major employers, including business activity, address, phone number, and hiring contact name. Many listings specify educational backgrounds being sought in potential employees. Each volume contains a solid discussion of each city's or state's major employment sectors. Organizations are also indexed by industry. Job Bank volumes are available for the following places: Atlanta, Boston, Chicago, Denver, Dallas–Ft. Worth, Florida, Houston, Ohio, St. Louis, San Francisco,

Seattle, Los Angeles, New York, Detroit, Philadelphia, Minneapolis, the Northwest, and Washington, D.C.

National Job Bank lists employers in every state, along with contact names and commonly hired job categories. Included are many small companies often overlooked by other directories. Companies are also indexed by industry. This publication provides information on educational backgrounds sought and lists company benefits.

Career-Specific Directories. VGM publishes a number of excellent series detailing careers for college graduates. In the *Professional Career Series* are guides to careers in the following fields, among others:

- ❑ Advertising

- ❑ Communications

- ❑ Business

- ❑ Computers

- ❑ Health Care

- ❑ High Tech

Each provides an excellent discussion of the industry, educational requirements for jobs, salary ranges, duties, and projected outlooks for the field.

Another VGM series, *Opportunities In . . .* , has an equally wide range of titles relating to specific majors, such as the following:

- ❑ *Opportunities in Banking*

- ❑ *Opportunities in Insurance*

- ❑ *Opportunities in Sports and Athletics*

- ❑ *Opportunities in Journalism*

- ❑ *Opportunities in Law*

- ❑ *Opportunities in Marketing*

- ❑ *Opportunities in Television and Radio*

Sports Market Place (Sportsguide) lists organizations by sport. It also describes trade/professional associations, college athletic organizations, multi-sport publications, media contacts, corporate sports sponsors, promotion/event athletic management services, and trade shows.

Periodicals and Newspapers. Several sources are available to help you locate which journals or magazines carry job advertisements in your field. Other resources help you identify opportunities in other parts of the country.

❑ *Where the Jobs Are: A Comprehensive Directory of 1,200 Journals Listing Career Opportunities* links specific occupational titles to corresponding periodicals that carry job listings for your field.

❑ *Social & Behavioral Sciences Jobs Handbook* contains a periodicals matrix organized by academic discipline and highlights periodicals containing job listings.

❑ *National Business Employment Weekly* compiles want ads from four regional editions of the *Wall Street Journal.* Most are business and management positions.

❑ *National Ad Search* reprints ads from seventy-five metropolitan newspapers across the country. Although the focus is on management positions, technical and professional postings are also included. *Caution:* Watch deadline dates carefully on listings, because deadlines may have already passed by the time the ad is printed.

❑ *The Federal Jobs Digest* and *Federal Career Opportunities* list government positions.

❑ *World Chamber of Commerce Directory* lists addresses for chambers worldwide, state boards of tourism, convention and visitors' bureaus, and economic development organizations.

This list is certainly not exhaustive; use it to begin your job search work.

Targeted Job Posting Publications. Although the resources that follow are national in scope, they are either targeted to one medium of contact (telephone), focused on specific types of jobs, or are less comprehensive than the sources previously listed.

❑ *Job Hotlines USA* pinpoints over 1,000 hard-to-find telephone numbers for companies and government agencies that use prerecorded job messages and listings. Very few of the telephone numbers listed are toll-free, and sometimes recordings are long, so callers beware!

❑ *The Job Hunter* is a national biweekly newspaper listing business, arts, media, government, human services, health, community-related, and student services job openings.

- *Current Jobs for Graduates* is a national employment listing for liberal arts professions, including editorial positions, management opportunities, museum work, teaching, and nonprofit work.

- *Environmental Opportunities* serves environmental job interests nationwide by listing administrative, marketing, and human resources positions along with education-related jobs and positions directly related to a degree in an environmental field.

- *Y National Vacancy List* shows YMCA professional vacancies, including development, administration, programming, membership, and recreation postings.

- *ARTSearch is* a national employment service bulletin for the arts, including administration, managerial, marketing, and financial management jobs.

- *Community Jobs* is an employment newspaper for the nonprofit sector that provides a variety of listings, including project manager, canvas director, government relations specialist, community organizer, and program instructor.

- *College Placement Council Annual: A Guide to Employment Opportunities for College Graduates* is an annual guide containing solid job-hunting information and, more importantly, displaying ads from large corporations actively seeking recent college graduates in all majors. Company profiles provide brief descriptions and available employment opportunities. Contact names and addresses are given. Profiles are indexed by organization name, geographic location, and occupation.

Videos. You may be one of the many job seekers who like to get information via a medium other than paper. Many career libraries, public libraries, and career centers in libraries carry an assortment of videos that will help you learn new techniques and get information helpful in the job search. A small sampling of the multitude of videos now available includes the following:

- *The Skills Search* (20 min.) discusses three types of skills important in the workplace, how to present the skills in an interview, and how to respond to problem questions.

- *Effective Answers to Interview Questions* (35 min.) presents two real-life job seekers and shows how they realized the true meaning of interview questions and formulated positive answers.

❑ *Employer's Expectations* (33 min.) covers three areas that are important to all employers: appearance, dependability, and skills.

❑ *The Tough New Labor Market of the 1990s* (30 min.) presents labor market facts as well as suggestions on what job seekers should do to gain employment in this market.

❑ *Dialing for Jobs: Using the Phone in the Job Search* (30 min.) describes how to use the phone effectively to gain information and arrange interviews by following two new graduates as they learn and apply techniques.

Locating Information Resources

The job market is changing, and the old guarantees of lifelong employment no longer hold true. Some of our major corporations, which were once seen as the most prestigious of employment destinations, are now laying off thousands of employees. Middle management is especially hard hit in downsizing situations. On the other side of the coin, smaller, more entrepreneurial firms are adding employees and realizing enormous profit margins. The geography of the new job market is unfamiliar, and the terrain is much harder to map. New and smaller firms can mean different kinds of jobs and new job titles. The successful job seeker will keep an open mind about where he or she might find employment and what that employment might be called.

In order to become familiar with this new terrain, you will need to undertake some research, which can be done at any of the following locations:

❑ Public libraries

❑ Business organizations

❑ Employment agencies

❑ Bookstores

❑ Career libraries

Each one of these places offers a collection of resources that will help you get the information you need.

As you meet and talk with service professionals at all these sites, be sure to let them know what you're doing. Inform them of your job search, what you've already accomplished, and what you're looking for. The more people who know you're job seeking, the greater the possibility that someone will have information or know someone who can help you along your way.

Public Libraries. Large city libraries, college and university libraries, and even well-supported town library collections contain a variety of resources to help you conduct a job search. It is not uncommon for libraries to have separate "vocational choices" sections with books, tapes, and associated materials relating to job search and selection. Some are now even making resume creation software available for use by patrons.

Some of the publications we name throughout this book are expensive reference items that are rarely purchased by individuals. In addition, libraries carry a wide range of newspapers and telephone yellow pages as well as the usual array of books. If resources are not immediately available, many libraries have loan arrangements with other facilities and can make information available to you relatively quickly.

Take advantage of not only the reference collections, but also the skilled and informed staff. Let them know exactly what you are looking for, and they'll have their own suggestions. You'll be visiting the library frequently, and the reference staff will soon come to know who you are and what you're working on. They'll be part of your job search network!

Business Organizations. Chambers of Commerce, Offices of New Business Development, Councils on Business and Industry, Small Business Administration (SBA) offices, and professional associations can all provide geographically specific lists of companies and organizations that have hiring needs. They also have an array of other available materials, including visitors' guides and regional fact books that provide additional employment information.

These agencies serve to promote local and regional businesses and ensure their survival and success. Although these business organizations do not advertise job openings or seek employees for their members, they may be very aware of staffing needs among their member firms. In your visits to each of these locations, spend some time with the personnel getting to know who they are and what they do. Let them know of your job search and your intentions regarding employment. You may be surprised and delighted at the information they may provide.

Employment Agencies. Employment agencies (including state and federal employment offices) professional "headhunters" or executive search firms, and some private career counselors can provide direct leads to job openings. Don't overlook these resources. If you are mounting a complete job search program and want to ensure that you are covering the potential market for employers, consider the employment agencies in your territory. Some of these organizations work contractually with several specific firms and may have access that is unavailable to you. Others may be particularly well-informed about supply and demand in particular industries or geographic locations.

In the case of professional (commercial) employment agencies, which include those executive recruitment firms labeled "headhunters," you should be cautious about entering into any binding contractual agreement. Before doing so, be sure to get the information you need to decide whether their services can be of use to you. Questions to ask include the following: Who pays the fee when employment is obtained? Are there any other fees or costs associated with this service? What is their placement rate? Can you see a list of previous clients and can you talk to any for references? Do they typically work with entry-level job seekers? Do they tend to focus on particular kinds of employment or industries?

A few cautions are in order, however, when you work with professional agencies. Remember, the professional employment agency is, in most cases, paid by the hiring organization. Naturally, their interest and attention is largely directed to the employer, not to the candidate. Of course, they want to provide good candidates to guarantee future contracts, but they are less interested in the job seeker than the employer.

For teacher candidates, there are a number of good placement firms that charge the prospective teacher, not the employer. This situation has evolved over time as a result of supply and demand and financial structuring of most school systems, which cannot spend money on recruiting teachers. Usually these firms charge a nonrefundable administrative fee and, upon successful placement, require a fee based on percentage of salary, which may range from 10 to 20 percent of annual compensation. Often, this can be repaid over a number of months. Check your contract carefully.

State and federal employment offices are no-fee services that maintain extensive "job boards" and can provide detailed specifications for each job advertised and help with application forms. Because government employment application forms are detailed, keep a master copy along with copies of all additional documentation (resumes, educational transcripts, military discharge papers, proof of citizenship, etc.). Successive applications may require separate filings. Visit these offices as frequently as you can, because most deal with applicants on a "walk-in" basis and will not telephone prospective candidates or maintain files of job seekers. Check your telephone book for the address of the nearest state and federal offices.

One type of employment service that causes much confusion among job seekers is the outplacement firm. Their advertisements tend to suggest they will put you in touch with the "hidden job market." They use advertising phrases such as "We'll work with you until you get that job," or "Maximize your earnings and career opportunities." In fact, if you read the fine print on these ads, you will notice these firms must state they are "Not an employment agency." These firms are, in fact, corporate and private outplacement counseling agencies whose work involves resume editing, counseling to provide leads for jobs, interview skills training, and all the other aspects of hiring preparation. They do this for a fee, sometimes in the thousands of dollars, which is paid by you, the client. Some of these firms have good reputations and provide excellent materials and techniques. Most, however, provide a service you as a college student or graduate can receive free from your alma mater or through a reciprocity agreement between your college and a college or university located closer to your current address.

Bookstores. Any well-stocked bookstore will carry some job search books that are worth buying. Some major stores will even have an extensive section devoted to materials, including excellent videos, related to the job search process. Several possibilities are listed in following sections. You will also find copies of local newspapers and business magazines. The one advantage that is provided by resources purchased at a bookstore is that you can read and work with the information in the comfort of your own home and do not have to conform to the hours of operation of a library, which can present real difficulties if you are working full-time as you seek employment. A few minutes spent browsing in a bookstore might be a beneficial break from your job search activities and turn up valuable resources.

Career Libraries. Career libraries, which are found in career centers at colleges and universities and sometimes within large public libraries, contain a unique blend of the job search resources housed in other settings. In addition, career libraries often purchase a number of job listing publications, each of which targets a specific industry or type of job. You may find job listings specifically for entry-level positions for liberal arts majors. Ask about job posting newsletters or newspapers specifically focused on careers in the area that most interests you. Each center will be unique, but you are certain to discover some good sources of jobs.

Most college career libraries now hold growing collections of video material on specific industries and on aspects of your job search process, including dress and appearance, how to manage the luncheon or dinner interview, how to be effective at a job fair, and many other specific titles. Some larger corporations produce handsome video materials detailing the variety of career paths and opportunities available in their organizations.

Some career libraries also house computer-based career planning and information systems. These interactive computer programs help you to clarify your values and interests and will combine that with your education to provide possible job titles and industry locations. Some even contain extensive lists of graduate school programs.

One specific kind of service a career library will be able to direct you to is computerized job search services. These services, of which there are many, are run by private companies, individual colleges, or consortiums of colleges. They attempt to match qualified job candidates with potential employers. The candidate submits a resume (or an application) to the service. This information (which can be categorized into hundreds of separate "fields" of data) is entered into a computer database. Your information is then compared with the information from employers about what they desire in a prospective employee. If there is a "match" between what they want and what you have indicated you can offer, the job search service or the employer will contact you directly to continue the process.

Computerized job search services can complement an otherwise complete job search program. They are *not*, however, a substitute for the kinds of activities described in this book. They are essentially passive operations that are random in nature. If you have not listed skills, abilities, traits, experiences, or education *exactly* as an employer has listed its needs, there is simply no match.

Consult with the staff members at the career libraries you use. These professionals have been specifically trained to meet the unique needs you present. Often you can just drop in and receive help with general questions, or you may want to set up an appointment to speak one-on-one with a career counselor to gain special assistance.

Every career library is different in size and content, but each can provide valuable information for the job search. Some may even provide some limited counseling. If you have not visited the career library at your college or alma mater, call and ask if these collections are still available for your use. Be sure to ask about other services that you can use as well.

If you are not near your own college as you work on your job search, call the career office and inquire about reciprocal agreements with other colleges that are closer to where you live. Very often, your own alma mater can arrange for you to use a limited menu of services at another school. This typically would include access to a career library and job posting information and might include limited counseling.

CHAPTER FOUR

NETWORKING

*N*etworking is the process of deliberately establishing relationships to get career-related information or to alert potential employers that you are available for work. Networking is critically important to today's job seeker for two reasons: it will help you get the information you need, and it can help you find out about *all* of the available jobs.

Getting the Information You Need

Networkers will review your resume and give you candid feedback on its effectiveness. They will talk about the job you are looking for and give you a candid appraisal of how they see your strengths and weaknesses. If they have a good sense of the industry or the employment sector for that job, you'll get their feelings on future trends in the industry as well. Some networkers will be very candid about salaries, job hunting techniques, and suggestions for your job search strategy. Many have been known to place calls right from the interview desk to friends and associates that might be interested in you. Each networker will make his or her own contribution, and each will be valuable.

Because organizations must evolve to adapt to current global market needs, the information provided by decision-makers within various organizations will be critical to your success as a new job market entrant. For example, you might learn about the concept of virtual organizations from a networker. Virtual organizations are those that are temporarily established to take advantage of fast-changing opportunities and then dissolved. This concept is being discussed and implemented by chief executive officers of many organizations, including Corning, Apple, and Digital. Networking can help you find out about this and other trends currently affecting the industries under your consideration.

Finding Out About All of the Available Jobs

Secondly, not every job that is available at this very moment is advertised for potential applicants to see. This is called the *hidden job market*. Only 15 to 20 percent of all jobs are formally advertised, which means that 80 to 85 percent of available jobs do not appear in published channels. Networking will help you become more knowledgeable about all the employment opportunities available during your job search period.

Although someone you might talk to today doesn't know of any openings within his or her organization, tomorrow or next week or next month an opening may occur. If you've taken the time to show an interest in and knowledge of their organization, if you've shown the company representative how you can help achieve organizational goals and that you can fit into the organization, you'll be one of the first candidates considered for the position.

Networking: A Proactive Approach

Networking is a proactive rather than a reactive approach. You, as a job seeker, are expected to initiate a certain level of activity on your own behalf; you cannot afford to simply respond to jobs listed in the newspaper. Being proactive means building a network of contacts that includes informed and interested decision-makers who will provide you with up-to-date knowledge of the current job market and increase your chances of finding out about employment opportunities appropriate for your interests, experience, and level of education.

An old axiom of networking says, "You are only two phone calls away from the information you need." In other words, by talking to enough people, you will quickly come across someone who can offer you help. Start with your professors. Each of them probably has a wide circle of contacts. In their work and travel they might have met someone who can help you or direct you to someone who can.

Control and the Networking Process

In deliberately establishing relationships, the process of networking begins with you in control—*you* are contacting specific individuals. As your network expands and you establish a set of professional relationships, your search for information or jobs will begin to move outside of your total control. A part of the networking process involves others assisting you by gathering information for you or recommending you as a possible job candidate. As additional people become a part of your networking system, you will have less knowledge about activities undertaken on your behalf; you will undoubtedly be contacted by individuals whom you did not initially approach. If you want to function effectively in surprise situations, you must be prepared at all times to talk with strangers about the informational or employment needs that motivated you to become involved in the networking process.

PREPARING TO NETWORK

In deliberately establishing relationships, maximize your efforts by organizing your approach. Five specific areas in which you can organize your efforts include reviewing your self-assessment, reviewing your research on job sites and organizations, deciding who it is you want to talk to, keeping track of all your efforts, and creating your self-promotion tools.

Review Your Self-Assessment

Your self-assessment is as important a tool in preparing to network as it has been in other aspects of your job search. You have carefully evaluated your personal traits, personal values, economic needs, longer-term goals, skill base, preferred skills, and underdeveloped skills. During the networking process you will be called upon to communicate what you know about yourself and relate it to the information or job you seek. Be sure to review the exercises that you completed in the self-assessment section of this book in preparation for networking. We've explained that you need to assess what skills you have acquired from your major that are of general value to an employer and to be ready to express those in ways employers can appreciate as useful in their own organizations.

Review Researching Job Sites and Organizations

In addition, individuals assisting you will expect that you'll have at least some background information on the occupation or industry of interest to you. Refer to the appropriate sections of this book and other relevant publications to acquire the background information necessary for effective networking. They'll explain how to identify not only the job titles that might be of interest to you, but also what kinds of organizations employ people to do that job. You will develop some sense of working conditions and expectations about duties and responsibilities—all of which will be of help in your networking interviews.

Decide Who It Is You Want to Talk To

Networking cannot begin until you decide who it is that you want to talk to and, in general, what type of information you hope to gain from your contacts. Once you know this, it's time to begin developing a list of contacts. Five useful sources for locating contacts are described here.

College Alumni Network. Most colleges and universities have created a formal network of alumni and friends of the institution who are particularly interested in helping currently enrolled students and graduates of their alma mater gain employment-related information.

∙∙∙∙∙∙∙∙∙∙∙∙∙∙∙∙∙∙∙∙∙∙∙∙∙∙∙∙∙∙∙∙∙∙∙∙∙∙∙

Because the mathematics major covers such a broad spectrum of human activity, you'll find mathematics majors employed in every sector of the economy: government, business, and nonprofit. The diversity of employment as evidenced by an alumni list from your college or university should be encouraging and informative to the mathematics graduate. Among such a diversified group, there are likely to be scores you would enjoy talking with and perhaps could meet. Some might be working quite far from you, but that does not preclude a telephone call or exchange of correspondence.

∙∙∙∙∙∙∙∙∙∙∙∙∙∙∙∙∙∙∙∙∙∙∙∙∙∙∙∙∙∙∙∙∙∙∙∙∙∙∙

It is usually a simple process to make use of an alumni network. You need only visit the alumni or career office at your college or university and follow the procedure that has been established. Often, you will simply complete a form indicating your career goals and interests and you will be given the names of appropriate individuals to contact. In many cases, staff members will coach you on how to make the best use of the limited time these alumni contacts may have available for you.

Alumni networkers may provide some combination of the following services: day-long shadowing experiences, telephone interviews, in-person interviews, information on relocating to given geographic areas, internship information, suggestions on graduate school study, and job vacancy notices.

∙∙∙∙∙∙∙∙∙∙∙∙∙∙∙∙∙∙∙∙∙∙∙∙∙∙∙∙∙∙∙∙∙∙∙∙∙∙∙

What a valuable experience! If you are interested in an operations research position with the government, you may be concerned about your degree preparation and whether you would be considered eligible to work in this field. Spending a day with an alumnus who works as an operations researcher for the government, asking questions about his or her educational preparation and training, will give you a more concrete view of the possibilities for your degree. Observing firsthand how this person does the job and exactly what the job entails is a far better decision criterion for you than just reading on the subject could possibly provide.

··

Present and Former Supervisors. If you believe you are on good terms with present or former job supervisors, they may be an excellent resource for providing information or directing you to appropriate resources that would have information related to your current interests and needs. Additionally, these supervisors probably belong to professional organizations, which they might be willing to utilize to get information for you.

··

If, for example, you were interested in working as an account representative for a telecommunications company, and you are currently working on the wait staff of a local restaurant, talk with your supervisor or the owner. He or she may belong to the local chamber of commerce, whose director might have information on members affiliated with the telecommunications industry in your area. You would probably be able to obtain the names and business telephone numbers of those people, which would allow you to begin the networking process.

··

Employers in Your Area. Although you may be interested in working in a geographic location different from the one where you currently reside, don't overlook the value of the knowledge and contacts those around you are able to provide. Use the local telephone directory and newspaper to identify the types of organizations you are thinking of working for or professionals who have the kinds of jobs you are interested in. Recently, a call made to a local hospital's financial administrator for information on working in health care financial administration yielded more pertinent information on training seminars, regional professional organizations, and potential employment sites than a national organization was willing to provide.

Employers in Geographic Areas Where You Hope to Work. If you are thinking about relocating, identifying prospective employers or informational contacts in this new location will be critical to your success. Many resources are available to help you locate contact names. These include the yellow pages directory, the local newspapers, local or state business publications, and local chambers of commerce.

Professional Associations and Organizations. Professional associations and organizations can provide valuable information in several areas: career paths that you may not have considered, qualifications relating to those career choices, publications that list current job openings, and workshops or seminars that will enhance your professional knowledge and skills. They can also be excellent sources for background information on given industries: their health, current problems, and future challenges.

There are several excellent resources available to help you locate professional associations and organizations that would have information to meet your needs. Two especially useful publications are the *Encyclopedia of Associations* and the *National Trade and Professional Associations of the United States.*

Keep Track of All Your Efforts

It can be difficult, almost impossible, to remember all the details related to each contact you make during the networking process, so you will want to develop a record-keeping system that works for you. Formalize this process by using a notebook or index cards to organize the information you gather. Begin by creating a list of the people or organizations you want to contact. Record the contact's name, address, telephone number, and what information you hope to gain. Each entry might look something like this:

Contact Name	Address	Phone #	Purpose
Mr. Tim Keefe	Wrigley Bldg.		
Dir. of Mines	Suite 72	555-8906	Resume screen

Once you have created this initial list, it will be helpful to keep more detailed information as you begin to actually make the contacts. Using the Network Contact Record form in Exhibit 4.1, keep good information on all your network contacts. They'll appreciate your recall of details of your meetings and conversations, and the information will help you to focus your networking efforts.

Exhibit 4.1

Network Contact Record

Name: Be certain your spelling is absolutely correct.

Title: Pick up a business card to be certain of the correct title.

Employing organization: Note any parent company or subsidiaries.

Business mailing address: This is often different from the street address.

Business telephone number: Include area code/alternative numbers/fax.

Source for this contact: Who referred you, and what is their relationship?

Date of call or letter: Use plenty of space here to record multiple phone calls or visits, other employees you may have met, names of secretaries/receptionists, etc.

Content of discussion: Keep enough notes here to remind you of the substance of your visits and telephone conversations in case some time elapses between contacts.

Follow-up necessary to continue working with this contact: Your contact may request that you send him or her some materials or direct you to contact an associate. Note any such instructions or assignments in this space.

Name of additional networker: Here you would record the
Address: names and phone numbers of
Phone: additional contacts met at this
Name of additional networker: employer's site. Often you will
Address: be introduced to many people,
Phone: some of whom may indicate
Name of additional networker: a willingness to help in your
Address: job search.
Phone:

Date thank-you note written: May help to date your next contact.

Follow-up action taken: Phone calls, visits, additional notes.

continued

continued

Other miscellaneous notes: Record any other additional
interaction you may find is
important to remember in working
with this networking client. You will
want this form in front of you when
telephoning or just before and after
a visit.

Create Your Self-Promotion Tools

There are two types of promotional tools that are used in the networking process. The first is a resume and cover letter, and the second is a one-minute "infomercial," which may be given over the telephone or in person.

Techniques for writing an effective resume and cover letter are covered in Chapter 2. Once you have reviewed that material and prepared these important documents, you will have created one of your self-promotion tools.

The one-minute infomercial will demand that you begin tying your interests, abilities, and skills to the people or organizations you want to network with. Think about your goal for making the contact to help you understand what you should say about yourself. You should be able to express yourself easily and convincingly. If, for example, you are contacting an alumnus of your institution to obtain the names of possible employment sites in a distant city, be prepared to discuss why you are interested in moving to that location, the types of jobs you are interested in, and the skills and abilities you possess that will make you a qualified candidate.

To create a meaningful one-minute infomercial, write it out, practice it if it will be a spoken presentation, rewrite it, and practice it again if necessary until expressing yourself comes easily and is convincing.

Here's a simplified example of an infomercial for use over the telephone:

•••

Hello, Mr. Hudson? My name is Mandie Dexter. I am a
recent graduate of Central College, and I wish to enter
the investment field. I feel confident I have many of the
skills I understand are valued for consultants in investment. I have a strong quantitative background, with good
research and computer skills. In addition, I have excellent

interpersonal skills and am known as a focused, goal-oriented individual. I understand these are valuable traits in your line of work!

Mr. Hudson, I'm calling you because I still need more information about the investment field and where I might fit in. I'm hoping you'll have time to sit down with me for about half an hour and discuss your perspective on careers in investment consulting with me. There are so many possible employers to approach, and I am seeking some advice on which might be the best bet for my particular combination of skills and experience.

Would you be willing to do that for me? I would greatly appreciate it. I am available most mornings, if that's convenient for you.

· ·

Other effective self-promotion tools include portfolios for those in the arts, writing professions, or teaching. Portfolios show examples of work, photographs of projects or classroom activities, or certificates and credentials that are job related. There may not be an opportunity to use the portfolio during an interview, and it is not something that should be left with the organization. It is designed to be explained and displayed by the creator. However, during some networking meetings, there may be an opportunity to illustrate a point or strengthen a qualification by exhibiting the portfolio.

BEGINNING THE NETWORKING PROCESS

Set the Tone for Your Contacts

It can be useful to establish "tone words" for any communications you embark upon. Before making your first telephone call or writing your first letter, decide what you want your contact to think of you. If you are networking to try obtain a job, your tone words might include words like *genuine, informed,* and *self-knowledgeable.* When trying to acquire information, your tone words may have a slightly different focus, such as *courteous, organized, focused,* and *well-spoken.* Use the tone words you establish for your contacts to guide you through the networking process.

Honestly Express Your Intentions

When contacting individuals, it is important to be honest about your reasons for making the contact. Establish your purpose in your own mind and be able and ready to articulate it concisely. Determine an initial agenda, whether it be informational questioning or self-promotion, present it to your contact, and be ready to respond immediately. If you don't adequately prepare before initiating your contacts, you may find yourself at a disadvantage if you're asked to immediately begin your informational interview or self-promotion during the first phone conversation or visit.

Start Networking Within Your Circle of Confidence

Once you have organized your approach—by utilizing specific researching methods, creating a system for keeping track of the people you will contact, and developing effective self-promotion tools—you are ready to begin networking. The best place to begin networking is by talking with a group of people you trust and feel comfortable with. This group is usually made up of your family, friends, and career counselors. No matter who is in this inner circle, they will have a special interest in seeing you succeed in your job search. In addition, because they will be easy to talk to, you should try taking some risks in terms of practicing your information-seeking approach. Gain confidence in talking about the strengths you bring to an organization and the underdeveloped skills you feel hinder your candidacy. Be sure to review the section on self-assessment for tips on approaching each of these areas. Ask for critical but constructive feedback from the people in your circle of confidence on the letters you write and the one-minute infomercial you have developed. Evaluate whether you want to make the changes they suggest, then practice the changes on others within this circle.

Stretch the Boundaries of Your Networking Circle of Confidence

Once you have refined the promotional tools you will use to accomplish your networking goals, you will want to make additional contacts. Because you will not know most of these people, it will be a less comfortable activity to undertake. The practice that you gained with your inner circle of trusted friends should have prepared you to now move outside of that comfort zone.

It is said that any information a person needs is only two phone calls away, but the information cannot be gained until you (1) make a reasonable guess about who might have the information you need and (2) pick up the telephone to make the call. Using your network list that includes alumni, instructors, supervisors, employers, and associations, you can begin preparing your list of questions that will allow you to get the information you need. Review the question list shown below and then develop a list of your own.

Questions You Might Want to Ask

1. In the position you now hold, what do you do on a typical day?

2. What are the most interesting aspects of your job?

3. What part of your work do you consider dull or repetitious?

4. What were the jobs you had that led to your present position?

5. How long does it usually take to move from one step to the next in this career path?

6. What is the top position to which you can aspire in this career path?

7. What is the next step in *your* career path?

8. Are there positions in this field that are similar to your position?

9. What are the required qualifications and training for entry-level positions in this field?

10. Are there specific courses a student should take to be qualified to work in this field?

11. What are the entry-level jobs in this field?

12. What types of training are provided to persons entering this field?

13. What are the salary ranges your organization typically offers to entry-level candidates for positions in this field?

14. What special advice would you give a person entering this field?

15. Do you see this field as a growing one?

16. How do you see the content of the entry-level jobs in this field changing over the next two years?

17. What can I do to prepare myself for these changes?

18. What is the best way to obtain a position that will start me on a career in this field?

19. Do you have any information on job specifications and descriptions that I may have?

20. What related occupational fields would you suggest I explore?

21. How could I improve my resume for a career in this field?

22. Who else would you suggest I talk to, both in your organization and in other organizations?

Questions You Might Have to Answer

In order to communicate effectively, you must anticipate questions that will be asked of you by the networkers you contact. Review the list below and see if you can easily answer each of these questions. If you cannot, it may be time to revisit the self-assessment process.

1. Where did you get my name, or how did you find out about this organization?

2. What are your career goals?

3. What kind of job are you interested in?

4. What do you know about this organization and this industry?

5. How do you know you're prepared to undertake an entry-level position in this industry?

6. What course work have you taken that is related to your career interests?

7. What are your short-term career goals?

8. What are your long-term career goals?

9. Do you plan to obtain additional formal education?

10. What contributions have you made to previous employers?

11. Which of your previous jobs have you enjoyed the most, and why?

12. What are you particularly good at doing?

13. What shortcomings have you had to face in previous employment?

14. What are your three greatest strengths?

15. Describe how comfortable you feel with your communication style.

General Networking Tips

Make Every Contact Count. Setting the tone for each interaction is critical. Approaches that will help you communicate in an effective way include politeness, being appreciative of time provided to you, and being prepared and thorough. Remember, *everyone* within an organization has a circle of influence, so be prepared to interact effectively with each person you encounter in the networking process, including secretarial and support staff. Many information or job seekers have thwarted their own efforts by being rude to some individuals they encountered as they networked because they made the incorrect assumption that certain persons were unimportant.

Sometimes your contacts may be surprised at their ability to help you. After meeting and talking with you, they might think they have not offered much in the way of help. A day or two later, however, they may make a contact that would be useful to you and refer you to it.

With Each Contact, Widen Your Circle of Networkers. Always leave an informational interview with the names of at least two more people who can help you get the information or job that you are seeking. Don't be shy about asking for additional contacts; networking is all about increasing the number of people you can interact with to achieve your goals.

Make Your Own Decisions. As you talk with different people and get answers to the questions you pose, you may hear conflicting information or get conflicting suggestions. Your job is to listen to these "experts" and decide what information and which suggestions will help you achieve *your* goals. Only implement those suggestions that you believe will work for you.

SHUTTING DOWN YOUR NETWORK

As you achieve the goals that motivated your networking activity—getting the information you need or the job you want—the time will come to inactivate all or parts of your network. As you do so, be sure to tell your primary supporters about your change in status. Call or write to each one of them and give them as many details about your new status as you feel is necessary to maintain a positive relationship.

Because a network takes on a life of its own, activity undertaken on your behalf will continue even after you cease your efforts. As you get calls or are contacted in some fashion, be sure to inform these networkers about your change in status, and thank them for assistance they have provided.

Information on the latest employment trends indicates that workers will change jobs or careers several times in their lifetime. If you carefully and thoughtfully conduct your networking activities now, you will have solid experience when you need to network again.

CHAPTER FIVE

INTERVIEWING

*C*ertainly, there can be no one part of the job search process more fraught with anxiety and worry than the interview. Yet seasoned job seekers welcome the interview and will often say, "Just get me an interview and I'm on my way!" They understand that the interview is crucial to the hiring process and equally crucial for them, as job candidates, to have the opportunity of a personal dialogue to add to what the employer may already have learned from a resume, cover letter, and telephone conversations.

Believe it or not, the interview is to be welcomed, and even enjoyed! It is a perfect opportunity for you, the candidate, to sit down with an employer and express yourself and display who you are and what you want. Of course, it takes thought and planning and a little strategy; after all, it *is* a job interview! But it can be a positive, if not pleasant, experience and one you can look back on and feel confident about your performance and effort.

For many new job seekers, a job, any job, seems a wonderful thing. But seasoned interview veterans know that the job interview is an important step for both sides—the employer and the candidate—to see what each has to offer and whether there is going to be a "fit" of personalities, work styles, and attitudes. And it is this concept of balance in the interview, that both sides have important parts to play, that holds the key to success in mastering this aspect of the job search strategy.

Try to think of the interview as a conversation between two interested and equal partners. You both have important, even vital, information to deliver and to learn. Of course, there's no denying the employer has some leverage, especially in the initial interview for recruitment or any interview scheduled by the candidate and not the recruiter. That should not prevent the interviewee from seeking to play an equal part in what should be a fair exchange of information. Too often the untutored candidate allows the interview to become one-sided. The employer asks all the questions and the candidate simply responds. The ideal would be for two mutually interested parties to sit down and discuss possibilities for each. For this is a *conversation of significance,* and it requires pre-interview preparation, thought about the tone of the interview, and planning of the nature and details of the information to be exchanged.

PREPARING FOR THE INTERVIEW

Most initial interviews are about thirty minutes long. Given the brevity, the information that is exchanged ought to be important. The candidate should be delivering material that the employer cannot discover on the resume and, in turn, the candidate should be learning things about the employer that he or she could not otherwise find out. After all, if you have only thirty minutes, why waste time on information that is already published? The information exchanged is more than just factual, and both sides will learn much from what they see of each other, as well. How the candidate looks, speaks, and acts is important to the employer. The employer's attention to the interview and awareness of the candidate's resume, the setting, and the quality of information presented are important to the candidate.

Just as the employer has every right to be disappointed when a prospect is late for the interview, looks unkempt, and seems ill-prepared to answer fairly standard questions, the candidate may be disappointed with an interviewer who isn't ready for the meeting, hasn't learned the basic resume facts, and is constantly interrupted for telephone calls. In either situation, there's good reason to feel let down.

There are many elements to a successful interview, and some of them are not easy to describe or prepare for. Sometimes there is just a chemistry between interviewer and interviewee that brings out the best in both, and a good exchange takes place. But there is much the candidate can do to pave the way for success in terms of his or her resume, personal appearance, goals, and interview strategy—each of which we will discuss. However, none of this preparation is as important as the time and thought the candidate gives to personal self-assessment.

Self-Assessment

Neither a stunning resume nor an expensive, well-tailored suit can compensate for candidates who do not know what they want, where they are going, or why they are interviewing with a particular employer. Self-assessment, the process by which we begin to know and acknowledge our own particular blend of education, experiences, needs, and goals, is not something that can be sorted out the weekend before a major interview. Of all the elements of interview preparation, this one requires the longest lead time and cannot be faked.

Because the time allotted for most interviews is brief, it is all the more important for job candidates to understand and express succinctly why they are there and what they have to offer. This is not a time for undue modesty or for braggadocio, either; but it is a time for a compelling, reasoned statement of why you feel that you and this employer might make a good match. It means you have to have thought about your skills, interests, and attributes; related those to your life experiences and your own history of challenges and opportunities; and determined what that indicates about your strengths, preferences, values, and areas needing further development.

A common complaint of employers is that many candidates didn't take advantage of the interview time, didn't seem to know why they were there or what they wanted. When candidates are asked to talk about themselves and their work-related skills and attributes, employers don't want to be faced with shyness or embarrassed laughter; they need to know about you so they can make a fair determination of you and your competition. If you lose the opportunity to make a case for your employability, you can be certain the person ahead of you has or the person after you will, and it will be on the strength of those impressions that the employer will hire.

If you need some assistance with self-assessment issues, refer to Chapter 1. Included are suggested exercises that can be done as needed, such as making up an experiential diary and extracting obvious strengths and weaknesses from past experiences. These simple, pen-and-paper assignments will help you look at past activities as collections of tasks with accompanying skills and responsibilities. Don't overlook your high school or college career office, as well. Many offer personal counseling on self-assessment issues and may provide testing instruments such as the Myers-Briggs Type Indicator (MBTI)®, the Harrington-O'Shea Career Decision Making® System (CDM), the Strong Interest Inventory (SII)®, or any of a wide selection of assessment tools that can help you clarify some of these issues prior to the interview stage of your job search.

The Resume

Resume preparation has been discussed in detail, and some basic examples of various types were provided. In this section, we want to concentrate on how best to use your resume in the interview. In most cases, the employer will have seen the resume prior to the interview, and, in fact, it may well have been the quality of that resume that secured the interview opportunity.

An interview is a conversation, however, and not an exercise in reading. So, if the employer hasn't seen your resume and you have brought it along to the interview, wait until asked or until the end of the interview to offer it. Otherwise, you may find yourself staring at the back of your resume and simply answering "yes" and "no" to a series of questions drawn from that document.

Sometimes an interviewer is not prepared and does not know or recall the contents of the resume and may use the resume to a greater or lesser degree as a "prompt" during the interview. It is for you to judge what that may indicate about the individual doing the interview or the employer. If your interviewer seems surprised by the scheduled meeting, relies on the resume to an inordinate degree, and seems otherwise unfamiliar with your background, this lack of preparation for the hiring process could well be a symptom of general management disorganization or may simply be the result of poor planning on the part of one individual. It is your responsibility as a potential employee to be aware of these signals and make your decisions accordingly.

••

In any event, it is perfectly acceptable for you to get the conversation back to a more interpersonal style by saying something like, "Ms. Gingue, you might be interested in some recent experience I gained in a volunteer position at our local homeless shelter that is not detailed on my resume. May I tell you about it?" This can return the interview to two people talking to each other, not one reading and the other responding.

••

By all means, bring at least one copy of your resume to the interview. Occasionally, at the close of an interview, an interviewer will express an interest in circulating a resume to several departments, and you could then offer to provide those. Sometimes, an interview appointment provides an opportunity to meet others in the organization who may express an interest in you and your background, and it may be helpful to follow that up with a copy of your resume. Our best advice, however, is to keep it out of sight until needed or requested.

Appearance

Although many of the absolute rules that once dominated the advice offered to job candidates about appearance have now been moderated significantly, conservative is still the watchword unless you are interviewing in a fashion-related industry. For men, conservative translates into a well-cut dark suit with appropriate tie, hosiery, and dress shirt. A wise strategy for the male job seeker looking for a good but not expensive suit would be to try the men's department of a major department store. They usually carry a good range of sizes, fabrics, and prices; offer professional sales help; provide free tailoring; and have associated departments for putting together a professional look.

For women, there is more latitude. Business suits are still popular, but they have become more feminine in color and styling with a variety of jacket and skirt lengths. In addition to suits, better-quality dresses are now worn in many environments and, with the correct accessories, can be most appropriate. Company literature, professional magazines, the business section of major newspapers, and television interviews can all give clues about what is being worn in different employer environments.

Both men and women need to pay attention to issues such as hair, jewelry, and makeup; these are often what separates the candidate in appearance from the professional workforce. It seems particularly difficult for the young job seeker to give up certain hair styles, eyeglass fashions, and jewelry habits, yet those can be important to the employer, who is concerned with your ability to successfully make the transition into the organization. Candidates often find the best strategy is to dress conservatively until they find employment. Once employed and familiar with the norms within your organization, you can begin to determine a look that you enjoy, works for you, and fits your organization.

Choose clothes that suit your body type, fit well, and flatter you. Feel good about the way you look! The interview day is not the best for a new hairdo, a new pair of shoes, or any other change that will distract you or cause you to be self-conscious. Arrive a bit early to avoid being rushed, and ask the receptionist to direct you to a restroom for any last-minute adjustments of hair and clothes.

Employer Information

Whether your interview is for graduate school admission, an overseas corporate position, or a reporter position with a local newspaper, it is important to know something about the employer or the organization. Keeping in mind that the interview is relatively brief and that you will hopefully have other interviews with other organizations, it is important to keep your research in proportion. If secondary interviews are called for, you will have additional time to do further research. For the first interview, it is helpful to know the organization's mission, goals, size, scope of operations, etc. Your research may uncover recent areas of challenge or particular successes that may help to fuel the interview. Use the "Where Are These Jobs, Anyway?" section of Chapter 3, your library, and your career or guidance office to help you locate this information in the most efficient way possible. Don't be shy in asking advice of these counseling and guidance professionals on how best to spend your preparation time. With some practice, you'll soon learn how much information is enough and which kinds of information are most useful to you.

INTERVIEW CONTENT

We've already discussed how it can help to think of the interview as an important conversation—one that, as with any conversation, you want to find pleasant and interesting and to leave you with a good feeling. But because this conversation is especially important, the information that's exchanged is critical to its success. What do you want them to know about you? What do you need to know about them? What interview technique do you need to particularly pay attention to? How do you want to manage the close of the interview? What steps will follow in the hiring process?

Except for the professional interviewer, most of us find interviewing stressful and anxiety-provoking. Developing a strategy before you begin interviewing will help you relieve some stress and anxiety. One particular strategy that has worked for many and may work for you is interviewing by objective. Before you interview, write down three to five goals you would like to achieve for that interview. They may be technique goals: smile a little more, have a firmer handshake, be sure to ask about the next stage in the interview process before leaving, etc. They may be content-oriented goals: find out about the company's current challenges and opportunities, be sure to speak of my recent research writing experiences or foreign travel, etc. Whatever your goals, jot down a few of them as goals for this interview.

Most people find that, in trying to achieve these few goals, their interviewing technique becomes more organized and focused. After the interview, the most common question friends and family ask is, "How did it go?" With this technique, you have an indication of whether you met *your* goals for the meeting, not just some vague idea of how it went. Chances are, if you accomplished what you wanted to, it informed the quality of the entire interview. As you continue to interview, you will want to revise your goals to continue improving your interview skills.

Now, add to the concept of the significant conversation the idea of a beginning, a middle, and a closing and you will have two thoughts that will give your interview a distinctive character. Be sure to make your introduction warm and cordial. Say your full name (and if it's a difficult-to-pronounce name, help the interviewer to pronounce it) and make certain you know your interviewer's name and how to pronounce it. Most interviews begin with some "soft talk" about the weather, chat about the candidate's trip to the interview site, national events, etc. This is done as a courtesy, to relax both you and the interviewer, to get you talking, and to generally try to defuse the atmosphere of excessive tension. Try to be yourself, engage in the conversation, and don't try to second-guess the interviewer. This is simply what it appears to be—casual conversation.

Once you and the interviewer move on to exchange more serious information in the middle part of the interview, the two most important concerns become your ability to handle challenging questions and your success at asking meaningful ones. Interviewer questions will probably fall into one of three categories: personal assessment and career direction, academic background, and knowledge of the employer. The following are some examples of questions in each category:

Personal Assessment and Career Direction

1. How would you describe yourself?
2. What motivates you to put forth your greatest effort?
3. In what kind of work environment are you most comfortable?
4. What do you consider to be your greatest strengths and weaknesses?
5. How well do you work under pressure?
6. What qualifications do you have that make you think you will be successful in this career?
7. Will you relocate? What do you feel would be the most difficult aspect of relocating?
8. Are you willing to travel?
9. Why should I hire you?

Academic Assessment

1. Why did you select your college or university?
2. What changes would you make at your alma mater?
3. What led you to choose your major?
4. What subjects did you like best and least? Why?
5. If you could, how would you plan your academic study differently? Why?
6. Describe your most rewarding college experience.
7. How has your college experience prepared you for this career?
8. Do you think that your grades are a good indication of your ability to succeed with this organization?
9. Do you have plans for continued study?

Knowledge of the Employer

1. If you were hiring a graduate of your school for this position, what qualities would you look for?

2. What do you think it takes to be successful in an organization like ours?

3. In what ways do you think you can make a contribution to our organization?

4. Why did you choose to seek a position with this organization?

The interviewer wants a response to each question but is also gauging your enthusiasm, preparedness, and willingness to communicate. In each response you should provide some information about yourself that can be related to the employer's needs. A common mistake is to give too much information. Answer each question completely, but be careful not to run on too long with extensive details or examples.

Questions About Underdeveloped Skills

Most employers interview people who have met some minimum criteria of education and experience. They interview candidates to see who they are, to learn what kind of personality they exhibit, and to get some sense of how this person might fit into the existing organization. It may be that you are asked about skills the employer hopes to find and that you have not documented. Maybe it's grant-writing experience, knowledge of the European political system, or a knowledge of the film world.

To questions about skills and experiences you don't have, answer honestly and forthrightly and try to offer some additional information about skills you do have. For example, perhaps the employer is disappointed you have no grant-writing experience. An honest answer may be as follows:

> No, unfortunately, I was never in a position to acquire those skills. I do understand something of the complexities of the grant-writing process and feel confident that my attention to detail, careful reading skills, and strong writing would make grants a wonderful challenge in a new job. I think I could get up on the learning curve quickly.

The employer hears an honest admission of lack of experience but is reassured by some specific skill details that do relate to grant writing and a confident manner that suggests enthusiasm and interest in a challenge.

For many students, questions about their possible contribution to an employer's organization can prove challenging. Because your education has probably not included specific training for a job, you need to review your academic record and select capabilities you have developed in your major that an employer can appreciate. For example, perhaps you read well and can analyze and condense what you've read into smaller, more focused pieces. That could be valuable. Or maybe you did some serious research and you know you have valuable investigative skills. Your public speaking might be highly developed and you might use visual aids appropriately and effectively. Or maybe your skill at correspondence, memos, and messages is effective. Whatever it is, you must take it out of the academic context and put it into a new, employer-friendly context so your interviewer can best judge how you could help the organization.

Exhibiting knowledge of the organization will, without a doubt, show the interviewer that you are interested enough in the available position to have done some legwork in preparation for the interview. Remember, it is not necessary to know every detail of the organization's history, but rather to have a general knowledge about why it is in business and how the industry is faring.

Sometime during the interview, generally after the midway point, you'll be asked if you have any questions for the interviewer. Your questions will tell the employer much about your attitude and your desire to understand the organization's expectations so you can compare it to your own strengths. The following are some selected questions you might want to ask:

1. What are the main responsibilities of the position?

2. What are the opportunities and challenges associated with this position?

3. Could you outline some possible career paths beginning with this position?

4. How regularly do performance evaluations occur?

5. What is the communication style of the organization? (meetings, memos, etc.)

6. Describe a typical day for me in this position.

7. What kinds of opportunities might exist for me to improve my professional skills within the organization?

8. What have been some of the interesting challenges and opportunities your organization has recently faced?

Most interviews draw to a natural closing point, so be careful not to prolong the discussion. At a signal from the interviewer, wind up your presentation, express your appreciation for the opportunity, and be sure to ask what the next stage in the process will be. When can you expect to hear from them?

Will they be conducting second-tier interviews? If you're interested and haven't heard, would they mind a phone call? Be sure to collect a business card with the name and phone number of your interviewer. On your way out, you might have an opportunity to pick up organizational literature you haven't seen before.

With the right preparation—a thorough self-assessment, professional clothing, and employer information—you'll be able to set and achieve the goals you have established for the interview process.

CHAPTER SIX

NETWORKING OR INTERVIEWING FOLLOW-UP

Quite often, there is a considerable time lag between interviewing for a position and being hired, or, in the case of the networker, between your phone call or letter to a possible contact and the opportunity of a meeting. This can be frustrating. "Why aren't they contacting me?" "I thought I'd get another interview, but no one has telephoned." "Am I out of the running?" You don't know what is happening.

CONSIDER THE DIFFERING PERSPECTIVES

Of course, there is another perspective—that of the networker or hiring organization. Organizations are complex, with multiple tasks that need to be accomplished each day. Hiring is but one discrete activity that does not occur as frequently as other job assignments. The hiring process might have to take second place to other, more immediate organizational needs. Although it may be very important to you and it is certainly ultimately significant to the employer, other issues such as fiscal management, planning and product development, employer vacation periods, or financial constraints, may prevent an organization or individual within that organization from acting on your employment or your request for information as quickly as you or they would prefer.

USE YOUR COMMUNICATION SKILLS

Good communication is essential here to resolve any anxieties, and the responsibility is on you, the job or information seeker. Too many job seekers and networkers offer as an excuse that they don't want to "bother" the organization by writing letters or calling. Let us assure you here and now, once and for all, that if you are troubling an organization by overcommunicating, someone will indicate that situation to you quite clearly. If not, you can only assume you are a worthwhile prospect and the employer appreciates being reminded of your availability and interest in them. Let's look at follow-up practices in both the job interview process and the networking situation separately.

FOLLOWING UP ON THE EMPLOYMENT INTERVIEW

A brief thank-you note following an interview is an excellent and polite way to begin a series of follow-up communications with a potential employer with whom you have interviewed and want to remain in touch. It should be just that—a thank-you for a good meeting. If you failed to mention some fact or experience during your interview that you think might add to your candidacy, you may use this note to do that. However, this should be essentially a note whose overall tone is appreciative and, if appropriate, indicative of a continuing interest in pursuing any opportunity that may exist with that organization. It is one of the few pieces of business correspondence that may be handwritten, but always use plain, good quality, monarch-size paper.

If, however, at this point you are no longer interested in the employer, the thank-you note is an appropriate time to indicate that. You are under no obligation to identify any reason for not continuing to pursue employment with that organization, but if you are so inclined to indicate your professional reasons (pursuing other employers more akin to your interests, looking for greater income production than this employer can provide, a different geographic location than is available, etc.), you certainly may. It should not be written with an eye to negotiation, for it will not be interpreted as such.

As part of your interview closing, you should have taken the initiative to establish lines of communication for continuing information about your candidacy. If you asked permission to telephone, wait a week following your thank-you note, then telephone your contact simply to inquire how things are progressing on your employment status. The feedback you receive here should be taken at face value. If your interviewer simply has no information, he or she will tell you so and indicate whether you should call again and when. Don't be discouraged if this should continue over some period of time.

If during this time something occurs that you think improves or changes your candidacy (some new qualification or experience you may have had), including any offers from other organizations, by all means telephone or write to inform the employer about this. In the case of an offer from a competing but less desirable or equally desirable organization, telephone your contact, explain what has happened, express your real interest in the organization, and inquire whether some determination on your employment might be made before you must respond to this other offer. If the organization is truly interested in you, they may be moved to make a decision about your candidacy. Equally possible is the scenario in which they are not yet ready to make a decision and so advise you to take the offer that has been presented. Again, you have no ethical alternative but to deal with the information presented in a straightforward manner.

When accepting other employment, be sure to contact any employers still actively considering you and inform them of your new job. Thank them graciously for their consideration. There are many other job seekers out there just like you who will benefit from having their candidacy improved when others bow out of the race. Who knows, you might, at some future time, have occasion to interact professionally with one of the organizations with whom you sought employment. How embarrassing to have someone remember you as the candidate who failed to notify them of taking a job elsewhere!

In all of your follow-up communications, keep good notes of who you spoke with, when you called, and any instructions that were given about return communications. This will prevent any misunderstandings and provide you with good records of what has transpired.

FOLLOWING UP ON THE NETWORK CONTACT

Far more common than the forgotten follow-up after an interview is the situation where a good network contact is allowed to lapse. Good communications are the essence of a network, and follow-up is not so much a matter of courtesy here as it is a necessity. In networking for job information and contacts, you are the active network link. Without you, and without continual contact from you, there is no network. You and your need for employment are often the only shared elements between members of the network. Because network contacts were made regardless of the availability of any particular employment, it is incumbent upon the job seeker, if not simple common sense, that unless you stay in regular communication with the network, you will not be available for consideration should some job become available in the future.

This brings up the issue of responsibility, which is likewise very clear. The job seeker initiates network contacts and is responsible for maintaining those contacts; therefore, the entire responsibility for the network belongs with him or her. This becomes patently obvious if the network is left unattended. It very shortly falls out of existence, as it cannot survive without careful attention by the networker.

A variety of ways are open to you to keep the lines of communication open and to attempt to interest the network in you as a possible employee. You are limited only by your own enthusiasm for members of the network and your creativity. However, you as a networker are well advised to keep good records of whom you have met and spoken with in each organization. Be sure to send thank-you notes to anyone who has spent any time with you, be it a quick tour of a department or a sit-down informational interview. All of these communications should, in addition to their ostensible reason, add some information about you and your particular combination of strengths and attributes.

You can contact your network at any time to convey continued interest, to comment on some recent article you came across concerning an organization, to add information about your training or changes in your qualifications, to ask advice or seek guidance in your job search, or to request referrals to other possible network opportunities. Sometimes just a simple note to network members reminding them of your job search, indicating that you have been using their advice, and noting that you are still actively pursuing leads and hope to continue to interact with them is enough to keep communications alive.

Because networks have been abused in the past, it's important that your conduct be above reproach. Networks are exploratory options, they are not back-door access to employers. The network works best for someone who is exploring a new industry or making a transition into a new area of employment and who needs to find information or to alert people to his or her search activity. Always be candid and direct with contacts in expressing the purpose of your call or letter and your interest in their help or information about their organization. In follow-up contacts, keep the tone professional and direct. Your honesty will be appreciated, and people will respond as best they can if your qualifications appear to meet their forthcoming needs. The network does not owe you anything, and that tone should be clear to each person you meet.

FEEDBACK FROM FOLLOW-UPS

A network contact may prove to be miscalculated. Perhaps you were referred to someone and it became clear that your goals and his or her particular needs did not make a good match. Or the network contact may simply not be in a position to provide you with the information you are seeking. Or in some unfortunate situations, the contact may become annoyed by being contacted for this purpose. In such a situation, many job seekers simply say "Thank you" and move on.

If the contact is simply not the right contact, but the individual you are speaking with is not annoyed by the call, it might be a better tactic to express regret that the contact was misplaced and then express to the contact what you are seeking and ask for his or her advice or possible suggestions as to a next step. The more people who are aware you are seeking employment, the better your chances of connecting, and that is the purpose of a network. Most people in a profession have excellent knowledge of their field and varying amounts of expertise on areas near to or tangent to their own. Use their expertise and seek some guidance before you dissolve the contact. You may be pleasantly surprised.

Occasionally, networkers will express the feeling that they have done as much as they can or provided all the information that is available to them. This may be a cue that they would like to be released from your network. Be alert to such attempts to terminate, graciously thank the individual by letter, and move on in your network development. A network is always changing, adding and losing members, and you want the network to be composed of only those who are actively interested in supporting your interests.

A FINAL POINT ON NETWORKING FOR MATH MAJORS

In any field a mathematics major might consider as a potential career path, your contacts will be critically evaluating all your written and oral communications. For some job seekers, this may be more crucial than others. Many of the jobs in the career paths that follow do, however, emphasize communication skills. While your study of mathematics has involved group projects and some classroom presentations that have helped polish your oral communication style, the mathematics major generally does not emphasize prose writing. You'll want to ensure your cover letters are well written and that you have samples of other writing available.

In your telephone communications, interview presentations, and follow-up correspondence, your written and spoken use of English will be part of the portfolio of impressions you create in those you meet along the way.

CHAPTER SEVEN

JOB OFFER CONSIDERATIONS

for many recent college graduates, the thrill of their first job and, for some, the most substantial regular income they have ever earned seems an excess of good fortune coming at once. To question that first income or be critical in any way of the conditions of employment at the time of the initial offer seems like looking a gift horse in the mouth. It doesn't seem to occur to many new hires even to attempt to negotiate any aspect of their first job. And, as many employers who deal with entry-level jobs for recent college graduates will readily confirm, the reality is that there simply isn't much movement in salary available to these new college recruits. The entry-level hire generally does not have an employment track record on a professional level to provide any leverage for negotiation. Real negotiations on salary, benefits, retirement provisions, etc., come to those with significant employment records at higher income levels.

Of course, the job offer is more than just money. It can be comprised of geographic assignment, duties and responsibilities, training, benefits, health and medical insurance, educational assistance, car allowance or company vehicle, and a host of other items. All of this is generally detailed in the formal letter that presents the final job offer. In most cases, this is a follow-up to a personal phone call from the employer representative who has been principally responsible for your hiring process.

That initial telephone offer is certainly binding as a verbal agreement, but most firms follow up with a detailed letter outlining the most significant parts of your employment contract. You may certainly choose to respond immediately at the time of the telephone offer (which would be considered a binding oral contract), but you will also be required to formally answer the letter of offer with a letter of acceptance, restating the salient elements of the employer's description of your position, salary, and benefits. This ensures that both parties are clear on the terms and conditions of employment and remuneration and any other outstanding aspects of the job offer.

IS THIS THE JOB YOU WANT?

Most new employees will write this letter of acceptance back, glad to be in the position to accept employment. If you've worked hard to get the offer, and the job market is tight, other offers may not be in sight, so you will say "Yes, I accept!" What is important here is that the job offer you accept be one that does fit your particular needs, values, and interests as you've outlined them in your self-assessment process. Moreover, it should be a job that will not only use your skills and education, but also challenge you to develop new skills and talents.

Jobs are sometimes accepted too hastily, for the wrong reasons, and without proper scrutiny by the applicant. For example, an individual might readily accept a sales job only to find the continual rejection by potential clients unendurable. An office worker might realize within weeks the constraints of a desk job and yearn for more activity. Employment is an important part of our lives. It is, for most of our adult lives, our most continuous productive activity. We want to make good choices based on the right criteria.

If you have a low tolerance for risk, a job based on commission will certainly be very anxiety provoking. If being near your family is important, issues of relocation could present a decision crisis for you. If you're an adventurous person, a job with frequent travel would provide needed excitement and be very desirable. The importance of income, the need to continue your education, your personal health situation—all of these have an impact on whether the job you are considering will ultimately meet your needs. Unless you've spent some time understanding and thinking about these issues, it will be difficult to evaluate offers you do receive.

More importantly, if you make a decision that you cannot tolerate and feel you must leave that job, you will then have both unemployment and self-esteem issues to contend with. These will combine to make the next job search tough going, indeed. So make your acceptance a carefully considered decision.

NEGOTIATING YOUR OFFER

It may be that there is some aspect of your job offer that is not particularly attractive to you. Perhaps there is no relocation allotment to help you move your possessions, and this presents some financial hardship for you. It may be that the medical and health insurance is less than you had hoped. Your initial assignment may be different than you expected, either in its location or in the duties and responsibilities that comprise it. Or it may simply be that the salary is less than you anticipated. Other considerations may be your official starting date of employment, vacation time, evening hours, dates of training programs or schools, etc.

If you are considering not accepting the job because of some item or items in the job offer "package" that do not meet your needs, you should know that most employers emphatically wish that you would bring that issue to their attention. It may be that the employer can alter it to make the offer more agreeable for you. In some cases, it cannot be changed. In any event, the employer would generally like to have the opportunity to try to remedy a difficulty rather than risk losing a good potential employee over an issue that might have been resolved. After all, they have spent time and funds in securing your services, and they certainly deserve an opportunity to resolve any possible differences.

Honesty is the best approach in discussing any objections or uneasiness you might have over the employer's offer. Having received your formal offer in writing, contact your employer representative and indicate your particular dissatisfaction in a straightforward manner. For example, you might explain that, while very interested in being employed by this organization, the salary (or any other benefit) is less than you have determined you require. State the terms you do need, and listen to the response. You may be asked to put this in writing, or you may be asked to hold off until the firm can decide on a response. If you are dealing with a senior representative of the organization, one who has been involved in hiring for some time, you may get an immediate response or a solid indication of possible outcomes.

Perhaps the issue is one of relocation. Your initial assignment is in the Midwest, and because you had indicated a strong West Coast preference, you are surprised at the actual assignment. You might simply indicate that, while you understand the need for the company to assign you based on its needs, you are disappointed and had hoped to be placed on the West Coast. You could inquire if that were still possible and, if not, would it be reasonable to expect a West Coast relocation in the future.

If your request is presented in a reasonable way, most employers will not see this as jeopardizing your offer. If they can agree to your proposal, they will. If not, they will simply tell you so, and you may choose to continue your candidacy with them or remove yourself from consideration as a possible employee. The choice will be up to you.

Some firms will adjust benefits within their parameters to meet the candidate's need if at all possible. If a candidate requires a relocation cost allowance, he or she may be asked to forgo tuition benefits for the first year to accomplish this adjustment. An increase in life insurance may be adjusted by some other benefit trade-off; perhaps a family dental plan is not needed. In these decisions, you are called upon, sometimes under time pressure, to know how you value these issues and how important each is to you.

Many employers find they are more comfortable negotiating for candidates who have unique qualifications or who bring especially needed expertise to the organization. Employers hiring large numbers of entry-level college graduates may be far more reluctant to accommodate any changes in offer conditions. They are well supplied with candidates with similar education and experience, so that if rejected by one candidate, they can draw new candidates from an ample labor pool.

COMPARING OFFERS

With only about 40 percent of recent college graduates employed three months after graduation, many graduates do not get to enjoy the experience of entertaining more than one offer at a time. The conditions of the economy, the job seekers' particular geographic job market, and their own needs and demands for certain employment conditions may not provide more than one offer at a time. Some job seekers may feel that no reasonable offer should go unaccepted, for the simple fear there won't be another.

In a tough job market, or if the job you seek is not widely available, or when your job search goes on too long and becomes difficult to sustain financially and emotionally, it may be necessary to accept an offer. The alternative is continued unemployment. Even here, when you feel you don't have a choice, you can at least understand that in accepting this particular offer, there may be limitations and conditions you don't appreciate. At the time of acceptance, there were no other alternatives, but the new employee can begin to use that position to gain the experience and talent to move toward a more attractive position.

Sometimes, however, more than one offer is received at one time, and the candidate has the luxury of choice. If the job seeker knows what he or she wants and has done the necessary self-assessment honestly and thoroughly, it may be clear that one of the offers conforms more closely to those expressed wants and needs.

However, if, as so often happens, the offers are similar in terms of conditions and salary, the question then becomes which organization might provide the necessary climate, opportunities, and advantages for your professional development and growth. This is the time when solid employer research and astute questioning during the interviews really pays off. How much did you learn about the employer through your own research and skillful questioning?

When the interviewer asked during the interview, "Do you have any questions?" did you ask the kinds of questions that would help resolve a choice between one organization and another? Just as an employer must decide among numerous applicants, so must the applicant learn to assess the potential employer. Both are partners in the job search.

RENEGING ON AN OFFER

An especially disturbing occurrence for employers and career counseling professionals is when a job seeker formally (either orally or by written contract) accepts employment with one organization and later reneges on the agreement and goes with another employer.

There are all kinds of rationalizations offered for this unethical behavior. None of them satisfies. The sad irony is that what the job seeker is willing to do to the employer—make a promise and then break it—he or she would be outraged to have done to them—have the job offer pulled. It is a very bad way to begin a career. It suggests the individual has not taken the time to do the necessary self-assessment and self-awareness exercises to think and judge critically. The new offer taken may, in fact, be no better or worse than the one refused. Job candidates should be aware that there have been incidents of legal action following job candidates reneging on an offer. This adds a very sour note to what should be a harmonious beginning of a lifelong adventure.

CHAPTER EIGHT

THE GRADUATE SCHOOL CHOICE

The reasons for continuing one's education in graduate school can be as varied and unique as the individuals electing this course of action. Many continue their studies at an advanced level because they simply find it difficult to end the educational process. They love what they are learning and want to learn more and continue their academic exploration.

. . . .

Continuing to work with a particular subject, such as number theory or elliptical equations and thinking, studying, and writing critically on what others have discovered can provide excitement, challenge, and serious work. Some mathematics majors have loved this aspect of their academic work and want to continue that activity.

Others go on to graduate school for purely practical reasons. They have examined employment prospects in their field of study and all indications are that a graduate degree is required. For example, you have a B.S. in mathematics, no particular "hard" skills, and many of the jobs you're interested in seem to demand an M.S. (master of science). You sense your opportunities to work at the level you prefer in mathematics would be limited without an M.S. Be certain to read Chapter 12 for a strategy to approach the graduate school decision.

Alumni who are working in the fields you are considering can be a good source of what degree level the field demands. Ask your college career office for some alumni names and give them a telephone call. Prepare some questions on specific job prospects in their field at each degree level. A thorough examination of the marketplace and talking to employers and professors will give you a sense of the scope of employment for a bachelor's, master's, or doctoral degree.

College teaching will require an advanced degree. The more senior executive positions in the career paths outlined in this book will require advanced education and perhaps some particular specialization in a subject area (statistics, operations research, etc.).

CONSIDER YOUR MOTIVES

The answer to the question of "Why graduate school?" is a personal one for each applicant. Nevertheless, it is important to consider your motives carefully. Graduate school involves additional time out of the employment market, a high degree of critical evaluation, significant autonomy as you pursue your studies, and considerable financial expenditure. For some students in doctoral programs, there may be additional life choice issues, such as relationships, marriage, and parenthood, that may present real challenges while in a program of study. You would be well-advised to consider the following questions as you think about your decision to continue your studies.

Are You Postponing Some Tough Decisions by Going to School?

Graduate school is not a place to go to avoid life's problems. There is intense competition for graduate school slots and for the fellowships, scholarships, and financial aid available. This competition means extensive interviewing, resume submission, and essay writing that rivals corporate recruitment. Likewise, the graduate school process is a mentored one in which faculty stay aware of and involved in the academic progress of their students and continually challenge the quality of their work. Many graduate students are called upon to participate in teaching and professional writing and research as well.

In other words, this is no place to hide from the spotlight. Graduate students work very hard and much is demanded of them individually. If you elect to go to graduate school to avoid the stresses and strains of the "real world," you will find no safe place in higher academics. Vivid accounts, both fiction and nonfiction, have depicted quite accurately the personal and professional demands of graduate school work.

The selection of graduate studies as a career option should be a positive choice—something you *want* to do. It shouldn't be selected as an escape from other, less attractive or more challenging options, nor should it be selected as the option of last resort (i.e., "I can't do anything else; I'd better just stay in school"). If you're in some doubt about the strength of your reasoning about continuing in school, discuss the issues with a career counselor. Together you can clarify your reasoning, and you'll get some sound feedback on what you're about to undertake.

On the other hand, staying on in graduate school because of a particularly poor employment market and a lack of jobs at entry-level positions has proven to be an effective "stalling" strategy. If you can afford it, pursuing a graduate degree immediately after your undergraduate education gives you a year or two to "wait out" a difficult economic climate while at the same time acquiring a potentially valuable credential.

Have You Done Some "Hands-On" Reality Testing?

There are experiential options available to give some reality to your decision-making process about graduate school. Internships or work in the field can give you a good idea about employment demands, conditions, and atmosphere.

∙∙

A master's degree is the frequent choice of mathematics majors who hope to advance their career. You'll want to read Chapter 12 in this book to understand how you can make the most of both your graduate education and your career, if a master's is in your plans. Publications like the *Wall Street Journal's Managing Your Career* newspaper often contain articles that continue the public discussions over the wisdom of the master's choice.

For mathematics majors who want to take their graduate education to the doctoral level, with an eye to college teaching or research, the need for some "hands-on" reality testing is vital. Begin with your own college professors and ask them to talk to you about their own educational and career paths that have taken them to their current teaching posts. They will have had actual experience with the current market for Ph.D.s in mathematics.

Whether it's an M.S. or a Ph.D. in mathematics that is in your future, the kind of reality tests that come through internships, co-op experiences, and, most importantly, talking to people who have attained the kinds of careers you are seeking, will give you the best kind of information to make your decision.

....

Do You Need an Advanced Degree to Work in Your Field?

Certainly there are fields such as law, psychiatry, medicine, and college teaching that demand advanced degrees. Is the field of employment you're considering one that also puts a premium on an advanced degree? You may be surprised. Read the want ads in a number of major Sunday newspapers for positions you would enjoy. How many of those require an advanced degree?

Retailing, for example, has always put a premium on what people can do, rather than how much education they have had. Successful people in retailing come from all academic preparations. A Ph.D. in English may bring only prestige to the individual employed as a magazine researcher. It may not bring a more senior position or better pay. In fact, it may disqualify you for some jobs because an employer might believe you will be unhappy to be overqualified for a particular position. Or your motives in applying for the work may be misconstrued, and the employer might think you will only be working at this level until something better comes along. None of this may be true for you, but it comes about because you are working outside of the usual territory for that degree level.

When economic times are especially difficult, we tend to see stories featured about individuals with advanced degrees doing what is considered unsuitable work, such as the Ph.D. in English driving a cab or the Ph.D. in chemistry waiting tables. Actually, this is not particularly surprising when you consider that as your degree level advances, the job market narrows appreciably. At any one time, regardless of economic circumstances, there are only so many jobs for your particular level of expertise. If you cannot find employment for your advanced degree level, chances are you will be considered suspect for many other kinds of employment and may be forced into temporary work far removed from your original intention.

Before making an important decision such as graduate study, learn your options and carefully consider what you want to do with your advanced degree. Ask yourself whether it is reasonable to think you can achieve your goals. Will there be jobs when you graduate? Where will they be? What will they pay? How competitive will the market be at that time, based on current predictions?

If you're uncertain about the degree requirements for the fields you're interested in, you should check a publication such as the U.S. Department of Labor's *Occupational Outlook Handbook*. Each entry has a section on training and other qualifications that will indicate clearly what the minimum educational requirement is for employment, what degree is the standard, and what employment may be possible without the required credential.

For example, for physicists and astronomers, a doctoral degree in physics or a closely related field is essential. Certainly this is the degree of choice in academic institutions. However, the *Occupational Outlook Handbook* also indicates what kinds of employment may be available to individuals holding a master's or even a bachelor's degree in physics.

Have You Compared Your Expectations of What Graduate School Will Do for You with What It Has Done for Alumni of the Program You're Considering?

Most colleges and universities perform some kind of postgraduate survey of their students to ascertain where they are employed, what additional education they have received, and what levels of salary they are enjoying. Ask to see this information either from the university you are considering applying to or from your own alma mater, especially if it has a similar graduate program. Such surveys often reveal surprises about occupational decisions, salaries, and work satisfaction. This information may affect your decision.

The value of self-assessment (the process of examining and making decisions about your own hierarchy of values and goals) is especially important in this process of analyzing the desirability of possible career paths involving graduate education. Sometimes a job requiring advanced education seems to hold real promise but is disappointing in salary potential or numbers of opportunities available. Certainly, it is better to research this information before embarking on a program of graduate studies. It may not change your mind about your decision, but by becoming better informed about your choice, you become better prepared for your future.

Have You Talked with People in Your Field to Explore What You Might Be Doing After Graduate School?

In pursuing your undergraduate degree, you will have come into contact with many individuals trained in the field you are considering. You might also have the opportunity to attend professional conferences, workshops, seminars, and job fairs where you can expand your network of contacts. Talk to them all! Find out about their individual career paths, discuss your own plans and hopes, and get their feedback on the reality of your expectations, and heed their advice about your prospects. Each will have a unique tale to tell, and each will bring a different perspective on the current marketplace for the credentials you are seeking. Talking to enough people will make you an expert on what's out there.

Are You Excited by the Idea of Studying the Particular Field You Have in Mind?

This question may be the most important one of all. If you are going to spend several years in advanced study, perhaps engendering some debt or postponing some lifestyle decisions for an advanced degree, you simply ought to enjoy what you're doing. Examine your work in the discipline so far. Has it been fun? Have you found yourself exploring various paths of thought? Do you read in your area for fun? Do you enjoy talking about it, thinking about it, and sharing it with others? Advanced degrees often are the beginning of a lifetime's involvement with a particular subject. Choose carefully a field that will hold your interest and your enthusiasm.

It is fairly obvious by now that we think you should give some careful thought to your decision and take some action. If nothing else, do the following:

- ❑ Talk and question (remember to listen!)

- ❑ Reality-test

- ❑ Soul-search by yourself or with a person you trust

FINDING THE RIGHT PROGRAM FOR YOU: SOME CONSIDERATIONS

There are several important factors in coming to a sound decision about the right graduate program for you. You'll want to begin by locating institutions that offer appropriate programs, examining each of these programs and their requirements, undertaking the application process by obtaining catalogs and application materials, visiting campuses if possible, arranging for letters of recommendation, writing your application statement, and finally following up on your applications.

Locate Institutions with Appropriate Programs

Once you decide on a particular advanced degree, it's important to develop a list of schools offering such a degree program. Perhaps the best sources of graduate program information are Peterson's *Guides to Graduate Study.* Use these guides to build your list. In addition, you may want to consult the College Board's *Index of Majors and Graduate Degrees,* which will help you find graduate programs offering the degree you seek. It is indexed by academic major and then categorized by state.

Now, this may be a considerable list. You may want to narrow the choices down further by a number of criteria: tuition, availability of financial aid, public versus private institutions, U.S. versus international institutions, size of student body, size of faculty, application fee (this varies by school; most fall within the $10 to $75 range), and geographic location. This is only a partial list; you will have your own important considerations. Perhaps you are an avid scuba diver and you find it unrealistic to think you could pursue graduate study for a number of years without being able to ocean dive from time to time. Good! That's a decision and it's honest. Now, how far from the ocean is too far, and what schools meet your other needs? In any case, and according to your own criteria, begin to build a reasonable list of graduate schools that you are willing to spend the time investigating.

Examine the Degree Programs and Their Requirements

Once you've determined the criteria by which you want to develop a list of graduate schools, you can begin to examine the degree program requirements, faculty composition, and institutional research orientation. Again, using a resource such as Peterson's *Guides to Graduate Study* can reveal an amazingly rich level of material by which to judge your possible selections.

In addition to degree programs and degree requirements, entries will include information about application fees, entrance test requirements, tuition, percentage of applicants accepted, numbers of applicants receiving financial aid, gender breakdown of students, numbers of full- and part-time faculty, and often gender breakdown of faculty as well. Numbers graduating in each program and research orientations of departments are also included in some entries. There is information on graduate housing, student services, and library, research, and computer facilities. A contact person, phone number, and address are also standard pieces of information in these listings. In addition to the standard entries, some schools pay an additional fee to place full-page, more detailed program descriptions. The location of such a display ad, if present, would be indicated at the end of the standard entry.

It can be helpful to draw up a chart and enter relevant information about each school you are considering in order to have a ready reference on points of information that are important to you.

Undertake the Application Process

The Catalog. Once you've decided on a selection of schools, send for catalogs and applications. It is important to note here that these materials might take many weeks to arrive. Consequently, if you need the materials quickly, it might be best to telephone and explain your situation to see whether the process can be speeded up for you. Also, check a local college or university library, which might have current and complete college catalogs in a microfiche collection. These microfiche copies can provide you with helpful information while you wait for your own copy of the graduate school catalog or bulletin to arrive.

When you receive your catalogs, give them a careful reading and make notes of issues you might want to discuss on the telephone or in a personal interview, if that's possible. Does the course selection have the depth you had hoped for?

....

> If you are interested in graduate work in statistics, for example, in addition to classic courses in probability theory and linear models, consider the availability of colloquiums, directed research opportunities, and specialized seminars.

....

What is the ratio of faculty to the required number of courses for your degree? How often will you encounter the same faculty member as an instructor?

If, for example, your program offers a practicum or off-campus experience, who arranges this? Does the graduate school select a site and place you there, or is it your responsibility? What are the professional affiliations of the faculty? Does the program merit any outside professional endorsement or accreditation?

Critically evaluate the catalogs of each of the programs you are considering. List any questions you have and ask current or former teachers and colleagues for their impressions as well.

The Application. Preview each application thoroughly to determine what you need to provide in the way of letters of recommendation, transcripts from undergraduate schools or any previous graduate work, and personal essays that may be required. Make a notation for each application of what you need to complete that document.

Additionally, you'll want to determine entrance testing requirements for each institution and immediately arrange to complete your test registration. For example, the Graduate Record Exam (GRE) and the Graduate Management Admission Test (GMAT) each have thee to four weeks between the last registration date and the test date. Your local college career office should be able to provide you with test registration booklets, sample test materials, information on test sites and dates, and independent test review materials that might be available commercially.

Visit the Campus If Possible

If time and finances allow, a visit, interview, and tour can help make your decision easier. You can develop a sense of the student body, meet some of the faculty, and hear up-to-date information on resources and the curriculum. You will have a brief opportunity to "try out" the surroundings to see if they fit your needs. After all, it will be home for a while. If a visit is not possible but you have questions, don't hesitate to call and speak with the dean of the graduate school. Most are more than happy to talk to candidates and want them to have the answers they seek. Graduate school admission is a very personal and individual process.

Arrange for Letters of Recommendation

This is also the time to begin to assemble a group of individuals who will support your candidacy as a graduate student by writing letters of recommendation or completing recommendation forms. Some schools will ask you to provide letters of recommendation to be included with your application or sent directly to the school by the recommender. Other graduate programs will provide a recommendation form that must be completed by the recommender. These graduate school forms vary greatly in the amount of space provided for a written recommendation. So that you can use letters as you need to, ask your recommenders to address their letters "To Whom It May Concern," unless one of your recommenders has a particular connection to one of your graduate schools or knows an official at the school.

Choose recommenders who can speak authoritatively about the criteria important to selection officials at your graduate school. In other words, choose recommenders who can write about your grasp of the literature in your field of study, your ability to write and speak effectively, your class performance, and your demonstrated interest in the field outside of class. Other characteristics that graduate schools are interested in assessing include your emotional maturity, leadership ability, breadth of general knowledge, intellectual ability, motivation, perseverance, and ability to engage in independent inquiry.

When requesting recommendations, it's especially helpful to put the request in writing. Explain your graduate school intentions and express some of your thoughts about graduate school and your appreciation for their support. Don't be shy about "prompting" your recommenders with some suggestions of what you would appreciate being included in their comments. Most recommenders will find this direction helpful and will want to produce a statement of support that you can both stand behind. Consequently, if your interaction with one recommender was especially focused on research projects, he or she might be best able to speak of those skills and your critical thinking ability. Another recommender may have good comments to make about your public presentation skills.

Give your recommenders plenty of lead time in which to complete your recommendation, and set a date by which they should respond. If they fail to meet your deadline, be prepared to make a polite call or visit to inquire if they need more information or if there is anything you can do to move the process along.

Whether or not you are providing a graduate school form or asking for an original letter to be mailed, be sure to provide an envelope and postage if the recommender must mail the form or letter directly to the graduate school.

Each recommendation you request should provide a different piece of information about you for the selection committee. It might be pleasant for letters of recommendation to say that you are a fine, upstanding individual, but a selection committee for graduate school will require specific information. Each recommender has had a unique relationship with you, and their letters should reflect that. Think of each letter as helping to build a more complete portrait of you as a potential graduate student.

Write Your Application Statement

....

For the mathematics major, the application and personal essay should be a welcome opportunity to express your deep interest in pursuing graduate study. Your understanding of the challenges ahead, your commitment to the work involved, and your expressed self-awareness

> **will weigh heavily in the decision process of the gradu-
> ate school admissions committee.**

·····································

An excellent source to help in thinking about writing this essay is *How to Write a Winning Personal Statement for Graduate and Professional School* by Richard J. Stelzer. It has been written from the perspective of what graduate school selection committees are looking for when they read these essays. It provides helpful tips to keep your essay targeted on the kinds of issues and criteria that are important to selection committees and that provide them with the kind of information they can best utilize in making their decision.

Follow Up on Your Applications

After you have finished each application and mailed it along with your transcript requests and letters of recommendation, be sure to follow up on the progress of your file. For example, call the graduate school administrative staff to see whether your transcripts have arrived. If the school required your recommenders to fill out a specific recommendation form that had to be mailed directly to the school, you will want to ensure that they have all arrived in good time for the processing of your application. It is your responsibility to make certain that all required information is received by the institution.

RESEARCHING FINANCIAL AID SOURCES, SCHOLARSHIPS, AND FELLOWSHIPS

Financial aid information is available from each school, so be sure to request it when you call for a catalog and application materials. There will be several lengthy forms to complete, and these will vary by school, type of school (public versus private), and state. Be sure to note the deadline dates for these important forms.

There are many excellent resources available to help you explore all of your financial aid options. Visit your college career office or local public library to find out about the range of materials available. Two excellent resources include Peterson's *Grants for Graduate Students* and the Foundation Center's *Foundation Grants to Individuals*. These types of resources generally contain information that can be accessed by indexes including field of study, specific eligibility requirements, administering agency, and geographic focus.

EVALUATING ACCEPTANCE

If you apply to and are accepted at more than one school, it is time to return to your initial research and self-assessment to evaluate your options and select the program that will best help you achieve the goals you set for pursuing graduate study. You'll want to choose a program that will allow you to complete your studies in a timely and cost-effective way. This may be a good time to get additional feedback from professors and career professionals who are familiar with your interests and plans. Ultimately, the decision is yours, so be sure you get answers to all the questions you can think of.

SOME NOTES ABOUT REJECTION

Each graduate school is searching for applicants who appear to have the qualifications necessary to succeed in its program. Applications are evaluated on a combination of undergraduate grade point average, strength of letters of recommendation, standardized test scores, and personal statements written for the application.

A carelessly completed application is one reason many applicants are denied admission to a graduate program. To avoid this type of needless rejection, be sure to carefully and completely answer all appropriate questions on the application form, focus your personal statement given the instructions provided, and submit your materials well in advance of the deadline. Remember that your test scores and recommendations are considered a part of your application, so they must also be received by the deadline.

If you are rejected by a school that especially interests you, you may want to contact the dean of graduate studies to discuss the strengths and weaknesses of your application. Information provided by the dean will be useful in reapplying to the program or applying to other, similar programs.

PART TWO

THE CAREER PATHS

CHAPTER NINE

INTRODUCTION TO THE MATHEMATICS CAREER PATHS

The four chapters that follow each present realistic options for candidates with a mathematics undergraduate degree. The authors have designed, investigated, and written each of these chapters with an eye both to the job market for math majors and our own experience counseling and advising students over the past two decades.

Before we begin the process of outlining each of the four paths and the jobs they contain, we want to offer one particular piece of advice that many of our clients have told us was immensely helpful. It is based on an important distinction between *contextual* skills and *portable* skills. Contextual skills are those that are particular to the industry in which you are working. For example, if you are an operations research analyst working in aircraft production, you can't help but learn a tremendous amount about how aircraft are built. That information is part of the context of your employment. But, consider the limitations of that knowledge, for example, if you change jobs and move to a job for a manufacturer of small motor equipment (snowblowers, chain saws, lawnmowers, etc.). You can't do much with that contextual information about aircraft.

What you can take with you to your new employer are your *portable* skills. Portable skills would include your critical thinking skills and your ability to diagnose problems, "What's wrong with this assembly line production set-up?" Your ability to conduct a needs assessment is a portable skill. "Tell me about what happens when the production line goes down and what you have to do to bring it back up." Your abilities to listen, design new systems, test prototypes, or build feedback systems are all examples of portable skills. It's these portable skills that you'll be able to bring to any new job you may take in the future.

Take advantage of the opportunities your employer gives you to learn portable skills. If computer training is offered, take it. If there's a chance to learn a new job through cross-training, grab it. Think about your resume right now. Think about taking one of the many jobs in any of the chapters that follow and working at that job for a year or two or three. How will your resume change? What new talents will you be able to document? How will a new employer be able to measure your success in your previous job?

THE MATH JOB YOU KNOW BEST: TEACHING

If you love your math studies, it's probably going to happen (if it hasn't happened already) that at some time during your college career you are going to ask yourself, "Could I teach mathematics?" Your math teachers have obviously played an important role in stimulating your interest and enthusiasm for math over your years of schooling, and many of those teachers probably conveyed to you some of their excitement about the possibilities and rewards of a teaching career.

If you could return and talk to some of those teachers, you'd find they'd tell you that good teaching (math or anything else) is about *communicating* to your students. We've all had teachers who knew their subject but somehow couldn't get it across. It's the "getting it across" part that will be your challenge in this career. Some of the ingredients for success will be genuinely appreciating your students and understanding where they are and what they need right now. Creativity is also important, if you are to engage your students' imagination and sense of fun and adventure as they explore new math concepts. Planning is also a critical skill. If students are going to succeed after they leave your class, that means you have to accomplish certain goals. If you're teaching Algebra I, you need to cover everything students will need before they enroll in Algebra II with a different teacher. That takes many hours of planning, mapping out your lesson plan strategy to get from September to June and not leave anything out!

Please don't fool yourself into thinking that a teaching career is static. When you read Chapter 10, you'll see that a career teaching mathematics is vital, ever-changing, and newsworthy. Right now, the country is very concerned with the sharp drop-off in math and science interest among young women during the junior high school years. There have been some exciting new initiatives in curriculums, schools, and teaching interventions to correct this problem, but there's still lots to do. You could be part of that change.

For those of you thinking about high school teaching, you should be aware of the recent IEA Third International Mathematics and Science Study administered around the world to high school seniors in 1995. The United States students fell far short of their European counterparts and other industrialized nations in statistics, physics, and principles of science. There's no question the results of this study will have educators and the government calling for a reenergizing of our math and science teaching curriculums. As career counselors, we see strong indications of the reemergence of demand for math and science graduates. If you're interested in being part of the preparation of today's youth for those careers, this is a wonderful time to enter the teaching field.

THE JOBS THAT CAN'T BE DONE WITHOUT A MATH DEGREE: MATH AS A PRIMARY JOB SKILL

Chapter 11 is a look at four possible career paths that require math as a primary job skill: actuary, mathematician, statistician, and operations research analyst. All four of these paths and the many jobs each path represents will not only use every bit of the math you've acquired thus far, but demand more and more of you. If that's an exciting prospect, then you'll want to give this chapter a close reading and then follow up by investigating both the jobs that we cite and the sources of information listed for each career.

While the jobs of actuary, mathematician, statistician, and operations research analyst all function in different areas of the economy and with very different job sites, they are clustered in Chapter 11 for several reasons. Each of these career paths demands specific personal attributes and skills. Over and over, you'll see that each of the four paths emphasizes working with teams, collaboration, a need for the ability to explain and teach things to those who don't have a math background or vocabulary. In fact, superb communication skills surface again and again. It's funny, many people don't associate being an accomplished mathematician or scientist with being a skilled communicator. Think of the physicist Dr. Stephen Hawking, or the late Dr. Carl Sagan, who have done so much to help us understand the mysteries of math and science. Dr. Alexander Wiles of Princeton University, whose quest to solve Pierre de Fermat's notoriously difficult formula has become popular reading and TV fare for many who otherwise would not approach the subject of prime numbers, or, if they did, would not expect that they could understand it in the way these books and films help us to.

Mathematicians not only can be strong communicators; they *must* be for these jobs. Actuaries, mathematicians, statisticians, and operations research analysts are frequently part of a management team. These management teams form and re-form constantly, but they are frequently called upon to help advise and determine organization policy and direction based on their projections and estimates of future behavior as predicted by the models they have established. Generally, they are the only ones on the management team who understand the math involved! To make your points clearly and to persuade effectively, you need to be very skilled at explaining complex information in simple language. Even though senior management positions for you are likely to be some years down the road, potential employers will still be looking at your resume, cover letter, and interviewing style for evidence of your communications skills even as you apply for entry-level positions.

THINKING ABOUT AN ADVANCED DEGREE?: MATH AS AN ESSENTIAL JOB SKILL

A master's degree? Perhaps a Ph.D.? It might happen. Sooner or later, someone will ask you if you have plans for an advanced degree. Even if you've selected mathematics education as your major in anticipation of teaching in the public schools, you'll find going on for an advanced degree is common there, as well.

As you already are well aware, mathematics is a huge body of knowledge with discoveries still being made. Since there will always be more to learn, you may feel you need to add to your math study after obtaining your bachelor's degree. Many undergraduates who are contemplating teaching positions in higher education will often, if they can afford it, continue straight on through graduate school. Others, especially those interested in using their math in business or government, aren't as sure about an advanced degree and would rather get a job and make that graduate school decision later.

What we advise in Chapter 12 is to think a bit strategically about the kinds of jobs you might take upon graduation that will do the best for you in terms of any future education. For example, the jobs we suggest as research or financial analysts (when you read this chapter, you'll discover the analyst jobs go by many different titles), will utilize your math skills to a high degree and allow you impressive professional development. These jobs bring the opportunity to work with colleagues of a high level of managerial skill and educational background. Most importantly, you have the opportunity to use your undergraduate degree in math, earn an excellent income, while at the same time positioning yourself for a possible return to graduate school.

"Stopping out" like this before graduate school allows you to take a breather, use your degree, meet people in the field, and reassess what you want in the long run. At the same time, choosing a first job as a research or financial analyst keeps your skills fresh, your income high, and also provides you with employee benefits for graduate education should you choose to return to school part-time. This path makes a lot of sense if you are hesitant about graduate school because it gives you the most options.

USING YOUR MATH BUYING AND SELLING IN THE WORKPLACE: MATH AS AN IMPORTANT JOB SKILL

The last chapter of this book for math majors is an attempt to recognize that some math majors chose their degree concentration because they were good at it and wanted a major that would allow them to succeed. Math may be something you do well—even very well, but it may not be all you want to do. Or, you may really enjoy mathematics and be very happy you majored in it, but perhaps your grades don't reflect that enthusiasm. Whatever your motivation, Chapter 13 contains a number of job options for the mathematically talented.

A word of caution is in order, however. Math is important in the jobs and career paths we discuss in this final chapter, but it is not a primary or even the essential skill. It is not necessarily more important than the ability to make a decision, to solve problems, to manage your time, or to communicate well. The jobs in this path are done best by those who are comfortable with quantitative thinking and problem solving, but they may also be done by people whose strongest skills are not in math.

Sales representative, retail buyer and purchasing agent are sophisticated jobs, responsible for decisions involving large sums of money. Interviewers and employers will be interested in your math skills, but more concerned about your ability to think on your feet and to be decisive and creative at solving problems. The jobs in this path can take you into any number of employment situations, including major department stores, federal government procurement offices, to any major industry or service organization from the airlines to financial institutions. The possibilities are endless.

If you are at all interested in broadening your horizons with your math degree and looking at a variety of fields that offer not only an opportunity to capitalize on your degree, but enormous flexibility and potential for movement as you advance in your career, please give this final chapter a read. We guarantee you'll be surprised at what these careers have to offer.

Most of us think we know all there is to know about careers in buying and selling. Like so many smug assurances, we're usually wrong. Sales and marketing jobs, including the purchasing agent positions we describe, have become extremely sophisticated, requiring strong computer skills, a demand for detailed product knowledge, and far more listening and consultation than persuasion. These jobs are worth your attention.

CHAPTER TEN

PATH 1: THE MATH JOB YOU KNOW BEST: TEACHING

T alk to any math teachers you know and they'll tell you a surprising fact about their profession. They don't teach math, they teach students! The art of teaching and the skill required in the dynamics of student interaction weigh far more heavily in this equation than love of the subject matter. Though the subject may be math, the overriding concerns in teaching are conveying and instilling an appreciation and enjoyment of math in all its myriad forms of expression. That's because learners come to a math classroom with different issues, at different ages, for different reasons, from different lifestyles and with dramatically different degrees of interest (and anxiety!) about math and maybe about the teacher!

Simply having a love of math yourself is not enough, though that is certainly important and desirable. How could you begin to teach something you didn't truly enjoy without conveying that disinterest through a mechanical approach to the subject? Teaching most subjects requires very different skills than the skills demanded by studying the particular discipline. The world is full of extremely skillful practitioners who, for one reason or another and quite often inexplicably, cannot teach someone how they do it! The practice of something is very different from professing it in a classroom.

Planning for learning outcomes is critical. Teaching math within an established curriculum, be it high school or college, means corresponding to some stated goals or course outline. In high school, it may be state standards, and in college, it may be a written course description in the catalog. That means you have certain learning outcomes that you *must* accomplish during the semester or year. To accomplish this body of learning within a set time period requires judicious planning. What will be done each day? How much time should be allowed between assignments or readings? Which materials should be required and which should only be recommended? You'll have to make countless decisions. What textbooks and ancillary materials will you use, and how will you evaluate your students?

Add to this the fact that students learn in different ways. Some are auditory learners who enjoy listening and gain most of their information in this way. Concentrated listening is how they best absorb material in the classroom. If they are required to take notes *and* listen, something may have to give, or it may be difficult for them to retain the material. Others prefer a visual approach with board work, handouts, their own notes, diagrams, books, and many visual materials. They retain these images and can call them up to remember the material.

Others need to participate through more activity and physical involvement with the material. These learners like to participate in team projects or contests such as building a pyramid or cube, going outside and estimating the height of a building, and other activities that physically involve them. They learn best this way. These are kinesthetic learners and they are often forgotten in planning and curriculum design. The teacher ensures that the learning styles of *all* students are satisfied through a judicious combination of modalities in teaching. Teachers need to analyze their own teaching style and seek to incorporate those elements that come less naturally to them in order to ensure that they reach all students.

The teaching and learning that takes place in a classroom is not static. The classroom is an emotionally charged environment for the student and instructor that may call into play questions of self-esteem and competency. Students are continually exploring themselves in relation to their capabilities, values, and achievement. A good teacher understands this and encourages a risk-free environment of mutual appreciation and participation. Both teacher and student are allowed to make mistakes and move on. The teacher strives to assist in establishing congruence between the real self (how we think of ourselves at that moment), the ideal self (who we want to be), and the learning environment created in the classroom. Hopefully, the classroom will be a place where the real self can rise up and begin to touch the ideal self.

While any classroom can cause us to call into question who we are or how competent we are, this is perhaps especially true for the mathematics classroom. Math is a series of building blocks, and certain skills must be mastered to move on to other, more advanced proficiencies in using math. Many people develop a strong sense of inadequacy early on about mathematics and their own levels of competence. You've heard this from your friends and family and you'll continue to hear people's "horror stories" about math every time you mention you're a math major.

One group that has been particularly hurt by this traditional resistance to math and science is young women. We now have an increasing number of gender-sensitive studies describing how, frequently during middle school years, young girls seem willing to cede superiority to the boys in their classes. For many years researchers have been interested in the educational and career barriers between females and the field of mathematics. Studies (Fennema and Sherman, 1977; Fox, 1980; Armstrong, 1979; Boswell and Katz, 1980) have shown that the development of attitudes that affect a female's math achievement begin about thirteen years of age. That this attitude is due to stereotyping and not aptitude is obvious, and these studies make clear that at this age, young, talented girls begin to be rewarded for social conformity and move away from math, which is seen as more masculine. Fortunately, studies such as these have alerted not only teachers and other educators to the problem, but employers, too, are working hard to encourage women to enter fields that center on math and science skills.

Any mention of competency, self-esteem, or self-worth naturally suggests another sensitive subject—grading and the evaluation teachers provide on quizzes, tests, and report cards. Grades are an expected and required part of many institutional academic settings. Establishing fair and consistent standards of evaluating your students and assigning grades is a significant challenge to many teachers who otherwise feel perfectly competent in the teaching role. Math teachers find that having regular assignments is helpful to monitor their students' progress. Daily homework, perhaps frequent quiz opportunities, and examinations result in good tracking for a student's progress and excellent feedback for the student. However, this results in a lot of work for the teacher, and much of that work is going to be done outside the classroom, during office hours or at home in the evening. Teaching is not a nine-to-five job, and the after-hours demands of grading homework is just the tip of the iceberg in discussing the lack of boundaries in this important profession.

The teacher of math is called upon to play other roles, too. Animating the class and inspiring attention and commitment to the material are all required in teaching. Part of this is the teacher's enthusiasm, teaching style, effective use of ancillary materials, and the ability to relate this material to a student's life. Of course math teachers present information, but hopefully they are giving students lots of examples of applications of this information. Math can become especially exciting if young people understand how they use it in their daily life and how they may use math to make their lives easier, more productive, and more satisfying. It takes a creative and energetic teacher to discover ways to bring that relationship of math applicability in the real world into the classroom and drive home math's usefulness to their students. Other roles teachers play include seeking to raise relevant questions, prompt dialogues within the class, and develop within students the discipline of self-questioning. Teachers also, of course, use their creativity with math to clarify a student's difficulties or to draw parallels or find relationships between examples.

A math teacher not only teaches math, but also how to learn. The skills involved in learning to question, to retain information, to be selective, to order information, to record information, and to solve problems are hopefully a priority of every math teacher.

A good teacher also uses the class and the material to model good work and study habits as well. It's important and motivating for students when teachers share their personal enthusiasm for ideas in discussions of the material under study. Most of all, an instructor will, by example, develop the student's capacity for self-evaluation through careful, caring feedback about the student's work. The instructor's own example of preparation, organization, evaluation standards, personal appearance, interest in students, and enthusiasm for the subject will remain an example long after the memory of the actual class content may have faded.

Teachers are very frequently cited as important factors in one's choice of a career. Very often teachers will remember one or two of *their* teachers who were strong influences on their decision to teach. Much of that influence was a result of their classroom persona. Those teachers served as models of people enjoying what they were doing and doing it skillfully. They were professional and correct, yet remained natural and approachable. We could watch and listen to them and think, "Maybe I could do that."

DEFINITION OF THE CAREER PATH

We'll look at two possible levels of teaching math: secondary school teaching with a bachelor's degree, and college teaching, possibly with a master's degree, but more frequently, requiring a doctoral degree as the essential credential.

Secondary School Teaching

If teaching at the middle or high school level is of interest to you, you'll need to major in math education so that, in addition to your math courses, you acquire the necessary education courses to meet state certification competencies. Following graduation, certified teachers apply for advertised positions in public middle and high schools that often look remarkably similar. Here's one from the Pacific Northwest, but it just as easily could have been from any part of the United States:

Middle School Math Teacher, Oregon: Bachelor's degree in related field and Oregon license required; annual salary $25,706 to $50,769; application deadline November 16. To request an application and more information, call 1-513-555-1234.

Teaching positions are well advertised, and all certified teacher graduates are qualified for entry-level math teaching assignments. Actually, in some situations the first-year teacher's inexperience can be a plus. With school budgets under terrific strain, principals, superintendents, and other hiring officials may be more attracted to a new teacher who will earn a lower salary than a more experienced teacher with a higher degree who would take a larger proportion of salary funds.

Is it possible to teach math at the high school level without state certification and with a bachelor of arts in math? Maybe. In some public school districts that have had difficulty securing teachers because of location or pay scales, there have been provisions made to grant temporary certification to noncredentialed teachers. This is, however, not very common and often occurs in geographic areas that, for reasons of locale or economic impact, do not otherwise attract a good supply of applicants. Consequently, those districts may not be attractive to you. Some private high schools might consider a noncertified teacher, although that is not universally true. Schools often have needs for a long-term substitute position for secondary math teachers due to illness or pregnancy and again, depending upon the pool of applicants, a noncertified teacher might secure a long-term substitute position in these cases.

Even if you secure a provisional situation or a long-term substitute job, if you are not certified, you will eventually have to confront the issue of state certification. Further complicating the job search is the varying state licensing standards which can make it difficult for teachers to move from state to state. Although some states have reciprocity agreements, teachers often must undergo additional training to qualify for certification in a new state. Even private schools can, and increasingly do, require teaching credentials that equal or are very close to those which public schools require. In fact, at some private schools, it is not uncommon for a majority of the math teachers to have master's degrees, and there exist numerous large city high schools that have attracted Ph.D.s, as well. As you pursue your job search in a particular geographic locale, you'll naturally become aware of certification standards and requirements.

Teaching with a Master's Degree

A master's degree in math may be helpful in securing a private school teaching position at the high school level, especially if the master's work in math corresponds to the school's needs, i.e., trigonometry, algebra, geometry, etc. Advanced degree work in a master's degree program frequently offers the opportunity to assist a faculty member in teaching an undergraduate class and may include experience designing exams and grading tests as well as staffing math help clinics, etc. Those graduates with master's degrees and no certification at the bachelor's level may also find employment in junior and community college settings or special college programs for adult learners. These schools may welcome the teacher with a master's degree, again, especially if the specialty is one that would be useful in their curriculum. The following is an actual advertisement for a community college level math instructor with a master's degree working in an advising center:

Mathematics: Faculty in Academic Support Center. Full-time tenure track position available beginning July 1. Teach and develop college level and developmental math courses. Master's degree required; experience in alternative learning and flexible formats desirable. Position involves a nontraditional role for faculty that includes a combination of teaching, curriculum development, supervision and mentoring of adjunct faculty, and other assignments commensurate with a growing institution.

Here is another posting for a master's degree candidate working as an instructor of mathematics in a two-year college:

Mathematics Instructor: Essential functions include teaching assignments which may range from developmental mathematics through differential equations. Master's degree in mathematics required. Preferential consideration given to candidates with at least two years of teaching experience and knowledge of graphing technology and computer assisted software.

Teaching with a Doctorate

The doctoral degree in math opens up the world of college teaching to the prospective educator. There is competition for these positions, certainly, although at the time of publication of this volume the number of college teaching positions and the number of new Ph.D.s in mathematics indicates better than average possibilities of securing employment. Positions are well advertised in vehicles such as *The Chronicle of Higher Education,* a weekly newspaper reporting on higher education issues and containing the most complete listing of faculty, staff, and leadership position openings for colleges and universities in the United States and some foreign countries. The following is an ad from *The Chronicle* that would be of interest to a new Ph.D. in math.

Mathematics: Four-year, Catholic, liberal arts college is seeking applications for a tenure-track position. Candidates should have a Ph.D. in mathematics (preferred) with expertise in applied mathematics and/or statistics and strong evidence of excellence in undergraduate teaching. The successful candidate will be capable of assuming a leadership position within the department in the future; will have experience in using current math pedagogy including technology; will be expected to teach all levels of undergraduate mathematics; will participate in student advising. Salary relative to experience.

This ad is interesting for a number of reasons. First, it requires an earned doctorate. To apply, you must have your degree in hand. It's a position that has been reserved for tenure line, so scrutiny for candidates will be intense. All the more so because the ad indicates the candidate must display the potential for assuming a leadership role, probably department chair, at some point in the future. Nevertheless, the undergraduate course load stated suggests the position is open to an exemplary new doctorate who may have accumulated significant teaching experience in graduate school.

Some advertisements will encourage the application of ABD (all but dissertation) candidates who have completed all required doctoral course work but have not yet written their dissertation.

Assistant Professor/Instructor of Mathematics: Ph.D. in mathematics preferred; consideration will be given to candidates with a master's degree in mathematics who have completed all course work toward the doctorate (ABD). College teaching experience required. Responsibilities include teaching lower level

continued

continued

through highest upper division major courses, advising,
committee work, and participation in university functions.
Applicants must possess a strong commitment to
college/university work undertaken.

The preceding advertisement also indicates that the successful candidate
will be balancing teaching with advising, committee work, and participation
in university functions. An ABD will generally not pay as well as an earned
doctorate and will not lead as directly or as quickly to possible tenure and
promotion. ABD candidates will also have to decide how they will finish their
degree (the dissertation often being the most time-consuming aspect of their
academics) *and* hold down a full-time job.

Teaching introductory college math courses is generally part of the teaching load of new college math teachers. Many of your students will be taking some variation of "Introduction to College Math" or whatever the
institution requires for students to meet the college's general education
requirements. Students enrolled in these courses are taking them because it
is a college requirement for graduation and not because they are math majors
or have chosen the course. The math department performs a general education service to the entire college in offering this course. Generally, even
senior faculty will teach at least one class of first-year college math, though
as you become more senior in the faculty, you can add courses more directly
related to your interests and educational background.

The point to remember here is that, despite your advanced degree and
specialized work in mathematics, you are very apt to have a teaching load
that is largely comprised of lower-level courses. You will undoubtedly have
opportunities to pursue your doctoral field in writing and research and
speaking at scholarly conferences, but you may have to teach for a few years
before your teaching schedule includes advanced students.

There is also in the ad cited above demand for documentation of college
teaching experience. This could come from teaching assistantships done
while working on the doctoral degree. Many students acquire this experience as graduate teaching assistants, part-time faculty, lecturers, or adjunct
faculty at other colleges.

The road to a doctorate is fairly long and arduous. It is hard work. Along
the way, you'll meet some wonderful people, some who'll be friends and colleagues the rest of your life. Even colleagues separated by long distances have
the opportunity to revisit at conferences and symposia. You'll have opportunities to write, teach, and perhaps publish—all before you finish your
degree. Take advantage of these opportunities when you can. However, it is

possible to become overly involved in some of these opportunities to the detriment of your degree progress.

There has been considerable discussion in academic circles of the number of individuals who begin doctoral programs and do not see them through to completion. In fact, Neil Rudenstein, the president of Harvard University, published a book on the issue of improving and tightening up the time requirements to earn a Ph.D., particularly in the humanities, where his research clearly demonstrated the longest time lines between initiating the degree and earning it, with a correspondingly high rate of mortality (dropouts) in candidates. In the science and math areas, he found a higher completion rate and shorter time-to-degree completion. The more defined parameters of the fields of science and math, with their emphasis on correct process, formula, and execution seem to lend themselves to a doctoral degree process that is crisp, well-defined, with clearly expressed expectations and deadlines.

WORKING CONDITIONS

High School

The working conditions for teachers of math are dramatically different according to the educational setting. The high school math teacher has a full complement of classes, perhaps as many as five or six a day, and may have study hall or lunchroom supervision duties during the week, responsibilities for some after-school detention centers, or even a sports activity to supervise. The place of discipline in the secondary curriculum has a major impact in the classroom and is perhaps the single most challenging element of the working conditions for any teacher. Having been a high school student yourself, you realize that attendance is for the most part not voluntary, so students sometimes exhibit some resistance, and acting-out through poor behavior is not uncommon.

The effective classroom teacher is one who has successfully mastered classroom management. For many young teachers, these are the most challenging lessons in teaching to accomplish and make for the most interesting stories as they grow in their profession! The balance between the time spent teaching math and maintaining classroom discipline is seldom in equilibrium and can be particularly frustrating, as when one disruptive student threatens the decorum of a class.

Most public high schools are fairly rigid systems of enforced behavior norms, and the principal agents of that enforcement are the faculty. To elect high school math education as your particular arena is to challenge your ability to maintain your poise and focus on the subject matter while at the same time enforcing and administering the necessary disciplinary elements mandated by your school. These include grades, referrals to the principal, detention, warnings, and parent conferences.

Teaching is a full day with clear starting and ending times and much at-home work. Many math teachers correctly incorporate grading of homework by students within class time to provide immediate feedback for work done. Lesson planning is also time consuming, as is maintaining required records of attendance, grades, warnings, progress reports, and other evaluation instruments that may be required in your school district. You will frequently find yourself speaking with parents by telephone from your home in the evenings.

High school teachers are required to accompany students on field trips, be speakers, chaperone dances, or advise yearbooks, literary journals, or other clubs in the school. These also can be very time demanding, and it is important that the teacher entering into secondary teaching understand that these assignments are not so much additions but typically part of what makes up a high school teaching professional's commitment.

College

A college teaching environment is significantly different from a middle or high school setting. There are classes, office hours, meetings, and research work to do. Since college campuses are often wonderful centers of art, music, and intellectual exchange there are frequently events to attend in the evening. Faculty members may act as advisors to fraternities, sororities, campus newspapers, or other clubs which will add to their day. A college day is certainly less rigid than a high school schedule, though it may be just as busy and long. The difference is that for high school teachers, their day is largely predetermined for them. The college teacher, on the other hand, may feel institutional and professional pressures to fulfill certain roles, but the actual determination of how to do that is up to the individual. There is less need to appease a number of outside publics. There is no school board, no parents, no parent-teacher groups to satisfy. The world of the college classroom is closed to outsiders and isn't violated by anyone outside the class. In fact, this convention is so well understood that it is rare to have a class interrupted by anyone outside of the room. Academic freedom protects professors in large part and allows them to express themselves within their class material with far greater freedom than is the case in high school.

Grading, evaluation procedures, numbers of tests, even the issue of whether to have textbooks is entirely up to the faculty member, and if a rationale supports these decisions, the college would not interfere. An added protection is the granting of tenure to established professors who have documented significant teaching histories and excellent student reviews, publications, campus committee work, and outreach to the community. The granting of tenure to established professors gains them an additional degree of job security and further supports their expression of academic freedom. All of these conditions make the classroom environment and the relations of faculty and students very different than earlier experiences in public school. Although the tenure system is under increased scrutiny, and there are movements to initiate measures to determine faculty productivity, these are in their infant stages of development.

In spite of these seeming freedoms, it is important to note here that the standards of accountability still apply, and some are not very different from that of the high school teacher who must meet state educational standards. If you are teaching a basic college course in algebra, it will be very apparent to your colleagues in your department if you are not covering the material adequately. When they receive your students in upper-level classes, they will expect you to have covered certain material. So while college teaching brings much freedom of choice in methods and pedagogy, it in no way frees you of accountability for accomplishing your teaching task.

The actual teaching day in a college or university setting involves fewer class hours taught per day and per week than a high school setting. At an institution that focuses on faculty research, the teacher would be responsible for teaching two to three courses that each meet approximately two hours per week. Colleges that emphasize teaching rather than research require instructors to teach three to four courses for a total of eight to twelve hours of class meetings per week. These class hours and some mandated office hours for advising class students and general advisees are the principle requirements for attendance on the faculty members' part. But as the ad below makes clear, there are other expectations:

Mathematics: Tenure track position in mathematics at the rank of assistant professor. Ph.D. in mathematical sciences is required. Strong commitment to teaching required. Proven teaching ability with experience in technology and a background in statistics is preferred. Responsibilities involve teaching a wide range of undergraduate mathematics and statistics courses; normal teaching load is twelve hours/semester. Besides teaching, the successful candidate will be expected to participate in academic advising, faculty committees, and to engage in professional development activities and community service. Salary is dependent upon educational preparation and years of experience.

In addition to courses and advising, scholarly research is an expectation even of those colleges for whom tenure is not based on publication. All colleges want their faculty to contribute to the scholarly dialogue in their discipline, and this is reviewed by chairs of departments and academic deans periodically throughout the instructor's career. It may be a determining element in granting tenure or promotion. It may also influence issues such as salary negotiations and merit increases.

Committee work is also important as the faculty at most colleges are the governing and rule-making bodies who determine and vote on governance and program changes. Committee work can be issue oriented, such as a commission on the status of women or a faculty pay equity survey; it may be programmatic, such as a committee to study the core curriculum for undergraduates or to devise a new graphic arts major; or it may be related to credentials as in a committee set up to prepare materials for an accreditation visit.

Some committees, such as academic standards, curriculum review, promotion and tenure, planning, and administrator review committees are permanent, though the members may change on a rotating basis. Other groups are formed for a limited time or until completion of some task. These committees are essential, and are one vehicle for guiding the direction of the college. Having the support of all the faculty and constantly fresh and interested members helps to ensure all voices are heard and many different opinions considered in making what are often long-reaching decisions.

TRAINING AND QUALIFICATIONS

Bachelor's Degree

To teach math at the secondary level requires a bachelor of science degree in mathematics education at the secondary level and state certification for the state in which you wish to teach. These programs are well-defined options within the education curriculum of many teacher training colleges and universities. They include student teaching, where you have the opportunity to leave campus and teach actual math classes under a supervising teacher for (usually) a semester. Certification for the state granting the degree is usually part of the degree process and may include the requirement to participate by taking some kind of national examination. You will hear of the National Teacher Examination (NTE) frequently. NTE, however, has become a generalized term that often refers, not just to the original NTE (a specific exam), but to other national professional assessment instruments such as the

Praxis series. If you are applying for certification in Arkansas, Connecticut, Delaware, Georgia, Hawaii, Minnesota, Nebraska, Nevada, New Jersey, North Carolina, Oklahoma, Pennsylvania, Tennessee, West Virginia, or Wisconsin, consult the state Department of Education for information about the test(s) needed in that state. Current state-by-state information is available on The Praxis Series website at *http://www.ets.org/praxis*. In states requiring testing, test preparation is usually now well incorporated into the curriculum.

Master's Conversion Program

Another option for the individual with a degree in math who desires to teach but lacks certification is to enroll in a conversion program at a college or university. These programs offer an opportunity to add the necessary state-mandated teaching requirements to your existing degree. Depending on your undergraduate degree and whether a change of institution is involved, this could require twelve to eighteen months of academic enrollment, and in some cases, a full two years.

Some conversion programs not only provide you with the necessary certification requirements but also confer a master's degree. These master's conversion programs are attractive, but can present some difficulties to the new teacher, depending upon supply and demand. Since your school district must pay you according to your degree, the new principal may find you somewhat less attractive than a comparable candidate with a bachelor's degree in math education and similarly limited experience. Now, if math teachers are in short supply, the hiring officials may be delighted to find you and pay the increase your new degree requires, but this is something to keep in mind.

Conversion programs can also exist independent of a collegiate institution. Some are the product of a consortium of school districts, such as The Upper Valley Teacher Training Institute in Lebanon, New Hampshire. This unique teacher qualifying program takes individuals with bachelor's degrees, many of whom have had other careers or significant work experience, and places them with master teachers in actual classrooms for a full year. Half the year is at one grade level and the remaining half of the year with another grade. The year includes much independent work and follows a contract established at the start of the year. This contract will specify how and when the student will "solo" in the classroom, though in fact, these partnerships between supervising teachers and interns allow for the intern to acquire significant teaching mastery. These learning outcomes ensure that the program delivers the requisite training and experience for certification. There may be a requirement to participate in an associated classroom training program to meet state certification requirements, as well.

College Teaching

College and university teaching requires the doctorate, or in some cases, all but the dissertation (ABD) completed. Salary and assignments will be affected by lack of an earned doctorate. In addition to the doctorate, as we have seen, there may be requirements for teaching experience, a specified degree of research and publication or practice in a particular genre or subject area in math, and some additional competencies. There is almost always the requirement of teaching introductory college math classes to first- and second-year students.

EARNINGS

Middle and Secondary School Teachers

The teachers of math at this level are paid according to the same salary schedules as other teachers in their school district, and these schedules are based on a combination of your degree level and your teaching experience. These salary schedules are public information, and you can obtain them from your state Department of Education or from the particular school district you have an interest in. Teacher salaries vary dramatically across the United States by tens of thousands of dollars depending upon the wealth of the school district and the particular contract teachers have in a district.

Secondary School Teachers

As reported in the *Occupational Outlook Quarterly, Spring 1997*, in the 1995 Current Population Survey (the most recent), secondary school teachers across the country had median earnings of $35,500, compared to $33,400 for elementary school teachers. Salaries vary dramatically from state to state, possibly reflecting differences in cost of living, state education budgets, and job markets. According to another survey, by the National Education Association, the estimated national average salary of all public elementary and secondary school teachers for the 1995–96 school year was $37,900. Public secondary school teachers averaged about $38,600 a year. In some schools teachers receive extra pay for coaching sports or working with students in extracurricular activities.

Public School

The average salary of a public school teacher in Connecticut is $50,400 a year, almost double the average salary of a public school teacher in South

Dakota at $26,300 a year. Salaries also differ by whether a school district is located in an urban, suburban, or rural area and whether it is public or private. The best source of current information on public school teacher salaries is the state Department of Education office for the state in which you hope to teach. Another source of information is the ERIC Clearinghouse on Teacher Education in Washington, D.C., and is located on the Internet at *http://coe.ohio-state.edu/cete/ericcve/*.

Private School

Private school teachers, who are not unionized and are not required to hold a state license, earn substantially less than public school teachers, although they may be provided with free housing and board which offsets the salary reduction. Teachers in public schools had average base salaries of $34,200, compared to $22,000 for teachers in private school.

Postsecondary

Math professors in higher education have significantly higher salaries, as you would expect with their advanced education and graduate degrees. As reported in the January 9, 1998, issue of *The Chronicle of Higher Education*, the American Mathematical Society, the Institute for Mathematics Society, and the Mathematical Association of America surveyed faculty salaries at top-ranked public institutions and found that professors earned an average salary of $80,370 in 1997–98, up from $78,586 the previous year. Assistant professors earned $47,451, up from $46,771. Full professors at top private colleges earned $93,123 in 1997, up from $89,518, while assistant professors made $47,561, up from $45,888.

According to a 1995–96 survey by the American Association of University Professors, salaries for full-time faculty at all institutions averaged $51,000. By rank, the average for professors was $65,400; associate professors, $48,300; assistant professors, $40,100; instructors and lecturers, $33,700 and $30,800 respectively. Faculty in four-year institutions earn higher salaries than those in two-year schools. Average salaries for faculty in public institutions, $50,400, were lower in 1995–96 than those for private independent institutions, $57,500, but better than those for religious-affiliated private institutions, $45,200. Remember, these are average figures, and some teachers may start at a much lower level of pay. Some faculty members are able to add to their base salary by consulting, teaching additional courses, researching, writing for publications, or other scholarly employment, during both the academic year and the summer.

CAREER OUTLOOK

As reported in the *Occupational Outlook Quarterly, Spring 1997*, the career outlook for teaching jobs has several major variables, including the supply of qualified teachers, student enrollments, the discipline being taught, and individual district replacement needs. Replacement needs are very much in the news recently. An article in *The Boston Globe* in March of 1998 outlined the prospect of over 50 percent of Boston public school teachers retiring over the next ten years and real concerns evidenced about the ability to fill all those positions with qualified faculty. Similar situations are predicted, to a varying degree, across the country.

Employment opportunities for teachers are directly tied to enrollments. By 2005, enrollment is expected to grow to 55 million. The fastest growth will be at the secondary level, where enrollment in grades 9 through 12 is expected to grow 21 percent over the 1994–2005 period, from 13 million to 38 million. Because of the projected increase in enrollments, the increase in teaching jobs is expected to be 26 percent over the 1994–2005 period. (The average rate of growth for all occupations is projected to be 14 percent.) Historically, the number of teachers employed has always continued to increase even during periods of declining enrollments.

Middle and Secondary School Teachers

As reported by the Bureau of Labor Statistics, the job market for elementary and secondary teachers varies by geographic area and by subject specialty, and currently school districts have difficulty hiring qualified teachers in mathematics. *Recruiting Trends Survey, 1995–1996*, a University of Michigan survey of education administrators in 294 public school districts, found that mathematics positions were one of the most difficult positions to fill. Both inner city and rural areas have difficulty attracting teachers. Mathematics teachers are in demand generally at the middle and secondary level, but if you are willing to relocate, your outlook for finding a teaching position at the elementary and secondary level improves dramatically. Overall employment of elementary and secondary school teachers is expected to increase about as fast as the average for all occupations through the year 2006. However, employment at the secondary level is expected to grow faster than average. Of course, one of the influences on the availability of teaching positions would be pressures from taxpayers to limit spending for education.

Postsecondary

As reported by the Bureau of Labor Statistics, employment for college and university faculty is expected to increase about as fast as the average for all occupations through the year 2006 as enrollments in higher education increase. This increase is due to projected faculty retirements as those faculty who began teaching in the very late 1960s and 1970s reach retirement age. Additionally, college enrollment is projected to rise from 14 million in 1996 to 16 million in 2006, an increase of 14 percent. Between 1996 and 2006, the traditional college-age population will begin to grow again, spurred by the leading edge of the children of baby boomers reaching college age. As these enrollments start increasing at a faster rate in the late 1990s, opportunities for college faculty may begin to improve somewhat. Still the *Occupational Outlook Handbook* reports that there is keen competition for faculty jobs because of the growing number of Ph.D. graduates competing for these jobs, the trend of hiring adjunct or part-time faculty due to the financial difficulties of colleges and universities, and reduced state funding for public higher education.

STRATEGY FOR FINDING JOBS

Your strategy for finding a mathematics teaching job will vary depending on your degree level, the grade you wish to teach, and the type of school where you plan to work. Different strategies will be required for finding jobs in a public school, private school, or in higher education. There are some common strategies, however:

Step 1

Find out where the positions are listed. For most general employment, only 20 percent of the listings nationwide are published, leaving 80 percent to be discovered by other means, such as the networking techniques we discuss in Chapter 4. But for teaching positions, especially those in public schools, *all* positions are advertised. This is because schools receive some federal funding and thus are required to widely publicize job openings and conform to federal guidelines for hiring.

Take a proactive approach to locating the listings that appeal to you. Make a regular routine of checking newspapers at your local or college library. Your college career office or education department will also have listings or possibly a database. If you have access to the Web (and many public libraries can provide that access), you can check regional and national postings. Keep a notebook listing your favorite website bookmarks and return to them on a regular basis. Take advantage of job fairs for educators. There are annual job fairs listed in your college career office that will be both regional and national. Find out the requirements to attend these fairs. This is a great opportunity to talk directly with principals and superintendents.

Here's how to begin a typical search for teaching positions on the Internet:

1. Make a list of organizations that might have job listings on the Internet: local schools/colleges/universities, school districts, state departments of education, teachers' unions, regional and national associations, local and regional newspapers or periodicals.

2. Call one of the organizations on your list to get its Internet address. Also ask if the organization has other Internet addresses as "links" from its homepage or if the person could give you other sites to check for math teaching positions.

3. When you look up the Internet address or website address you will come to the homepage, and on this page we have found that the job listings fall under such categories as: "career opportunities," "job listings," or "classifieds."

4. Under these categories you can begin a word or topic search with such words as "mathematics," "teaching," "secondary," or "elementary." Some websites have job listings embedded under other headings or require that you be a member of the organization in order to gain access to the job listings.

In most cases, when you arrive at the job posting site, you can print the pages you have identified as meaningful to your job search. Occasionally, you will find some sites that do not allow the printing of Web pages.

The proactive approach also requires researching teacher supply and demand of the geographic areas you're interested in, identifying the schools within that geographic area, and calling the school districts to find out how and where the positions are posted. Don't neglect the professional associations listed at the close of this chapter that might post positions for members.

If there is little demand within your preferred geographic location then you may want to consider relocating. For more information about supply and demand check the Internet site for the Bureau of Labor Statistics, *http://stats.bls.gov/*. If you are mobile and willing to teach anywhere, you will have a significant advantage in the job market, since you can relocate to where job openings are available and avoid areas where the competition for jobs is more intense. Varying state licensing standards, which make it difficult for teachers to move from state to state, further complicate the job market. Although some states have reciprocity agreements, teachers often must undergo additional training to qualify to receive a license in a new state.

Step 2

Prepare your job search materials and techniques. These include:

❑ Your resume

❑ A cover letter

❑ Interviewing skills

Find the position that matches your teaching skills and experience. As you review the listings compare your interests, abilities, values, experiences, and skills to those listed in the position description. If there is a match then you can begin to prepare a resume and cover letter that speak directly to the position you have selected.

Chapter 2 will be a good resource for the resume and cover letter, and you'll find we've included some samples of each. Have your resume fine-tuned and ready to be submitted at a moment's notice. Sometimes you might hear about positions that have a deadline within twenty-four hours!

Write a cover letter that focuses on the benefits of hiring you and describes how your credentials match with the employer's needs. The hiring official reviews your credential packet and compares it with the qualifications outlined in the position description. If there is a match, then you will likely be asked to be interviewed. The final goal is getting an interview with the hiring official—and of course, being hired too!

Register with your college's credential file service. These credential files contain your resume, recommendations, and other pertinent information that would help you qualify for teaching positions. There may be a small setup fee for this credential file. If there is, think about the advantage of the convenience of credentials being in one location and being mailed from a central location. When you begin your search, the credentials can be sent as a packet directly to the school or superintendent that is advertising the teaching position.

The interview is a conversation between you and the hiring official, and this conversation allows you let the hiring official know why you are there, what you are looking for as a math teacher, and what you have to offer your students and the organization. In addition, you have the opportunity to support the information you wrote in your resume and cover letter. Chapter 5 offers some detailed tips on successful interview strategy. The more interviews you have, the more skilled you become at interviewing and the greater your chance of gaining a teaching contract. Putting your education to work gives you a wonderful feeling of accomplishment.

Step 3

Use networking to your advantage. Make sure those in your personal and professional network know that you are seeking a teaching position, what your interests are, and the geographic area in which you wish to work, so that they can keep you informed of any positions that might become available. In addition, while attending professional conferences or meetings, start networking with your colleagues by asking what might be available at their institutions. The best sources of information for schools seeking to fill a position are the recommendations of colleagues and former teachers. These recommendations are considered referrals when the candidates' credentials are reviewed by the search committee.

Networking is an art, and it is easily abused. In Chapter 6, we discuss how to carefully build a helpful network, and, even more important, how to close that network down when you have found a teaching position. You never know when you might need those contacts again. In many cases, you'll encounter your network contacts at conventions, training sessions, and workshops during your career.

Strategies for Finding Public School Jobs

Send a cover letter and resume to the schools that interest you. The state departments of education provide listings of all public schools in each state which give you the name of the superintendents, principals, personnel officers, or other administrative contacts. Not only do these listings give the names but the telephone numbers and addresses are listed as well. Check with your career services office for these directories published by the state Department of Education.

Strategies for Finding Private School Jobs

Private schools seldom advertise positions in newspapers in order to have a more select pool of candidates and to maintain a lower public profile than their public school counterparts. Finding a job teaching math in private schools requires more research work and diligence than looking for teaching positions in public schools. You'll need to check with your library or career services office for a directory of private schools. These directories (a good example is *The Handbook of Private Schools*, 1997 edition) list important information about grade levels, tuition, number of students and their gender, faculty, special facilities, and a short history of the institution. Send a resume and cover letter to each school where you would like to work.

For a private school job search we also suggest you consider placement agencies. As career counselors, we very seldom suggest third-party services.

However, many private schools use teacher recruitment services for their discretion and the efficiencies of time and money they offer. Be sure to investigate the services provided and any fees required by you before signing on the dotted line.

POSSIBLE EMPLOYERS

Directories

Patterson's Elementary Education and *Patterson's American Education* contain listings of school districts, superintendents, public and private schools. Private schools are found in *Peterson's Guide to Independent Secondary Schools* or the *Handbook of Private Schools*. These may be found in your career services office or a public or university library. If you are considering teaching at the college level, look at college guides to two- or four-year colleges, such as: *Peterson's Guide to Two Year Colleges, Peterson's Guide to Four Year Colleges, Peterson's Guide to Graduate Study*. In addition, Peterson's offers a series of publications, *Peterson's Job Opportunities for Health and Science Majors . . .* , which offers job opportunities in education.

Career Office Postings

Career offices post openings directly from organizations and subscribe to various regional and national listings as well. Math teaching positions can be found in publications such as *Current Jobs for Graduates in Education, Community Jobs, The Job Hunter, Current Jobs for Graduates, The Chronicle of Higher Education*. These publications have homepages where you may preview the listings free or subscribe to the them on the Internet!

Math Departments

Sometimes postings are sent directly to the mathematics departments, where they are posted on a bulletin board or in a binder in the department office. Give a phone call to the departmental secretary.

Professional Associations

Professional associations often publish their own newsletter or journal where openings are listed in a section of their publication. Review the list of professional associations in the last section of this chapter and contact those associations to see if they provide a listing either by telephone, fax, e-mail, or Internet.

POSSIBLE JOB TITLES

Most job titles will have the word "teacher," and advertisements might list them as:

Cooperating teacher	High school math teacher
Educator	Math instructor
Elementary school math teacher	Math/science teacher

In higher education, the status of the position becomes part of the title, such as:

Assistant professor	Instructor of mathematics
Associate professor	Professor of mathematics

In addition, teachers of mathematics find positions in:

Banking	Information science (technology)
Defense contract companies	Management and public relations
Disease control and prevention centers	Mapping agencies
	Research and testing
Engineering	Science, engineering, and technical services
Federal government	
Health insurance companies	State government

RELATED OCCUPATIONS

Mathematics teachers share the ability to communicate information and ideas with other types of occupations. Here are some related occupations that require a degree in or knowledge of mathematics. Investigate these and other positions that use this skill base:

Consultants	Policy analysts
Cryptologists	Statisticians
Employee development specialists	Trainers
Librarians	Writers
Lobbyists	

PROFESSIONAL ASSOCIATIONS

Listed below are some of the associations that relate to teachers of mathematics. For more information about these professional associations either check the websites listed or use the *Encyclopedia of Associations* published by Gale Research Inc. Review the members/purpose section for each organization and decide whether the organization pertains to your interests. Membership in one of these organizations might help in terms of job listings, networking opportunities, and employment search services. Some provide information at no charge. If you want to receive their publications that list job opportunities, you might need to join the organization. Check for student member rates. See if these associations can assist you in your job search:

American Association of Colleges for Teacher Education
One Dupont Circle, NW, Suite 610
Washington, DC 20036-1186
Website: http://www.aacte.org/
Members/Purpose: Colleges and universities concerned with the preparation and development of professionals in education and human resources. Seeks to improve the quality of institutional programs of the education profession.
Journals/Publications: *AACT Annual Directory; AACTE Briefs; Journal of Teacher Education*

American Federation of Teachers
555 New Jersey Avenue, NW
Washington, DC 20001
Website: http://www.aft.org//index.htm
Members/Purpose: Works with teachers and other educational employees at the state and local level in organizing, collective bargaining, research, educational issues, and public relations. Conducts research in areas such as educational reform, bilingual education, teacher certification, and evaluation.
Journals/Publications: *AFT Action: A Newsletter for AFT Leaders; American Educator; American Teacher; Healthwire*

American Mathematical Association of Two Year Colleges
Technical Institute of Memphis
5983 Macon Cove
Memphis, TN 38134
Website: http://www.amatyc.org/
Members/Purpose: Two-year college mathematics and computer science professors; four-year college mathematics professors concerned with lower

division mathematics education. Encourages development of effective mathematics programs; allows for the interchange of ideas on the improvement of mathematics education and mathematics-related experiences of students in two-year colleges or at the lower division level.
Journals/Publications: *AMATYC News; AMATYC Review*

American Mathematical Society
P.O Box 6248
Providence, RI 02940-6248
Website: http://www.ams.org
Members/Purpose: Professional society of mathematicians and educators which promotes the interests of mathematical scholarship and research. Holds institutes, short courses, and symposia to further mathematical research; compiles statistics. Maintains biographical archives; offers placement services; compiles statistics.
Journals/Publications: *Abstracts of Papers Presented to the AMS; Assistantships and Fellowships in the Mathematical Sciences; Bulletin of the MMS; Combined Mathematical List; Current Mathematical Publications; Employment Information in the Mathematical Sciences; Journal of the American Mathematical Society; Leningrad Mathematical Journal; Mathematical Reviews*

Association for Women in Mathematics
4114 Computer and Space Science Building
University of Maryland
College Park, MD 20742-2461
Website: http://www.math.neu.edu/awm/
Members/Purpose: Mathematicians employed by universities, government, and private industry; students. Seeks to improve the status of women in the mathematical profession, and to make students aware of opportunities for women in the field. Membership is open to all individuals regardless of gender.
Journals/Publications: Newsletter: *Association for Women in Mathematics; Directory of Women in the Mathematical Sciences; Careers for Women in Mathematics; Careers That Count, Careers in Mathematics; Profiles of Women in Mathematics: The Emmy Noether Lecturers*

Association of State Supervisors of Mathematics
c/o Mari Muri, President
CSDE P.O. Box 2219
Hartford, CT 06145
Website: http://www.maa.org/cbms/members/assm.html

Members/Purpose: Individuals serving on the education agency staff of any U.S. state or possession, the District of Columbia, the U.S. Department of Education, or any Canadian province or territory. Promotes high standards in the teaching of mathematics; encourages interest in mathematics and its teaching. Facilitates exchange of ideas and information among members; promotes cooperation among educational agencies. Identifies the needs of the future and makes recommendations for improving mathematics education.
Journals/Publications: *ASSM Newsletter*

Conference Board of the Mathematical Sciences
1529 Eighteenth Street, NW
Washington, DC 20036
Website: http://www.maa.org/cbms/cbms.html
Members/Purpose: Is an umbrella organization consisting of fifteen professional societies all of which have a primary objective to increase knowledge in one or more of the mathematical sciences. Its purpose is to promote understanding and cooperation among these national organizations so that they work together and support each other in their efforts to promote research, improve education, and expand the uses of mathematics. The fourteen professional societies include AMATY (American Mathematical Association of Two-Year Colleges, AMS (American Mathematical Society), ASA (American Statistical Association), ASL (Association for Symbolic Logic), AWM (Association for Women in Mathematics), ASSM (Association of State Supervisor of Mathematics), BBA (Benjamin Banneker Association), INFORMS (Institute for Operations Research and the Management Sciences), IMS (Institute of Mathematical Statistics), MAA (Mathematical Association of America), NAM (National Association of Mathematicians), NCSM (National Council of Supervisors of Mathematics), NCTM (National Council of Teachers of Mathematics), SIAM (Society for Industrial and Applied Mathematics), SOA (Society of Actuaries).
Journals/Publications: none
Convention/Meeting: semiannual council meeting

Mathematical Association of America
1529 Eighteenth Street, NW
Washington, DC 20036-1385
Website: http://www.maa.org
Members/Purpose: College mathematics teachers; individuals using mathematics as a tool in a business profession.

Journals/Publications: *American Mathematical Monthly; College Mathematics Journal; Mathematical Association of America; Mathematics Magazine*

Math/Science Network
Mills College
5000 MacArthur Boulevard
Oakland, CA 94612-1301
Website: http://www.elstad.com/alta.html
Members/Purpose: Mathematicians, scientists, counselors, parents, community leaders, and representatives from business and industry who are interested in increasing the participation of girls and women in mathematics, science, and technology.
Journals/Publications: *Broadcast/ Beyond Equals: To Promote the Participation of Women in Mathematics; Expanding Your Horizons in Science and Math; A Handbook for Conference Planners*

National Council of Supervisors of Mathematics
P.O. Box 10667
Golden, CO 80401
Website: http://www.maa.org/cbms/members/ncsm.html
Members/Purpose: Supervisors of curriculum and personnel in mathematics departments at the elementary, secondary, and college levels. Seeks to develop solutions to problems in all areas of mathematics supervision and curriculum development; provides a forum for the exchange of ideas and current research results. Works with other groups to improve the teaching of mathematics.
Journals/Publications: Membership Directory; Newsletter

National Council of Teachers of Mathematics
1906 Association Drive
Reston, VA 22091-1593
Website: http://www.nctm.org
Members/Purpose: Teachers of mathematics in grades K–12, two-year colleges, and teacher education personnel on college campuses.
Journals/Publications: *Arithmetic Teacher; Journal for Research in Mathematics Education; Mathematics Teacher; National Council of Teachers of Mathematics—Yearbook; NCTM News Bulletin*

National Education Association
1201 Sixteenth Street, NW
Washington, DC 20036-3290
Website: http://www.nea.org

Members/Purpose: Professional organization and union of elementary and secondary school teachers, college and university professors, administrators, principals, counselors, and others concerned with education.

Journals/Publications: *ESP Annual; ESP Progress; Handbook; NEA Today; Almanac of Higher Education; NEA Higher Education Advocate; Thought and Action*

School Science and Mathematics Association
Bloomsburg University
400 E. Second Street
Bloomsburg, PA l7815-1301
Website: http://hubble.bloomu.edu/~ssma

Members/Purpose: Science and mathematics teachers at elementary through college levels and persons involved in teacher education. Objectives are to facilitate the dissemination of knowledge in mathematics and the sciences; to encourage critical thinking of knowledge in mathematics and the sciences; to encourage critical thinking and use of the scientific method; to emphasize the interdependence of mathematics and the sciences in education, research, writing, curriculum development; to provide the means for dialogue among teachers of mathematics and the sciences; to identify and help solve problems common to science and mathematics education.

Journals/Publications: *School Science and Mathematics; School Science and Mathematics Association Convention Program; SSMARRT Newsletter*

Society for Industrial and Applied Mathematics
3600 Market Street
Philadelphia, PA 19104-2688
Website: http://www.siam.org

Members/Purpose: Mathematicians, engineers, computer scientists, physical scientists, bioscientists, educators, social scientists, and others utilizing mathematics for the solution of problems. Purposes are to promote research in applied mathematics and computational science; further the application of mathematics to new methods and techniques useful in industry and science; provide for the exchange of techniques useful in industry and science; provide for the exchange of information between the mathematical, industrial, and scientific communities.

Journals/Publications: *CBMS-NSF Regional Conference Series in Applied Mathematics; Classics in Applied Mathematics and Proceedings; Frontiers in Applied Mathematics;* Membership List; *Review; SIAM Journal on Applied Mathematics; SIAM Journal on Computing; SIAM Journal on Control and Optimization; SIAM Journal on Discrete Mathematics; SIAM Journal on Mathematical Analysis; SIAM Journal on Matrix Analysis and Applications;*

SIAM Journal on Numerical Analysis; SIAM Journal on Scientific Computing; SIAM News

Women and Mathematics Education
c/o Charlene Morrow
Mt. Holyoke College
302 Shattuck Hall
South Hadley, MA 01075
Website/e-mail: none
Members/Purpose: Individuals concerned with promoting the mathematical education of girls and women. Serves as a clearinghouse for ideas and resources in the area of women and mathematics. Establishes communications for networks focusing on doctoral students, elementary and secondary school teachers, and teacher educators. Encourages research in the area of women and mathematics, especially research that isolates factors contributing to the dropout rate of women in mathematics. Emphasizes the need for elementary and secondary school programs that help reverse the trend of avoidance of mathematics by females.
Journals/Publications: *Women and Mathematics; Women and Education*

CHAPTER ELEVEN

PATH 2: MATH AS A PRIMARY SKILL: ACTUARY, MATHEMATICIAN, STATISTICIAN, AND OPERATIONS RESEARCH ANALYST

No self-respecting career guide for math majors would leave out the jobs in this chapter: actuary, mathematician, statistician, and operations research analyst. These jobs are the crème de la crème of jobs for new graduates with a math major. Opportunities for math majors in these traditional occupational roles have been covered exhaustively in countless fine career guides, including another recent publication by VGM Career Books entitled *Jobs for Number Crunchers and Other Quantitative Types* by Rebecca Burnett. This is a superb guide to career opportunities in math and includes a strong section on actuarial careers. We recommend it.

The positions outlined in this chapter, like the teaching jobs addressed in the previous chapter, keep you within the world of mathematics on a day-to-day basis. Teaching does that, too, of course, but teaching also demands a tolerance for the distractions of classroom management, lesson planning, committee work, and even lunchroom duty!

Not every lover of mathematics is called to teach. And many in the teaching profession would be the first to admit that those other issues such as discipline and ancillary duties mean teaching is a profession designed for those who can maintain the balance between all of these competing demands. In Path 2, we consider a series of jobs that are representative of career situations that see your math education as *essential.* Many career guides will treat the jobs in this chapter as the *only* positions available for math majors who want to use math daily in their work. This book and the other career options it presents are evidence to the contrary.

The authors know that math majors are people, too. You're as different as any other group of bright, talented individuals. You all want different things out of your lives and workdays. Just because you're talented at math doesn't necessarily mean you want to live, breathe, and dream math. Some of you do and others may simply want to use their gifts to earn a living. Regardless of your motives, the authors want to give you as much information as possible to help you make a positive start to your career.

So while the good advice about the four areas of employment covered in this chapter should be available in any career guide, we'll endeavor to put a different spin on these traditional occupations. To do that, we'll be frank and direct about the pluses and minuses of each job and we'll also attempt to give you an opportunity to learn about a broad array of employers and job sites where these occupations can be found.

In every case, however, in the positions described below and in others suggested later in this chapter, your math degree will be *the* critical hiring qualification. More to the point, your math expertise will be something you utilize every day. It will figure as a major influence on your career from your first interview and could easily be the aptitude you credit with your advancement and promotion in any of these fields. The job ad below for an entry-level statistician is a good example of the emphasis employers will place on your math expertise:

Statistician/Project Analyst: Qualified candidate will learn all phases of the model building process, including submitting SAS jobs, generating distributions, and generating reports for

continued

> continued
>
> customer presentations (i.e., industry tables/performance charts). Requires a B.S./B.A. degree in statistics, mathematics, economics, computer science, or related field. Experience in data manipulation and model building using statistical software and/or other mainframe software necessary. Knowledge of SAS and MS Office applications essential. Must possess analytical skills to evaluate, understand, and interpret data from both our organization and the customer's perspective. Openings in Orange, CA, and Atlanta, GA.

Our first piece of straight talk in this chapter has to do with your value to the employment market. The latest issue of *Recruiting Trends* from the Michigan State Collegiate Employment Research Institute cites the estimated average starting salary for new graduates in mathematics as $33,180. That's a full $10,000 over the average starting salary for your classmates in education, and it's higher than business majors, communications majors, advertising, accounting, and other so-called, "glamour" majors.

If the expression "Money talks!" has any meaning for career counselors, it's a sure sign that the graduates of that major are in demand. There are two principal reasons for this demand: one is supply, the other is needed skills. Look around your math department and look at some of the other departments on your campus. Our guess is there are far more business, education, and accounting majors than math majors. That's one reason you're so much in demand. There simply aren't enough graduates to meet demand, and when the supply is thin, the price goes up.

But the other reason is more complex and has a tremendous impact on your entry into the fields in this chapter and your entire career progress. And it's something that needs to be made very clear. Let's return to that quoted starting salary for your major and ask very pointedly, "Which of your fellow graduates is ready to sit right down at a desk or conference table or go out on a consulting call and *do something*?" The math major.

The point we're trying to stress here in this book and especially in this chapter is that of the many college majors offered, math is one of the few that actually delivers up graduates who have specific skills and knowledge that can be put to work immediately with minimal training and grooming. Math may be science, but it's also incredibly practical, and that makes it easier for math majors to answer that famous question, "What are you going to do with that?"

Let's take a fresh look at those four standard career options for math majors to see what they might offer you.

ACTUARY

If you haven't appreciated the role of the actuary in today's business community, you will soon. The assumption of your own insurance payments when you graduate from college (if you haven't already) may expose you to some issues that actuaries have played a role in shaping and responding to. Why do young women pay less for the same coverage on their automobiles than young men do? How can term life insurance be so inexpensive and still be a good thing? How can they sell such enormous life insurance policies so cheaply at airports? The answers to these and many other questions about probabilities have been answered by actuaries.

Actuaries make a crucial contribution to any insurance organization that is attempting to stay competitive with other similar organizations and yet maintain insurance rates that will allow the necessary cash reserves to pay claims that come against the organization. There are all kinds of actuaries, with most actuaries specializing in a particular area—life insurance, health insurance, property or liability insurance, for example. There is a very large and growing field of pension actuaries who manage the risk involved in retirement planning.

The reason actuarial jobs are often mentioned for math majors is that their work involves lots of math. But here's our next piece of frank advice. Math skill is critical, however, actuaries are problem solvers who need to put their talents to work in a number of different settings. So they need to be good listeners in order to understand the issues involved. They need to be well-read and keep up on current trends and issues in business, the social sciences, law, and economics. They have a professional interest in news stories such as the risks of second-hand smoke, the length of hospital stays for pregnancy, studies on teenage depression, or any of a number of social and cultural factors that can affect longevity and risk management in insurance. Here's an entry-level job—the employer is a major life insurance annuity business that stresses just those factors:

Actuarial Student/Assistant Actuary: Responsibilities include preparing quarterly reserve information, maintaining segmented asset models, providing various projections related to the company's assets, preparing mortality studies, calculating reserve factors, and working on special projects as needed. Requirements: B.S. in mathematics, strong computer skills, high level of general information, detail oriented, and strong verbal and written skills. Competitive salary and comprehensive benefits.

Math may be crucial, but, hopefully, you are getting the point that actuaries really need to be very well-rounded. While they may have high salaries, they earn them. To be successful, they must have a combination of depth of math knowledge and breadth of general knowledge in regard to business and social trends.

Like any member of a management team, actuaries have to be good communicators—but with a difference. The truly valuable actuary is the man or woman who can take the complicated situations and variables to project probabilities of sickness, death, injury, disability, unemployment, retirement, or property loss and explain these in terms nonactuaries can understand.

And for anyone who might have the nerve to suggest this is a dull profession, we'll offer a bit of advice. There is perhaps no one as involved in the changing face of our culture as actuaries. Let's take AIDS for example. Think of the changes that have taken place in the number of people affected by this disease and the almost daily changing projection for their health and longevity as new treatments and medications come on the market. Actuaries dealing with these kinds of health issues are probably as well informed as anyone in the world regarding the cutting edge of AIDS treatment.

This brings up another important point. Actuaries just don't sit around figuring out when we're going to die. Remember, what actuaries do is create and maintain valuable statistics that help organizations predict the future and offer the best service at the most competitive price. Many students we talk with protest they don't want a "desk job." Well, we don't really know about too many jobs for college graduates that could classify as "desk jobs." Actuarial jobs often involve a lot of time away from the office. The example below is an entry-level job where the actuary trainee will help consult on welfare benefit teams for different companies:

Health and Welfare Benefits Consultant: Opportunities in Dallas, Chicago, and Cleveland. Must have a math degree from an accredited four-year college, strong analytical and written communication skills, actuarial studies/exams or technical benefits–related work experience a plus, good computer knowledge, including Microsoft Word, Excel, and Powerpoint, the ability to work as part of a team in a fast-paced environment and the ability and desire to travel 50 percent of the time.

In this way, you can easily see how this is a helping profession. Without actuaries, we would have no idea of what to charge policyholders for the coverage they want and, more importantly, might not be prepared to pay out claims for the very damages insurance was purchased to indemnify.

Below is a short checklist of qualities that you need to be a successful actuary. If most of these are true for you, probably you should seriously investigate the actuarial field:

- ❑ Do you truly enjoy problem-solving? Actuaries are the not the kind of people who just want a problem to "go away." They enjoy looking at problems from different perspectives and finding new and creative ways of solving them. Is that you?

- ❑ Are you a curious person who enjoys learning? Do you read the newspaper, watch the news, and generally stay abreast of how the world works? Is your level of general information fairly high? Actuaries are very much in the world.

- ❑ Are your math skills superior? This question will be true for every job in this chapter, but it's particularly apt for actuaries. Math is the very heart and soul of this job, and you need to ask yourself not only "Am I good?" but "Is math something I can see myself doing every day?" If the answer is yes, give some serious thought to actuarial work.

MATHEMATICIAN

Mathematics is our oldest science and its history is fabulous, mysterious, and deeply engaging to many. To wit, right now on bookstore shelves we see featured two bestsellers on the same mathematical mystery, *Fermat's Enigma* and *Fermat's Last Theorem*. Pierre de Fermat lived in Toulouse, France, in 1601. In 1637, scribbling in the margin of a book, he indicated he had solved a celebrated theory of numbers but lamented that the book's margin did not contain enough space to record the solution! For over 300 years mathematicians have labored to solve this problem. Just recently (1993) Andrew Wiles of Princeton announced his solution, only to have someone discover it was flawed. Professor Wiles went back to work for another year (he had already worked seven years on the problem) to firmly establish his solution. High drama, indeed!

At the same time, we have a runaway hit movie entitled *Contact,* starring Jodie Foster playing an astronomer devoted to listening for signs of extraterrestrial life in the universe. When she eventually makes contact with another planet, it is through prime numbers. She is least surprised by this, for as she says, "Mathematics is the international language!" While this movie is a fiction, the use of numbers and mathematics as a possible means to communicate with another life form has been present since our earliest days of space exploration.

A third sign of the place of mathematics in our lives is yet another new book, this one entitled *The Number Sense: How the Mind Creates Mathematics* by Stanislas Dehaene. This is an important study that says we humans can count before we can speak. Dehaene sees math not as something we acquire from someplace else, but something inherent in our mind and brains. He then goes on to show how culture, and especially language, can enhance or impede that mathematical sense.

So, obviously the work of mathematics goes on and there is much, much more to learn. Mathematicians do research in fundamental mathematics or in the application of mathematics to areas such as economics, social science, engineering, and other fields. They try to learn more about what math has to tell us or apply direct mathematical solutions to various fields. All the areas of math are involved, including algebra, geometry, number theories, logic, and topology. Generally, the work of mathematics is either applied or theoretical, but there are many math occupations that blur the distinction between the two.

Essentially, those working in theoretical math occupations are seeking to enhance our understanding of math. Their concern as they work is not how this understanding might affect our lives, but simply to know more. Theoretical mathematicians have given us many great achievements in science and engineering.

Those working in the field of applied mathematics are using their math skills to develop mathematical models or computational methods that can be used to solve real world problems—often in business, government, science, engineering, and a host of other disciplines. Sophisticated advertising agencies are increasingly developing mathematical models to account for the variables that affect a product's life cycle and the effects of increased expenditures for advertising or promotion.

Here's a sample job announcement for a mathematician straight out of college who might have some work experience or internship using data management:

Mathematician/SAS Analyst: Provide technical support to an epidemiological research group performing large, data-intensive studies of the health of military personnel. Requires at least one year of experience in data management and analysis using SAS. Must be able to perform frequency and univariate analyses on study data. Working knowledge of various desktop PC software. Formal training in statistics, biostatistics, or epidemiology a plus.

Contrary to popular opinion, mathematicians make news, too! In November of 1996, *The Boston Globe* banner headlined "$200 Million Error—in Your Favor." Burt Feinberg, a mathematician for the Massachusetts State Rating Bureau, a division of the state's Division of Insurance, discovered that consumers had been overcharged since 1991 because of the manner in which industry expenses had been calculated in annual rate cases. As was quoted in the newspapers over the many days this story ran, "This is an extremely complicated, arcane thing. From a consumer's standpoint, it's not an understatement to say that Burt's a hero on this issue."

What's algebra worth? About $200 million to the people of the state of Massachusetts. Mr. Feinberg was profiled as being born to working-class parents in Long Beach, New York, in an environment where playing with numbers was a way of life. "I guess I was just always ahead in math. Mom would feed me simple arithmetic problems. I saw it as fun." His boss reported in the newspapers that in addition to being good at math, Mr. Feinberg was also good at "stepping back and looking at the big picture."

Mathematicians use computers extensively in model making, analyzing and correlating relationships, and simply processing large amounts of data. The point here is that, in addition to your math skills, the most valuable hires in both theoretical and applied math settings are those individuals who have taken the time to learn a number of relevant software packages and may even have been involved in writing programs.

Later in this chapter you'll see that mathematicians have a great variety of job titles. The reason for this is that both theoretical and applied math occur in many settings. And in these settings mathematicians may be called researchers, analysts, specialists, and titles that are more reflective of the field they are working in. A cryptologist (the branch of mathematics that deals with designs to transmit secret information), an agricultural economist, and an operations researcher are all mathematicians. Name your field!

STATISTICIAN

The *Dictionary of Occupational Titles (DOT)* is perhaps not an exciting book (except maybe to a career counselor), and while its job descriptions are not written in a very dynamic way, they have proved to be remarkably accurate. Here's the *DOT*'s write-up of *statistician*:

> Statistician, Mathematical. Conducts research into mathematical theories and proofs that form basis of science of statistics and develops statistical methodology: Examines

theories, such as those of probability and inference, to discover mathematical bases for new or improved methods of obtaining and evaluating numerical data. Develops and tests experimental designs, sampling techniques, and analytical methods, and prepares recommendations concerning their utilization in statistical surveys, experiments, and tests. Investigates, evaluates, and prepares reports on applicability, efficiency, and accuracy of statistical methods used by physical and social scientists.

This dry-as-dust description doesn't begin to suggest the variety, the interest, and the scope of the statisticians' possible work settings. In the government and private sector, statisticians analyze consumer prices, employment patterns, and population trends. The results of their work will have a major impact on public policy, the administration of many social programs, and the practices and policies of many private businesses.

But that's not all. Scientific research of all kinds uses statistical information and the mathematicians who qualify to handle that material. It may be radiocarbon dating of volcanoes, or biochemical work in new drug trials. It could easily involve new agricultural techniques or human behavior studies that help us understand what we do and why we do it.

Private industry may use the work of statisticians to ensure they are neither understocked nor holding too much inventory. Statisticians may be asked to predict consumer behavior, to maintain quality of production, or ensure the viability of retirement investment accounts. The list goes on and on, and the applications of statistical mathematics are too vast for this small career guide.

Once again, however, you can easily see that mathematics and those who practice it are on the cutting edge of the issues and concerns of our society. The search for new and improved medical therapies for cancer, Alzheimer's, cystic fibrosis, and many of the medical challenges of the twenty-first century is being performed by teams of scientists that include statisticians. Likewise, in our increasing concern for the environment, we need the skill of statisticians to help us understand and see the impact of human behavior on life on this fragile planet.

Big questions such as those listed above occupy the working time of many statisticians. But statisticians are also working in many other fields each day with smaller but equally important questions for marketers (What are people buying at the grocery store?), advertisers (What is America watching on TV this week?), developers (Where should we site this new fast-food franchise?), social scientists (How many emergency room admissions are the result of gang violence?).

Ask yourself the following questions to test your interest in being a statistician:

❑ Are you good at and do you enjoy both math and computers?

❑ Do you like working with real-life problems?

❑ Much of the work of the statistician is done as part of a larger group effort. Do you have any experience with and would you enjoy working as part of a team?

❑ Are you a good listener? Statisticians frequently need to talk with people who don't understand statistics but need statistical information. To understand people's needs, you need to be a good listener.

❑ How do you feel about a steady diet of new problems, new challenges, and learning new things?

If you answered these questions in the affirmative, it's probably a good indication that you should continue to explore the careers offered to statisticians.

OPERATIONS RESEARCH ANALYST

Our fourth category of jobs using mathematics as a primary skill is operations research analyst. This is yet another fascinating job category where your math skills can take you to almost any field of human endeavor. To have a sense of what some operations research analysts do, a visit to Chicago's O'Hare International Airport would be both overwhelming and illustrative. The video monitors with many visual displays of arrivals and departures of aircraft from all over the world attest to a staggering amount of scheduling.

Add to that the incredibly complex system of baggage handling and routing as passengers for different flights all check in at the same counter within minutes of each other. Think, too, of food and beverage preparation and stocking requirements for all these aircraft. Most importantly, and crucially, are the on-ground maintenance checks and quick repairs that must often be done to keep the aircraft flight worthy. Consider the logistics involved in making sure those parts are available, that your favorite beverage is on board, and that your luggage arrives when you do.

Running any complex organization requires incredible coordination of people, machines, and materials. Operations research analysts, sometimes called management science analysts, help large organizations mount and run systems such as our airport example. They do this by applying mathematical concepts to organizational problems, generating a number of possible solutions, and then choosing solutions that meet the organization's goals, finances, mission, and philosophy.

Here's an ad for an entry-level operations research analyst that will serve as an excellent example because the industry advertising (small package transportation market) shares many similarities to our baggage example!

Operations Research Analyst: XYZ, Inc., a rapidly growing leader in the small package transportation market, is seeking candidates in business planning and operations research. These positions are located at our Boston corporate headquarters. Duties include developing and utilizing mathematical models and analytical tools to improve current operation and reduce operating costs, create and implement new tools to monitor and improve performance, provide operational support for planning and maintaining/implementing existing and new services, enhance/implement operational research techniques. This position requires a B.S. in mathematics or operations research. Must have excellent written and spoken communication skills, 1–2 years experience, good working knowledge of PC, SAS, Excel, Lotus, and be able to work independently at problem solving in a dynamic work environment.

Predicting how systems will work involves mathematical modeling, extensive use of the computer, and lots of consultation with other people, especially people on-site who will be involved in making these systems operational. Computer use, listening skills, teamwork, and the computer. Sound familiar? Like every other job type mentioned in this chapter, operations research analysts share these common needs.

Basically, you'll begin your problem solving by doing a needs assessment. You'll begin by talking to working professionals and trying to understand the problems and nature of their work. Maybe your job is to try to assess economic order quantities (EOQs) for materials purchases. Over-ordering means risking damage or loss or stock becoming out-of-date; under-ordering means you risk a stock-out and/or a production shutdown.

You'll take your problem and isolate all its elements and ensure you understand and have information on each of these elements. For example, you might want to learn about alternate shipping methods for transporting parts, direct computer links to the parts suppliers, etc.

Then you'll begin to design a series of analytical techniques using any number of mathematical models to construct a system that solves the problem at hand. These methods might include simulations, linear optimization, networks, waiting lines, and game theory.

Generally, use of the computer involves significant work with databases. Operations research analysts need to master database collection, management, and programming to be successful. Many of the mathematical models employed by operation research analysts are very large and multilayered and use major amounts of computer resources to process.

WORKING CONDITIONS

All of the paths we discuss in this chapter generally work regular hours in an office environment, although there may be frequent team meetings and project committee work. None of these jobs are desk bound; some, including actuaries, may travel to branch offices of their own employer or to the offices of clients. Frequently, there are deadlines to be met, and that means occasionally working under pressure. As all of these jobs are management-level, salaried employees, it is not uncommon to work more than a forty-hour week to accomplish specific tasks or during certain times of the year. Because new information is vital to all of these jobs, there is typically frequent opportunity for professional development which may include traveling to seminars and conferences.

TRAINING AND QUALIFICATIONS

A strong background in math and computers is certainly essential for all of the jobs listed in this chapter. All of these positions also require you to think logically, work well with people, and have good oral and written communication skills. Each job category, however, presents its own unique set of training and qualification demands.

Actuaries

Again, the authors need to be frank here. There are math majors and there are math majors. All of the jobs in this chapter require superior math skills. Not only that, but it would not be uncommon during the interview process to discuss mathematical issues with you. Not on the first interview, perhaps, but if you return for a second interview with any employer for an actuarial, statistician, operations research analyst, or mathematician-type position, you may be shown some work-in-progress and asked to comment on it. You might be asked to spend some time on a sample problem or case study involving mathematical processes. So your math must be top-notch. Though in many of the *Great Jobs* series, we have indicated employers seldom look at college transcripts, in your case that is not true. Your transcript and your performance in your major courses will probably be of real interest to these employers, since many of them took the same courses. All of these interview procedures help the employer to understand your strengths and weaknesses and have a richer appreciation for how you might be utilized in the organization.

The rewards of a career in actuarial work (and there are many rewards) are probably directly related to the passing of the many levels of qualifying examinations to achieve professional standing. All professional actuaries begin by taking the same three initial examinations and then, following specialization, go on to take their own specific course of additional examinations in their professional specialty. It's not unusual for some college students to have taken and passed one or two of these exams prior to graduation. Generally speaking, it takes from five to ten years to pass the entire series. With the passage of different exams, you move from actuary trainee, to actuary, to actuary associate.

Statisticians

Math majors also can find employment with their bachelor's degree as statisticians. Many of you will have taken a significant number of the courses offered in your math departments at college. Those will be important, of course, but your employer will also be interested in what and how many statistics courses you took as well. Try to take as many specific courses in statistics as your math department offers.

Don't neglect the opportunity to take additional hours of quantitative courses in any other discipline your college might offer, as well. For example, there may be statistics courses in an engineering, education, premed, social science, or biology department. Depending upon your own interests and the prerequisites for those courses, you might want to try your hand at some of those. It will come in handy in your job search. Statistician jobs occur in a variety of settings.

Job candidates for federal positions will need to document at least six semester hours in statistics courses and nine semester hours in other math courses. Higher-level positions with the government have commensurately higher demands for advanced math courses.

Like all the positions in this chapter, employers seeking statisticians want good communicators, and those hiring in the private sector want job candidates who have a solid working knowledge of business, economics, and management practices.

Operations Research Analysts

You'll begin your career doing routine assignments under the supervision of an experienced supervisor who most likely will have an advanced degree. Many employers prefer operational research analysts to have at least a master's degree. There are entry-level positions in this field, but you'll have to work hard to prove yourself as the premium candidates generally have advanced degrees. Your entry-level title may be as a coordinator or project manager. As bachelor's degree candidates advance with their employer in operational management, they may begin to attend university classes to gain their advanced degree at the employer's expense. That, however, may be more of an unspoken demand than an option if you want to advance beyond the lower rungs of the employment ladder. The great thing about working on a master's degree while employed is that, although it certainly impacts your social life and sleep, your job gives you wonderful day-to-day laboratory of experiences that make the learning come alive.

In addition to your continuing professional improvement, your qualifications should include some demonstrations of your ability to think logically, to work well with people, and some samples of your written work. Your communication skills during your interview will also be judged. Your resume should include a section devoted to your computer skills, indicating systems and software you are familiar with or proficient in, as computer expertise is yet another important qualification for operations research analysts.

Here's a job ad for a project analyst (a common entry-level job title in operations research) that touches on many of these skill and attribute demands:

Project Analyst: The Dynamic Group is a $6.2 billion firm owned by the PBC Corporation, parent company of Air National Airlines. We are the leading provider of business decision-support tools for the transportation and travel industry. Using innovative operations research techniques and cutting-edge technology, we provide creative solutions for our clients' toughest problems. Success in the role of project analyst generally requires a B.S. in mathematics or operations research, industrial engineering, computer science or an equally analytical discipline, though our analysts come from a variety of college majors. Analysts are the primary point of contact for our clients and function in a variety of

continued

---

continued

ways. They are responsible for the implementing of our software at clients' sites, training users, technical writing, troubleshooting, and ongoing customer support. This position requires strong problem-solving skills, excellent communication skills, a teamwork ethic, and the ability to juggle multiple tasks and clients. Some travel is required.

Mathematicians

For mathematicians, there are many jobs for the bachelor's degree recipient. In federal government (the largest employer of math majors), you must have a four-year degree with a math major for entry-level positions as a mathematician. Courses you should consider taking include calculus, differential equations, and linear and abstract algebra. Beyond this, courses in mathematical analysis, topology, numerical analysis, probability theory, and statistics are also worthwhile.

As with operations research analysts, taking mathematics courses in other disciplines at your college would be very advantageous if you can meet the prerequisites and have an interest in the subject matter. Look into the math offerings in the computer, engineering, physical and social sciences, as well as economics departments.

In the private sector, too, there will be positions available for every degree level, however, the entry-level positions may be entitled something other than mathematician. You may be called a researcher, programmer, systems analyst, or systems engineer. Generally, the full title of mathematician is reserved for those holding advanced degrees.

EARNINGS

Actuaries

Earnings are excellent for math graduates with a bachelor's degree. In 1995, according to the most recent edition of the *Occupational Outlook Handbook* (citing a survey by the National Association of Colleges and Employers), entry-level salaries averaged about $36,000. With the passing of different stages of your qualifying examinations, many firms will raise your salary level and/or accompany your test success with a bonus. Newly designated Associates in the Society of Actuaries average about $46,000, according to the 1994 salary survey of insurance and financial companies conducted by the Life Office Management Association. Senior Fellows in the Society of Actuaries who have ten years experience as Senior Fellows average over $100,000.

Statisticians

Salary is a funny aspect of a job. If you hate your work, a high salary may be reward enough to hold you in a job you don't enjoy because you have the resources to utilize your nonwork time as you wish. You can compensate. If you are unhappy with the job and your coworkers, it's been our experience that in those cases, money becomes very unimportant and people will do anything to change jobs, including taking a pay cut.

Salaries for statisticians are going to average the highest of all the salaries possible in this book. At the time this book went to press, the average salary for statisticians was $61,000, and that includes statisticians working in supervisory or managerial jobs. For practicing mathematical statisticians, the average was $65,000. Although these are averages, they give you a sense of the pay levels. Of course, those statisticians who earn master's degrees and other more advanced degrees received even higher salaries.

Operations Research Analysts

The average salary for operations and systems researchers was $42,400 a year in 1996. The middle range of that average had salaries between $33,000 and $55,000. As with most private employers, there is quite a range of pay possible for people doing the same job at the same level of experience. Federal government positions generally pay within a narrower range than private employment, therefore the average salary in 1997 was $66,760. You need to remember, however, in considering these salaries that it includes those who have a master's degree since advanced degrees predominate in this particular path.

Mathematicians

The National Association of College and Employers (NACE) reports from a 1997 survey that starting salaries averaged about $31,800 a year for mathematics graduates with a bachelor's degree and $38,300 for a master's degree.

These are very high starting salaries. Stop by your career office and look at their estimates of starting salaries for business majors, accountants, marketing types, and other employment-oriented fields, and you'll find your average starting salary in math is among the highest.

According to the Bureau of Labor Statistics, the average annual salary for mathematicians who worked for the federal government in supervisory, non-supervisory, and managerial positions was $62,000; for mathematical statisticians, $65,660; and for cryptanalysts, $56,160.

EMPLOYMENT OUTLOOK

Actuaries

The general trend in the economy now is to coalesce businesses, to merge and to gain efficiencies by downsizing. All of these activities have affected the number of actuarial positions and mean increased competition for jobs in this career path. Insurance trends have an effect on job growth as well, and as our country moves towards fewer, larger insurers and health maintenance organizations, we will see a trend toward the increasing geographical concentration of the actuarial's job site.

But the actuarial field is a big one, and despite slower-than-average growth predictions, there are pockets of opportunity. As you are probably well aware from the media, malpractice claims, product liability lawsuits, and claims surrounding catastrophic occurrences continue to grow in this country, and casualty actuaries may, as a result, have increased employment opportunities within this particular sector of actuarial employment.

Mathematicians

The employment of mathematicians is expected to increase more slowly than the average for all occupations through the year 2006. The number of jobs available for workers whose educational background is solely mathematics is not expected to increase significantly. The reduction of defense-related research will affect the employment of mathematicians in the federal government. However, as technology advances and leads to the expansion of the application of mathematics, more workers with math skills will be needed. Many job titles reflect the end product and not the discipline of mathematics that is often used in that work.

Earning a bachelor's degree in mathematics does not generally qualify you for most jobs as a mathematician. However, if you can expand your background to include some computer science, electrical or mechanical engineering, or operations research, you'll find this opens up opportunities in industry. Bachelor's degree candidates meeting state teacher certification might become eligible for high school mathematics teaching positions.

Master's degree candidates in mathematics face a strong competition for jobs in theoretical research. Jobs are more numerous, however, in applied mathematics and related areas such operations research, engineering, and computer programming.

Statisticians

The outlook here is an interesting combination of supply and demand. While actual numbers of jobs may not grow particularly fast for statisticians, it is still predicted to be a favorable job outlook for those with the degree and talent. That's largely because we are simply not producing an overabundance of qualified statistics professionals.

Both the government and private industry will remain strong employers, with private industry placing a special emphasis on those with advanced degrees. Car manufacturers, drug companies, engineering firms, producers of chemicals and foodstuffs are all possibilities as is the increasing use of statisticians by marketing firms and advertising agencies to forecast and track sales and solve product positioning problems.

Operations Research Analysts

Your best bet in this field is to get a job as a research assistant of some sort (job titles will vary from employer to employer) where the decided emphasis in your job is on quantitative analysis. Learn as much as you can and keep an eye out for the opportunity to advance your education. Growth in operations research or management science graduates does not meet the number of positions available. Even so, employers will place a special premium on those with master's and doctoral degrees.

STRATEGY FOR FINDING JOBS

The strategy for finding jobs that use math as a primary skill, such as actuaries, mathematicians, statisticians, and operations research analysts, depends upon the supply and demand in these fields, the type of industry, and the geographical location. In these occupations, your math education is essential for breaking into the field and for continued growth.

There are some common strategies that exist for all four of these occupational areas. First, find out where the jobs are (resources, geographic, industry). If there is little demand within your preferred geographic location, you may need to consider relocation. Second, find the position that matches your mathematical skills and experience. Third, design a resume that speaks to that position description in the posting. And fourth, write a cover letter that focuses on the benefits of hiring you and describes the credentials that match the needs in the position you are seeking. If hiring officials are able to match the qualifications stated in your resume and cover letter with their needs, then there is a good chance you will be asked to come in for an interview. During the interview, the match between the qualifications is further supported so the final goal is achieved—getting hired!

The best strategy is a proactive strategy because only 20 percent of all the jobs are advertised—that leaves 80 percent that are unadvertised. Using a proactive strategy you will use your research skills to find the unadvertised jobs. It is these unadvertised postings that are referred to as the hidden job market. The key is finding these hidden opportunities in organizations that currently employ individuals who have a degree in mathematics. Begin your search by thinking about networking from known contacts to new contacts. Start a personal and professional network of contacts. The known contacts include those students who are in your mathematics classes at college, the professors who teach mathematics courses, and the clubs and organizations on campus. Be proactive by searching the directories of employers by occupation, field, and geographic areas. Use the Internet to search for websites that offer addresses for job opportunities. Search the yellow pages of your local telephone directory. Pick up the phone and call organizations to find out what they have for opportunities and where they advertise when they do have openings. Use the skill that most mathematicians have—"research" all possibilities!

At the end of this chapter, there are several associations and organizations that not only have websites listed but publish newsletters, journals, and on-line listings of positions from bachelor's degree level to Ph.D. In addition, they offer hot tips on job search strategies. Review the on-line newspapers and journals for possible career positions. Find out if there are local, regional, or national job fairs being offered. Sometimes employers send their part-time and full-time listings directly to the math department and organizations on campuses. If you happen to find an internship listing that suggests the type of organization and skills you are seeking, then check with that employer to find out if they have full-time listings.

Here are some strategies and possible employers that would relate specifically to actuaries, mathematicians, statisticians, and operations research.

Strategies for Actuaries

Find out where actuaries work. About 50 percent of the actuaries are employed in the insurance industry, while others work for firms providing services such as management, or public relations, or in actuarial consulting firms. A small number of actuaries work for security and commodity brokers, government agencies, and computer software developers.

Actuaries most often specialize in life, health, or property and casualty insurance, while other actuaries specialize in pension plans. To learn various actuarial operations and phases, beginning actuaries often rotate between jobs, and they may move from one company to another in their early years to find growth and more responsibility. As reported in the *Occupational Outlook Handbook*, employment of actuaries is expected to grow more slowly than the average for all occupations, however, employment of consulting actuaries is expected to grow faster than actuaries employed by insurance carriers.

Possible Employers. To find possible employers who have actuarial positions, use your research skills, take a proactive approach to search for openings with insurance companies, educational institutions, government agencies, financial institutions, computer software companies, consulting firms, and public relations firms. Use your telephone directories, the Internet, the campus career services, and actuarial associations.

Check out your careers library resources, the campus library, career office postings, the mathematics department bulletin board, and professional associations. All of these physical locations might have information on websites as well. For instance, *Peterson's Job Opportunities for Business Majors* and *Peterson's Job Opportunities for Engineering and Computer Science Majors* have information on overviews of organizations, key statistics about the organization, expertise/education sought by the organization, international assignments, alternatives to assignments (internships), a contact name, and an organization's URL (website) for many of their listing for actuaries. Here is an example of a partial listing taken from this particular directory:

XYZ Life Insurance Company, New York, NY; Overview: Provides life, health, and disability insurance; Established: 1860; Ownership: private; Key Statistics: Annual Sales: $6.2 billion; Number of Employees: 5,322; Expertise/Education sought: actuarial, accounting, computer programming, finance, industrial engineering, law, marketing, underwriting; Alternatives to full-time employment: part-time jobs, paid internships; Contact Linda Talbert, Employment Supervisor; Phone 212-555-8491; Fax: 212-555-8492; Company URL: http://www.XYZlife.com.

Strategies for Mathematicians

Because of the two broad classes in which mathematicians fall (theoretical and applied), a different job strategy must be used for each. The job search for mathematicians starts with a broad search that needs to be narrowed by developing a strategy, and that strategy will be for you to decide:

1. Where, geographically, do you want to work?

2. Choose the industry where you would like to work:
   - Government (the federal government employs 75 percent of the mathematicians)—take a look on the Internet at the Office of Personnel Management for positions with the federal government: *http://www.usajobs.opm.gov/*
   - Manufacturing (drug industries are the key employers)
   - Private sector (management and publication services, educational services, research testing, security and commodity exchanges, and employers such as insurance companies and banks)

Mathematicians work as an integral part of an interdisciplinary team that may include engineers, computer scientists, physicists, technicians, and economists.

3. Search the industries using various avenues with a reactive approach (advertisements that are printed in newspapers, magazines, or journals), or proactive approach (searching for employers that are in your geographic area but have not advertised that they have openings by searching on the Internet, placing telephone calls, contacting professional organizations that have their own job listings.

Possible Employers. Use some of the same job search strategies for mathematicians as for actuaries: possible employers are found in industries such as government, manufacturing, education, and the private sector. Research your college's careers library resources, the campus library, career office postings, the mathematics department bulletin board on campus, and the professional associations for mathematician job postings. Mathematics is the skill used and not the descriptive occupational title used in job listings as it was for statistician and actuaries, who have their own specialty in a branch of mathematics!

Peterson's Job Opportunities for Business Majors and *Peterson's Job Opportunities for Engineering and Computer Science Majors* have information on overviews of organizations, key statistics about the organization, expertise/education sought by the organization, international assignments, alternatives to assignments (internships), a contact name, and the organization's URL (website) for many of their listing in the area of actuarial, mathematics, operations research, and statistics. Here is only one example taken from these two guides:

XYZ Foundation, VA; 104 Longfellow Boulevard, Alexandria, VA. Overview: promotes science, engineering, and technical programs; Hiring History: number of professional employees hired in 1996: 30, 1995: 30; Expertise/Education Sought: mathematics, actuarial, engineering, computer science, contracts administration/management, behavioral sciences, education, biology, geology; Alternatives to full-time employment: part-time jobs, paid internships; Contact: Donna Cadwell; Recruitment Coordinator; Phone: 703-555-2121; Fax 703-555-2122. E-mail: dcadwell@xyz.job

Taking a look on the Internet for job opportunities quickly confirms the keyword is more than "mathematician" in your search. The authors found that by entering the words "theoretical mathematician," job titles such as analyst, technician, engineer, research associate, system designer, scientist were popping up on the lists. Entering the job title of "applied mathematician" again brings the same listings with a more applied nature such as programmer, developer, finance associate, maintenance technician, quality assurance engineer, applied systems sales, architect, consultant, and business solutions specialist.

Strategies for Statisticians

It is not enough to just be good at statistics. Communication skills, a good understanding of business and the economy, and the ability to explain technical processes to those who are not statisticians are all important to make you more attractive to any industry. Advancement comes with experience gained in the field and a more advanced degree.

As reported in the *Occupational Outlook Handbook*, employment for statisticians is expected to grow little through the year 2006. Those with bachelor's degrees will discover that they will be finding jobs that don't have the title of "statistician," especially in the areas of engineering, economics, biology, or psychology. To get a great start as a statistician, students will need to have a strong background in mathematics, engineering, or computer science. With this experience, you should have the best prospects of finding jobs, especially in the federal government (where 25 percent of the job are found)—and even then, there will be strong competition to meet the minimum qualifications. If you get state certification, there are opportunities to teach high school statistics. Look for full-time opportunities in private industry: pharmaceuticals, manufacturers, research and development, businesses, and consulting firms.

Remember, statistics is a science—as a statistician you have learned the skills for good job search strategies such as

1. Decide where and how to gather the data (for your job search—proactive or reactive)

2. Determine the type and size of a sample group (the industry)

3. Develop a reporting form (your contact list)

4. Implement your plan—call, write, e-mail, and search the Internet, directories, and your career services library!

Possible Employers. Where do statisticians work? What employers do you explore? Use your research skills, take a proactive approach to search for openings in the field of medicine, psychology, engineering, business, manufacturing, and biology. Many positions in statistics in private industry and colleges and universities require a master's or a doctorate. The title "statistician" is often incorporated into the title, as in "econometrician," or it may be hidden altogether. Use your telephone directories, the Internet, the campus career services library, and actuarial associations.

Don't forget your college's careers library resources, the campus library, career office postings, the mathematics department bulletin board on campus, and the professional associations. Find out if these physical locations offer websites as well. There is a series of job hunter's guides published by Adams Publishing, *www.adamsonline.com*, that might help locate associations, employment services, industry publications, and advice on job hunting for students interested in becoming statisticians: *The Boston JobBank, The Atlanta JobBank, The Los Angeles JobBank, The Metropolitan New York JobBank,* and there are others published as well. A similar geographic job hunter's guide would be the series by Camden and Palmer published by Surrey Books: *How to Get a Job in Southern California, How to Get a Job in Washington, D.C.,* and other geographic areas. There are *Peterson's Job Opportunities for Business Majors* and *Peterson's Job Opportunities for Engineering and Computer Science Majors,* which have information on overviews of organizations, key statistics about the organization, expertise/education sought by the organization, international assignments, alternatives to assignments (internships), a contact name, and the organization's URL (website) for many of their listings in the area of actuarial, mathematics, operations research, and statistics. Here is an example:

Center XYZ, 4884 Wilson Highway, Atlanta, GA 30388; Overview: Monitors and controls physical and psychological disease; Key Statistics: Number of Employees; 7,000; Hiring History: Number of professional employees hired in 1996: 500;

continued

> continued
>
> Expertise/Education Sought: Statistics, mathematics, behavioral sciences, sociology, public health, biology, pharmacology, epidemiology; Alternatives to full-time employment: part-time jobs, paid internships; International Assignments are available to employees. Contact: For college students and recent graduates: Lois Huntington, College Relations Coordinator; Phone 770-555-8441; Fax: 770-555-8442. For individuals with previous experience: Human Resources Department; Phone 770-555-8446; Job Hotline: 888-555-8111; Company URL: http://www.xyzjob.com.

Strategies for Operations Research Analysts

When employers are seeking to fill an operation research analyst position, they are seeking two primary skills: 1) the ability to think logically and work well with people, and 2) the ability to use the computer, which is the most important tool for quantitative analysis—and a background in programming. Employers also prefer applicants with at least a master's degree in operations research, industrial engineering, or management science, coupled with a bachelor's degree in computer science, economics, or statistics.

Where are the jobs? Because operations research analysts help organizations coordinate and operate in the most efficient manner by applying mathematical principles to organizational problems, the jobs are located in various industries, especially those that help with the problems occurring in large business and government organizations. As reported in the *Occupational Outlook Handbook*, individuals with a master's or Ph.D. in management science or operations research should find good job prospects through the year 2006, despite projected slower-than-average employment growth. Some operations research analysts are generalists, some specialize in one type of applications. Sometimes their work is embedded in the work of economists, system analysts, mathematicians, and industrial engineers. However, operations research analysts are employed in most industries.

An analyst begins working under supervision of a more experienced analyst, is then assigned more responsibilities to design models and solve problems. They advance by becoming technical specialists and working as a supervisor. With only a bachelor's degree, you can find opportunities as research assistants in a variety of related fields that allow you to use your mathematical skills.

Possible Employers. Operations research analysts are employed by the federal government, engineering and management services firms, insurance carriers, financial institutions, computer and data processing services, telecommunications companies, and air carriers. As reported in the *Occupational Outlook Handbook,* 20 percent work for management, research, public relations, and testing agencies that do operations research consulting.

Check with your college's careers library resources, the campus library, career office postings, the Mathematics Department bulletin board, and the professional associations and their websites as well. There are directories or job hunter's guides of employers which are organized geographically, such as: *How to Get a Job in Chicago* and *The Greater Philadelphia JobBank.* For information on overviews of organization, *Peterson's Job Opportunities for Business Majors* and *Peterson's Job Opportunities for Engineering and Computer Science Majors,* have key statistics about the organization, expertise/education sought by the organization, international assignments, alternatives to assignments (internships), a contact name, and the organization's URL (website) for many of their listings in the area of actuarial, mathematics, statistics, and operations research. Here is an example:

> XYZ Administration, 2011 Pennsylvania Avenue, Washington, DC 23498; Overview: Division of the United States Department of Transportation; Key Statistics: Number of Employees: 52,442; Expertise/Education Sought: Operations research, accounting, finance, business management, aviation, electrical engineering, security, safety, computer science; International Assignments are available to employees; Contact: Luvie Tuller, Recruitment Leader; Phone: 202-555-8491; Fax 202-555-8111; Job Hotline: 202-555-8844; Company URL: http://www.xyz.com

POSSIBLE JOB TITLES

As we have discovered through the industry listings, the job titles frequently do not contain the specific words *actuary, mathematician, statistician,* or *operations research analyst.* They expand or overlap into *technician, consultant, engineer, associate, designer,* and more—as you will see from the following list:

Mathematician
Possible job titles include:

Theoretical Mathematician

Accounting analyst

Marketing associate

Operations research analyst—
operations specialist

Product quality engineer

Research associate

Systems level designer

Applied Mathematician

Applied systems sales

Contracts specialist

Director of information technology

Finance associate

Quality assurance engineer

Quality engineer

Program manager

Project analyst

Project/program analyst

Relations manager

Software engineer/programmer

Systems analyst/programmer

Test technician

Statistician
Possible job titles include:

Assistant professor–statistics

Biostatistician

Clinical trials statistician

Department chair, public health
sciences

Epidemiologist

Financial analyst

Programmer analyst

Quality assurance analyst

Research associate

Risk management analyst

Senior analyst

Senior marketing analyst

Senior mathematical statistician

Senior researcher for survey
methodology

Statistical analyst

Statistical programmer

Statistician

Operations Research Analyst

Possible job titles include:

Business analyst

Director of management science

Economics analyst

Global manufacturing analyst

Manager of marketing science

Operations research analyst

Principal analyst

Product marketing manager

Project manager

Quality and customer satisfaction consultant

Research analyst

Risk management manager

Senior financial analyst

Senior project analyst for strategic financial management

System analyst

RELATED OCCUPATIONS

This list of related occupations shows that not all occupations in this chapter have job titles that feature *actuary, mathematician, statistician,* or *operations research analyst.*

Related Occupations for Actuaries

Accountants

Computer programmer

Economists

Financial analyst

Mathematicians

Statisticians

Systems analyst

Systems engineer

All of the above have related skills and a strong knowledge of mathematics is desired.

Related Occupations for Statisticians

Actuaries

Computer programmers

Computer systems analysts

Economists

Engineers

Financial analysts

Information scientists	Operations research analysts
Life scientists	Physical scientists
Mathematicians	Social scientists

Related Occupations for Mathematicians

Actuary	Statistician
Computer programmer	Systems analyst
Operations research analyst	Systems engineer

Related Occupations for Operations Research Analysts

Computer scientists	Mathematicians
Economists	Statisticians
Engineers	

Use the *Occupational Outlook Handbook* or VGM's *Career Encyclopedia* to read job descriptions for these titles.

PROFESSIONAL ASSOCIATIONS

The following list shows some of the associations that relate to actuary, mathematician, statistician, and operations research analyst. Review the "Members/Purpose" section for each organization and decide whether the organization pertains to your interests. For additional information, use the *Encyclopedia of Associations* published by Gale Research Inc. Memberships in one of these organizations might help in terms of job listings, networking opportunities, and employment search services. Some provide information at no charge. If you want to receive their publications that list job opportunities, you might need to join the organization. Check for student member rates. Check the websites of these organizations for further career information or links to other sites that provide other information related to actuaries, mathematicians, statisticians, and operations research analysts. See if these associations can assist you in your job search:

Actuaries

American Academy of Actuaries
1100 Seventeenth Street NW, Seventh Floor
Washington, DC 20036
Website: http://www.actuary.org
Members/Purpose: Qualified actuaries. Seeks to facilitate relations
between actuaries and government bodies; conduct public relations
activities; promulgate standards of practice for the actuarial profession.
Journals/Publications: *Actuarial Update; American Academy of Actuaries
Yearbook; Contingencies; Directory of Actuarial Memberships; Enrolled
Actuaries Report*

American Society of Pension Actuaries
4350 N. Fairfax Drive, Suite 820
Arlington, VA 22203-1619
Website: http://www.aspa.org
Members/Purpose: Individuals involved in consulting, administrative, and
design aspects of the employee benefit business; promotes high standards in
the profession; provides nine-part educational program.
Journals/Publications: *American Society of Pension Actuaries—Yearbook;
Pension Actuary*

Casualty Actuarial Society
1100 N. Glebe Road, Suite 600
Arlington, VA 2201
Website: http://www.casact.org
E-mail: office@casact.org
Members/Purpose: Professional society of insurance actuaries promoting
actuarial and statistical science as applied to insurance problems (such as
casualty, fire, and social) other than life insurance. Examination required
for membership.
Journals/Publications: *Proceedings; Year Book*; also publishes papers and
study notes on actuarial topics

Conference of Consulting Actuaries
1110 W. Lake Cook Road, Suite 235
Buffalo Grove, IL 60089-1968
Website: http://www.ccactuaries.com/
E-mail: info@ccactuaries.com
Members/Purpose: Full-time consulting actuaries or government actuaries;
providing services in the life, health, casualty, and pension fields. Mission is

to advance the practice of actuarial consulting by serving the professional needs of actuaries.

Journals/Publications: *Consulting Actuary; Proceedings of the Conference of Consulting Actuaries*

Insurance Accounting and Systems Association
1795 University Drive, Suite 280
Durham, NC 27707
Website: http://www.iasa.org
Members/Purpose: Insurance companies writing all lines of insurance. Associate members are statisticians, statistical organizations, actuarial consultants, independent public accountants, management consultants, and other organizations related to the insurance industry that are not eligible for active membership.
Journals/Publications: *The Interpreter; Proceedings; Life Accounting Textbook; Property and Liability Accounting Textbook*

Societies of Actuaries
475 N. Martingale Road, Suite 800
Schaumburg, IL 60173-2226
Website: http://www.soa.org
Members/Purpose: Professional organization of individuals trained in the application of mathematical probabilities to the design of insurance, pension, and employee benefit programs. Sponsors series of examinations leading to designation of fellow or associate in the society; maintains 3,100-volume library on actuarial science and statistics.
Journals/Publications: *The Actuary; The Future Actuary; The North American Actuarial Journal; Society of Actuaries Monograph Series; Directory of Actuarial Memberships; Society of Actuaries—Record; Society of Actuaries—Transactions; Society of Actuaries Yearbook; Index to Publications*

MATHEMATICIANS

American Mathematical Society
P.O. Box 6248
Providence, RI 02940-6248
Website: http://www.ams.org
Members/Purpose: Professional society of mathematicians which promotes the interests of mathematical scholarship and research; holds institutes, short courses, and symposia to further mathematical research; compiles statistics; maintains biographical archives; offers placement services; compiles statistics.

Journals/Publications: *Abstracts of Papers Presented to the AMS; Assistantships and Fellowships in the Mathematical Sciences; Bulletin of the MMS; Combined Mathematical List; Current Mathematical Publications; Employment Information in the Mathematical Sciences; Journal of the American Mathematical Society; Leningrad Mathematical Journal; Mathematical Reviews*

Association for Symbolic Language

University of Illinois
Department of Mathematics
1409 W. Green Street
Urbana, IL 61801
Website: http://www.maa.org/cbms/members/asl.html
Members/Purpose: Professional society of mathematicians, computer scientists, linguists, and philosophers interested in formal or mathematical logic and related fields. Promotes research in symbolic logic and provides for the exchange of ideas within the mathematical industry.
Journals/Publications: *Journal of Symbolic Logic*

Association for Women in Mathematics

4114 Computer and Space Science Building
University of Maryland
College Park, MD 20742-2461
Website: http://www.math.neu.edu/awm/
Members/Purpose: Mathematicians employed by universities, government, and private industry. Seeks to improve the status of women in the mathematical profession, and to make students aware of opportunities for women in the field. Membership is open to all individuals regardless of gender.
Journals/Publications: Newsletter: *Association for Women in Mathematics; Directory of Women in the Mathematical Sciences; Careers for Women in Mathematics; Careers That Count, Careers in Mathematics; Profiles of Women in Mathematics: The Emmy Noether Lecturers*

Conference Board of the Mathematical Sciences

1529 Eighteenth Street, NW
Washington, DC 20036
Website: http://www.maa.org/cbms/cbms.html
Members/Purpose: An umbrella organization consisting of fifteen professional societies all of which have a primary objective to increase the knowledge in one or more of the mathematical sciences. Its purpose is to promote understanding and cooperation among these national organizations so that they work together and support each other in their efforts to

promote research, improve education, and expand the uses of mathematics. The fourteen professional societies include AMATY (American Mathematical Association of Two-Year Colleges, AMS (American Mathematical Society), ASA (American Statistical Association), ASL (Association for Symbolic Logic), AWM (Association for Women in Mathematics), ASSM (Association of State Supervisors of Mathematics), BBA (Benjamin Banneker Association), INFORMS (Institute for Operations Research and the Management Sciences), IMS (Institute of Mathematical Statistics), MAA (Mathematical Association of America), NAM (National Association of Mathematicians), NCSM (National Council of Supervisors of Mathematics), NCTM (National Council of Teachers of Mathematics), SIAM (Society for Industrial and Applied Mathematics), SOA (Society of Actuaries).

Journals/Publications: none

Convention/Meeting: semiannual council meeting

Industrial Mathematics Society

P.O. Box 159

Roseville, MI 48066

Website/e-mail: none

Members/Purpose: Mathematicians, scientists, engineers, and economists extend the understanding and application of mathematics in industry; supports study group on mathematics of gear design. Areas of interest include applied mathematics, engineering mechanics, power generation, computers, statistics, automatic control, operations analysis, and biomechanics.

Journals/Publications: *Industrial Mathematics*

Institute of Mathematical Statistics

3401 Investment Boulevard, Suite 7

Hayward, CA 94545

Website: http://www.imstat.org/

E-mail: ims@stat.berkeley.edu

Members/Purpose: Professional society of mathematicians and others interested in mathematical statistics and probability theory.

Journals/Publications: *Annals of Applied Probability; Annals of Probability; Annals of Statistics; Institute of Mathematical Statistics Bulletin; Statistical Science*

International Association for Mathematical Geology

c/o Dr. Richard B. McCammon

U.S. Geological Survey

National Center 920

Reston, VA 22992

Website: http://www.iamg.org/
Members/Purpose: Professional geologists, mathematicians, statisticians, and interested individuals. Promotes cooperation in the application and use of mathematics and statistics in geological research and technology.
Journals/Publications: *Mathematical Geology; Computers and Geosciences; IAMG Newsletter; Studies in Mathematical Geology*

Mathematical Association of America
1529 Eighteenth Street, NW
Washington, DC 20036-1385
Website: http://www.maa.org
Members/Purpose: College mathematics teachers; individuals using mathematics as a tool in a business profession or another profession.
Journals/Publications: *American Mathematical Monthly; College Mathematics Journal; Mathematical Association of America; Mathematics Magazine*

Math/Science Network
Mills College
5000 MacArthur Boulevard
Oakland, CA 94613-1301
Website: http://www.elstad.com/alta.html
Members/Purpose: Mathematicians, scientists, counselors, parents, community leaders, and representatives from business and industry who are interested in increasing the participation of girls and women in mathematics, science, and technology.
Journals/Publications: *Broadcast/ Beyond Equals: To Promote the Participation of Women in Mathematics; Expanding Your Horizons in Science and Math; A Handbook for Conference Planners*

National Association of Mathematicians
Department of Mathematics and Computer Science
Elizabeth City State University
Elizabeth City, NC 27909
Website: http://www.maa.org/cbms/members/nam.html
Members/Purpose: To promote excellence in the mathematical sciences and to promote the mathematical development of underrepresented American minorities; conducts annual National Meeting in January; supports an annual invited address at the Joint Mathematical Summer Meetings; sponsors annual faculty conference on research and teaching excellence; sponsors a Summer Institute in Computational Science for undergraduate mathematics majors and selected faculty.
Journals/Publications: Newsletter

Society for Industrial and Applied Mathematics
3600 University City Science Center
Philadelphia, PA 19104-2688
Website: http://www.siam.org
Members/Purpose: To promote research in applied mathematics and computational science; further the application of mathematics to new methods and techniques useful in industry and science; provide for the exchange of information between the mathematical, industrial, and scientific communities.
Journals/Publications: *CBMS-NSF Regional Conference Series in Applied Mathematics; Classics in Applied Mathematics and Proceedings; Frontiers in Applied Mathematics; SIAM Journal on Applied Mathematics; SIAM Journal on Computing; SIAM Journal on Control and Optimization; SIAM Journal on Discrete Mathematics; SIAM Journal on Mathematical Analysis; SIAM Journal on Matrix Analysis and Applications; SIAM Journal on Numerical Analysis; SIAM Journal on Scientific Computing; SIAM News; SIAM Review; Studies in Applied Mathematics; Theory of Probability and Its Applications*

Special Interest Group on Numerical Mathematics
c/o G. W. "Pete" Stewart
University of Maryland
Computer Science Department
Building 115, A.V. Williams Building
College Park, MD 20742-3255
Website: http://www.cs.umd.edu/~stewart/
Members/Purpose: A special interest group of the Association for Computing Machinery. Individuals interested in computing mathematics. Encourages communication between members and with other professional organizations; arranges representation on international standards committees.
Journals/Publications: Newsletter: *The Constant Society*

Young Mathematicians Network
College of Arts and Sciences
Department of Mathematics
University of Kentucky
715 Patterson Office Tower
Lexington, KY 40506-0027
Website: www.ms.uky.edu/~cyeomans/
Members/Purpose: A mathematicians' group keeping the mathematical community honest about the job market and its future; provides information about job searches from both inside and the outside; is a

support group for those on the job market; provides information on publishing, grant proposals, obtaining industry jobs, and other things which many didn't get in graduate school; informs the mathematical community of the interests and concerns of the younger mathematicians.
Journals/Publications: *Concerns for Young Mathematicians*

Statisticians

American Statistical Association
1429 Duke Street
Alexandria, VA 22314-3415
Website: http://www.amstat.org
Members/Purpose: Professional society of persons interested in the theory, methodology, and application of statistics to all fields of human endeavor. Sections: Bayesian Statistical Science; Biometrics; Biopharmaceutical; Business and Economic Statistics; Education; Epidemiology; Government Statistics; Physical and Engineering Sciences; Quality and Productivity; Social Statistics; Statistical Computing; Statistical Consulting Education; Statistical Graphics; Statistics and the Environment; Statistics in Marketing; Survey Research Methods; Teaching of Statistics in the Health Sciences.
Journals/Publications: *American Statistician; AMSTAT News; Directory of Statisticians; Current Index to Statistics; Journal of Business and Economic Statistics; Journal of Computational and Graphical Statistics; Journal of Educational Statistics; Proceedings; Technometrics; STATS*

Casualty Actuarial Society
1100 N. Glebe Road, Suite 600
Arlington, VA 22201
Website: http://www.casact.org
Members/Purpose: Professional society of insurance actuaries promoting actuarial and statistical science as applied to insurance problems (such as casualty, fire, and social) other than life insurance. Examination required for membership.
Journals/Publications: *Proceedings; Year Book*; also publishes papers and study notes on actuarial topics

Caucus for Women in Statistics
c/o Cynthia Struthers
200 University Avenue West
Waterloo, Ontario N23G1
Canada
Website/e-mail: none

Members/Purpose: Primarily statisticians united to improve employment and professional opportunities for women in statistics. Conducts technical sessions concerning statistical studies related to women.
Journals/Publications: *Caucus for Women in Statistics Directory;*
Newsletter: *Caucus for Women in Statistics*

Econometric Society
Northwestern University
Department of Economics
Evanston, IL 60208-2600
Website: www.econometricsociety.org
Members/Purpose: Statisticians, mathematicians, and economists. Promotes studies that are directed toward unification of the theoretical and empirical approaches to economic problems and advancement of economic theory in its relation to statistics and mathematics.
Journals/Publications: *Econometrica*

Institute for Econometric Research
2200 SW Tenth Street
Deerfield, FL 33442
Website: http://www.mfmag.com
Members/Purpose: Fosters scientific research into stock markets and related financial phenomena. Conducts seminars; compiles statistics.
Journals/Publications: *Income and Safety; The Insiders; Market Logic; Mutual Fund Forecaster; New Issues*

Institute of Mathematical Statistics
3401 Investment Boulevard, Suite 7
Hayward, CA 94545-3819
Website: http://www.imstat.org
Members/Purpose: Professional society of mathematicians and others interested in mathematical statistics and probability theory.
Journals/Publications: *Annals of Applied Probability; Annals of Probability; Annals of Statistics; Institute of Mathematical Statistics Bulletin; Statistical Science*

Insurance Accounting and Systems Association
1705 University Drive, Suite 280
Durham, NC 27707
Website: http://www.iasa.org
Members/Purpose: Insurance companies writing all lines of insurance. Associate members are statisticians, statistical organizations, actuarial consultants, independent public accountants, management consultants, and

other organizations related to the insurance industry that are not eligible for active membership.

Journals/Publications: *The Interpreter; Proceedings; Life Accounting Textbook; Property and Liability Accounting Textbook*

International Society of Statistical Science in Economics

536 Oasis Drive
Santa Rosa, CA 95407
Website/e-mail: none
Members/Purpose: Statisticians, economists, and econometricians in twenty-one countries. Seeks to create a union of statisticians and economists in order to clarify statistics and mathematical applications and misapplications. Provides statistical training and education for economists. Sponsors research programs on the improvement of statistical methods; conducts seminars; compiles statistics; offers computerized services.
Journals/Publications: *International Society of Statistical Science in Economics—Directory;* Newsletter; *Proceedings; Quantity and Quality in Economic Research: The Latest Developments in Statistics*

Operations Research Analysts

Operations Research Society of America
Institute for Operations Research and Management Sciences

901 Elkridge Landing Road, Suite 400
Linthicum, MD 21090
Website: http://www.informs.org
E-mail: informs@informs.org
Members/Purpose: Scientists, educators, and practitioners engaged or interested in methodological subjects such as optimization, probabilistic models, decision analysis, and game theory. Also involved in areas of public concern such as health, energy, urban issues, and defense systems through industrial applications including marketing, operations management, finance, and decision support systems. Operates a visiting lecturers program; sponsors competitions. Offers placement service; compiles statistics.
Journals/Publications: *Mathematics of Operations Research; Interfaces; Marketing Science; Operations Research; OR/MS Today; Operations Research Letters; ORSA Journal on Computing; ORSA/TIMS Bulletin; RRSA/TIMS Membership Directory; Stochastic Models; Transportation Science*

PATH 3: WORKING TOWARD AN ADVANCED DEGREE: MARKETING, RESEARCH, OR FINANCIAL ANALYST

*T*his chapter is all about making your decision to get a master's degree in whatever field you choose—a choice that will require some thought and not only enable you to get the most out of the degree, but also to enhance your job prospects in the process.

Where Are You in This Picture?

First of all, consider the following scenarios to see if any fit your current thinking or situation:

Scenario 1: You've enjoyed your math major and done pretty well academically, but you're not certain about exactly what kind of work you should look for. You majored in math because you were good at it, but really haven't given a lot of thought to how you'll use it. You're confused about what you can do in the workforce and who will hire you.

Scenario 2: You're approaching graduation or you've just graduated. You've tested the job market and it doesn't seem like a good time to be employed. Jobs are hard to come by, low paying, and don't seem to value your degree. Maybe you think it would be better to stay in school, get an advanced degree, and then try the job market.

Scenario 3: Perhaps you've done the kinds of job search activities suggested in the opening chapters of this book and seen all the better jobs and big money go to those who have a master's. You think, "Okay, I'll get a master's," but you're worried about your own lack of work experience in a professional environment. Most of the math jobs you are attracted to require a master's degree. You wonder if you could get one of these jobs if you could get through the degree. You have to ask yourself if you have what it takes.

The Reason for Any Confusion

You may begin to feel as confused and frustrated as Shakespeare's Hamlet, wrestling over the question of whether to continue your education with a master's or get out of school and go to work. Certainly, given the uncertainties of the job market and the shifting paradigms of employers and employee bases, it might seem a wise investment to continue to add to your math education, earn an advanced degree, and hope to make yourself more competitive than the typical undergraduate job candidate.

Graduate school has always been a popular option for those who could afford it when the job market is demanding. Enroll in grad school, wait a couple of years, and then hopefully enter the market at a more propitious time. The strategy is that, hopefully, not only will your chances of employment be better, but once you have an advanced degree you may be a candidate for more and different jobs than you would have been previously and at a higher salary.

DEFINITION OF THE CAREER PATH

Thinking About Which Master's Degree?

Reading this book, talking to your friends or faculty advisors, you're sure to hear suggestions about taking an advanced degree. As a math major, your options are many when it comes to graduate school. If your undergraduate degree was in math education and you are pursuing a career in teaching, then you might consider the master of arts in teaching or a master of education. Naturally, a master's degree in mathematics or some specialty within mathematics would seem obvious, especially for some of the directly related math positions discussed in the previous chapter. However, you have many other choices with your undergraduate mathematics degree. For example, you may be interested in using your undergraduate mathematics degree in a business field, so you might want to consider a master of business administration (the M.B.A.) or a master's degree in economics (M.A. Ec.). But there are many other choices than these two. There are master of arts in finance (M.A.F.), master of applied mathematical science (M.A.M.S.) or a master's in applied statistics (M.Ap.Stat.). Here's a list of a few others to get you thinking:

Master of Arts in Management (M.A. Mgt.)

Master of Arts in Teaching Mathematics (M.A.T.M.)

Master of Biomathematics (M. Biomath.)

Master of Computer Science (M.C.S.)

Master of Finance and Banking (M.F.B.)

Master of Information Systems (M.I.S.)

Master of Mathematics (M. Math.)

Master of Probability and Statistics (M. Prob. S.)

Master of Science in Operations Research (M.S.O.R.)

Master of Statistics (M. Stat.)

Think About the School

However, not all master's degrees are created equal. Graduate programs, curricula, and faculty (not to mention costs) can vary dramatically from school to school. The master's degree has been referred to as the working professional degree as so many management and leadership positions demand an advanced education. Every graduate school program comes with its own faculty, and that faculty has particular professional interests. You'll want to be certain that the research interests of the faculty match your needs in pursuing graduate education. Many of you may attend graduate school at night and on weekends as part of the educational benefits offered by your employer. You'll be working two jobs, in effect, your day job and your education after hours. When you think of the energy demands that will require, you'll want to be assured you're getting the kind of education that will serve you best.

THE TRAINING THAT WILL ENHANCE YOUR MASTER'S

The Question of Experience

There's no question that, in most cases, an advanced degree brings more responsibility and greater rewards, especially financial. But those rewards are not based entirely on the degree, they are also based on the breadth and depth of experience you bring to an employer. If you stay on for graduate school and earn your master's degree immediately, you'll find yourself in the unenviable position of being top-heavy with education and but weak in practical experience.

Most of the positions that require an advanced degree, such as a master's, include responsibilities such as budget management, staff supervision, or strategic planning responsibilities. Those positions are going to be reserved for individuals who have *both* the master's degree and the work experience to go with it.

Of course, there are exceptions to this rule. There are some isolated research or staff positions where your educational exposure is of a higher priority than your work history. However, if you've been giving this book a close reading, you'll have understood how many of the positions we have cited in the career paths outlined involve working on teams and collaborative approaches. So while there may be some autonomous positions out there, you'll have to ask yourself two questions: 1) Where are they? and once you find them, 2) Do you want them?

The other exception to moving on immediately to graduate work may be those individuals who already have acquired exceptional work experience through high-level internships in their chosen field, or teaching assistant or research assistant positions while undergraduates. As career counselors, we occasionally see undergraduate resumes that are startlingly rich in high-quality work experiences.

But in most cases, a master's degree without the attendant or expected experiential component means a job where you're given work that requires your degree but your pay and responsibilities match those with an undergraduate mathematics degree. We find our clients who have weak experience but advanced degrees have no trouble securing interviews and offers. Of course. Who wouldn't be happy to have all that talent, especially when you only have to pay bachelor's degree rates for it? Employers are unwilling to hire and pay for a master's degree without an accompanying high level of practical experience.

Finding a job is hard work, whatever shape the job market's in. It means putting yourself on the line, answering tough questions, going out on your own, day after day, and facing a lot of rejection and wondering why. For these reasons, a graduate degree starts to look good to all those math graduates who feel that getting another degree will add something to their resume and maybe, while they're doing that, the job market conditions will change and things will somehow be easier. This is *not* a wise strategy! You continue to add unproven education without experience. Sadly, many of your peers who have taken master's degrees with no real-world experience will tell you their salaries and job descriptions are little different from those of another employee with a bachelor's degree. In our own career counseling practice, we have seen this type of client all too frequently.

Gaining Admission to Graduate School

For the candidate who approaches the admissions office of a graduate school, two elements of that application can be particularly important: a strong personal essay and an interview (even if not required). Both are good indicators of your readiness for a graduate program. With each, admissions committees will be looking for maturity, drive, and focus. The personal essay required by your application should clearly enunciate your

- ❑ motivation

- ❑ goals

- ❑ degree of readiness

An excellent guide to writing this essay is *How to Write a Winning Personal Statement for Graduate and Professional School* by Richard J. Stelzer. Examining these issues in preparation for such a personal essay is a valuable experience in and of itself.

If it is at all possible, even when not required, try to have a personal interview at the school. The interview will allow the admissions staff to question you and probe for the elements listed above, and it will provide an opportunity for you to explain your reason for seeking an advanced degree and to discuss your commitment to your education.

A Suggested Career Path to the Master's Degree

An ideal job for the math undergraduate contemplating graduate school would be a position of some sophistication utilizing your math education and providing you with opportunities to learn more, a reasonable salary, and the chance to gain the kinds of experiences that will help you if you choose to go on to graduate school. Such positions *do* exist. Typical position titles would be market analysts (MAs) or financial analysts (FAs) and research analysts or research associates (RAs). They may also be called business analysts, associate consultants, or just associates.

Most of these positions are in business consulting firms, financial services, or banking. Whether it be banking or consulting, the analyst's role is generally the same. Analysts help to provide the expert advice that will help their employer or their employer's clients to invest wisely with the best return on their money or solve business problems.

Market and Financial Analysts. Your work will involve evaluating the marketplace as a whole. You'll study information on shifts in the gross national production, the cost of living, personal income growth, rates of employment, construction starts, fiscal plans of the federal government, growth and inflation rates, balance of payments, market trends, and even indexes of common stocks.

But your job is even more complex than the above list would suggest because you need to be aware of national and international events that could precipitate some serious reaction in the marketplace. As we write this chapter, the United States is contemplating a possible action against Iraq—the effects of which would reverberate throughout the marketplace. International crises such as that, political actions, large-scale tragedies all can cause the market to shift direction. So, you see, you need to keep an eye both on the data on your screen as well as on the pulse of the world. It's a fascinating job for a math graduate.

Here is an actual ad for a market analyst that was posted as this book went to press. It's a fairly specific job listing that contains some important hints about the nature of the work and the qualifications being sought:

Market/Financial Analyst—Entry Level

XYZ Analysis, Inc., is a management consulting company that applies sophisticated analytical techniques to real-world problems in the public and private sectors. XYZ's strength is high-quality work in areas such as strategic planning, decision analysis, operations management, analysis of public policy, forecasting markets for new products, R&D planning, and basic research. Recent clients include General Motors, IBM, Xerox, Samsung, Kaiser Permanent, the Electric Power Research Institute, the Department of Energy, and the Environmental Protection Agency. XYZ offers competitive salaries and opportunities for career growth.

XYZ is seeking applicants with bachelor's degrees for positions in

continued

---

continued

our analytical staff. Candidates should have: a degree in mathematics, operations research, decision analysis, computer science, engineering, or other technical field; a GPA of 3.3 or higher; an interest in solving important, complex problems; skills in a broad range of mathematical techniques; communication skills to present analytical results in a clear, concise manner; a high level of enthusiasm for challenging work in an informal atmosphere.

Analysts at XYZ work on teams with other XYZ consultants on a variety of projects. Analysts are involved in tasks such as data analysis, formulating and programming mathematical models, working with clients, preparing, presenting, and assisting with report and proposal writing.

If you are interested in learning more about this position, please send a cover letter, college transcript, and resume to Amelia Talbert. XYZ requires all three of these items in order to consider your application. E-mail to: xyz@mail.com; Fax: 203-555-2424; Mail: XYZ Analysis, Inc., 221 N. Washington, Detroit, MI 03384.

Several things are clear in this ad. There are high expectations for your performance, but the rewards are commensurate. As we've discussed throughout this book and this ad corroborates, you need to know your mathematics, and this employer specifies a high GPA to ensure that. At the same time, there is a clear indication that working conditions are relaxed and interesting. Note the emphasis on communication skills and the fact that you'll be involved in client negotiations, public presentations, and a number of writing assignments as well. If your math courses have not demanded much research or analytical writing, you might want to consider a technical writing class in your English department or an organizational communications course in the business department of your college.

Research Analysts and Associates. Generally, you will be doing library research, collecting data in organized forms, and conducting some data manipulations. Research associates and research analysts assist in helping to put together proposals, case studies, or analyses designed to help the consultant's client solve problems, determine future strategies, or implement programs. As you gain expertise, some responsibilities will be added, in most cases having to do with additional and more sophisticated research capabilities, quantitative manipulation of data using computer software, and the presentation of findings to your work team.

There is a limit on what you can do, on the decisions you will be allowed to make, and in how far you can go on your own. These positions have been structured to work under more senior positions. Senior workers have those decision-making responsibilities because important financial consequences may be the end result. The positive aspect of this supervision is that you'll work closely with true professionals who will have much to teach you, both explicitly and implicitly.

Now let's examine another actual research analyst position for someone just out of college to learn how an employer expresses the demands and qualifications of the position:

Research Analyst Entry Level

XYZ is an innovative world leader in telecommunications and networking. We are a high-tech, high-growth company in a rapidly changing global industry. XYZ is a diverse company and the world's best at bringing people together. Our global network provides voice, data, video, Internet access, satellite TV, and messaging. With XYZ it's all within your reach! XYZ has entry-level opportunities for individuals who seek employment involved with the development of business systems. Selected candidates will participate in an intensive nine-week training course. At the conclusion of this formal training, you will be assigned to one of the company's internal organizations to enhance your skills while providing business analysis support to resolve business problems. Once your performance has been evaluated to be sufficient, you will be promoted to intermediate-level analyst.

Key topics in the classroom training are:

- Problem analysis
- Function/task analysis
- Data analysis
- Systems design/test plan techniques

We require candidates to possess a B.A./B.S. degree in either math (with computer option), information systems, or quantitative/systems analysis along with a minimum GPA of 3.0.

Our major competitive value rests with our people, so we are aggressive in our goal to attract the best with generous salaries,

continued

continued

benefits, and growth potential. Qualified individuals should send their resume and cover letter as one message, resume first, via e-mail to job@xyz.com using a flat ASCII text only file without attachments or enclosures. Scannable resume and cover letter, original copy only, may be sent to XYZ Resume Center, Room 1234, Suite 122, Boston, Massachusetts 00211. You *must* include XYZ Ad Code IN272636 in the cover letter.

We are an equal opportunity employer. We welcome and encourage diversity in the workplace.

This position description shares some similarities with the market research position listed earlier. There's a real sense of high expectations about your performance, and like the previous advertisement, this firm also is demanding a specific level of GPA. Both firms have obviously decided that grades are as reasonable an indicator of your ability to master an environment as any other. Though you may disagree with this thinking, these ads are proof positive that for some employers, grades count.

This ad also emphasizes a higher degree of analytical functions compared to the market analyst position and specifically enumerates a number of kinds of analysis that will be part of your training. The emphasis on training is good news. Professional training by employers is often exceptional in its quality and stays with your career beyond any one job. It also is a guarantee of stability, as organizations that spend resources training employees have a vested interest in retaining those employees and seeing them grow and develop.

One final note here of importance is that the submission of resume and cover letter as e-mail (with submission specifications) or as a "scannable" document means this firm is on the cutting edge of technology. If either the e-mail submission or preparing a scannable resume is new to you, stop by your career office and get some assistance. Joyce Lain Kennedy has an excellent book on the market entitled *Electronic Resume Revolution* that addresses not just writing the best scannable resumes, but using electronic databases to help keep yourself visible. Another publication, the *Guide to Internet Job Searching* by Osserman, Riley, and Roehm and published by VGM Career Horizons, provides a good explanation of how to connect to the Internet and instructions for posting a resume electronically, as well as extensive listings of Internet sites with job ads and resume databases.

These positions are featured in this chapter because they particularly appeal to graduates contemplating advanced education. There's a fairly steady turnover in these analyst jobs as people choose to return to school or are promoted within the firm. More people move on, however, than move up because an advanced degree is often de rigeur to move up in these kinds of organizations. So, since these positions are not designed to fulfill career aspirations in and of themselves, they should appeal to you if you're contemplating graduate school. Though they come with excellent salary and benefits, they have more in common with postgraduate internships than typical entry-level positions because they typically involve so much education and training. In fact, these analyst positions are often part of special hiring "programs" for recent college graduates. Since the jobs do generally turn over rather quickly, many entry-level candidates are recruited and hired. The training and mentoring involved for the new analysts is considerable. The responsibilities for training are generally located with one individual or centered in one office that manages the research associate/analyst "program." The defined boundaries of the experience and the structure of the internal training process should be highly acceptable to the mathematics student with a bachelor's degree seeking to gain valuable skills and experience before entering graduate school.

Strategic Advantages

Job candidates applying for these positions do not have to misrepresent their intentions of leaving for a graduate degree. In fact, if you should desire to stay, you would find upon investigation that senior responsibility and authority is reserved for the higher-degreed specialists.

Many analysts do, in fact, return to the consulting firms and banks that initially hired them, *after* obtaining their master's in any of a number of majors, such as quantitative analysis or business administration. At this point they begin new career paths, in positions with titles such as associate-to-consultant, investment manager, perhaps chartered financial analyst (a designation similar to CPA received after passing equally rigorous examinations).

Whatever your choice upon coming to a decision following some time spent as a research associate, you are in a very different position of experience than when you graduated from college. You have significant, important business experience that will have transformed the value of your undergraduate degree. You are well situated to apply to one of the top graduate programs and feel confident about your ability to succeed.

Whatever graduate program you do enter, you arrive better prepared to make the most of the degree. When you do graduate with your new degree, you offer your new employer excellent justification for a responsible, decision-making position with all the appropriate rewards of such a job.

An Alternative Strategy

Perhaps in reading through this strategy, you've begun to have some doubts about its suitability in your case. Though you agree with the proposition, you don't feel like the ideal candidate for an advanced degree. Your objections might be on any number of grounds: your grades in college may not have been good enough for you to be competitive for some of these analyst positions; or, maybe your objection is you are not interested in resettling for any amount of time in the urban areas often occupied by this type of business. It may be the nature of the work of research associates as described does not interest you. Some folks just get tired of school and have no wish to return immediately. You still have options.

The basic premise of this book has been to give the math major frank advice about the worth of this degree and how best to use it in forging a productive and enjoyable career. One way you can ensure that without exercising the option of graduate school is by focusing on the development and acquisition of "portable" skills; that is, skills that you can carry from job to job. Content skills are pertinent to one job and not easily transferable to another. For example, if you work in the investment department of a bank and monitor the bank's portfolio of investments, you acquire two kinds of knowledge in this job. The first, your content knowledge, is what you learn about those specific stocks and their performance. Unless you encounter those stocks again in another job (not likely), the information doesn't "carry over" to new employment. Portable skills, however, follow you throughout your career. The portable skills you learned in portfolio management would be your data analysis, your work with relational databases, your knowledge of the market and trends in general. In today and tomorrow's ever-changing job market, portable skills offer you the best measure of job security.

But if, for the reasons listed above, or perhaps some other reasons, this path to a graduate degree isn't for you, you can still accomplish the same goals in a slightly different way. Seek out positions after graduation that provide the same kind of preparation as these analyst jobs can give you, but without some of the "thorns." For example, you can find these positions without relocating to an urban area. You can locate analyst positions in firms with less turnover and less competition for these lower-level entry jobs. You certainly can locate firms that will value your talents at that job and not be eager for you to leave. Let's look at some recent job announcements for positions that would be ideal for you:

Financial Analyst: Join us, the largest natural gas distribution company in the state. We currently have a challenging

continued

---

continued

opportunity available for a financial analyst with a bachelor's degree and excellent PC skills.

Budget Analyst/Nonprofit: To provide financial oversight of mental health and substance abuse programs. Responsibilities include tracking revenues and expenses, preparing budget reports, developing spending plans with program administrators. B.A., knowledge of spreadsheets and word processing required.

Market Analyst: As a key member of our marketing team focused on wholesale gasoline operations, you'll collect and interpret market data, advise management about market trends and critical regional market activities, develop and analyze rebate/reward sales programs, and track/report competitive information. To qualify, you should have a B.A./B.S., facility in mathematics, excellent PC and creative skills; Windows-related software proficiency—Quattro Pro for Windows 5.0; and the ability to manage multiple projects simultaneously.

These are, of course, career positions and not the fast-track kinds of positions described in the career path. These jobs certainly do not rule out the possibility of your advancing your education at some point in the future. You may decide to go to graduate school at night and hold on to your position. In fact, the employer may offer you educational benefits as an inducement to that course of action. And, of course, you may decide your job is so interesting with so many possibilities for personal enrichment that you decide not to go to graduate school, at least for the foreseeable future. Whatever your decision, you will have begun to build upon your undergraduate education with valuable work experience that benefits both your career and any possibility of future professional education.

WORKING CONDITIONS

Staying Abreast of Current Affairs

The work is time consuming, there is no question of that. This is due to the fact that analysts read so much. The best analysts read constantly—newspapers (more than one a day), annual reports, trade publications, journals, biographies, even novels—whatever keeps them abreast of the developments and changes in the marketplace. As a math major, this may come as a surprise, a delight, or a concern. So much of your work in your major involved processing and problem solving and not a significant amount of prose reading. And college life often leaves busy undergraduates little time to stay abreast of current affairs. If you are a reader and enjoy staying current, then you'll be delighted to find a career path that marries that interest with your degree. It will be a concern if you're not only out of practice reading, but not a particularly avid reader when you do have time.

Find the Concentration of Employers

Whether you are working for a consulting firm of the size that can afford a number of research or financial associate positions, or an investment bank or the investment department of a commercial bank large enough to have such a department, you should be thinking in terms of a major metropolitan area or the highway belt around such an area. This is where you will find the concentration of employers hosting these kinds of positions. To generalize a bit further, one could say these positions are concentrated in Boston, Chicago, New York City, and San Francisco. The major brokerage houses have branch offices in over eight hundred cities across the United States.

Explore Living in the Metropolitan Area

As career counselors, we have discovered there are a variety of reactions to living in a metropolitan area—some people love the idea and others don't. Most will admit, however, that metropolitan living offers more *choices* than any other locale: more choices in living , more choices about shopping, more choices in entertainment, and many more opportunities to meet people. When our own alumni who work in the city return to campus to visit, they tell us that living in the city can resemble a neighborhood. They see the same people on their way in and out of work, shopkeepers know their name, waitresses know their breakfast order, and so forth. City dwellers are quick to list the advantages and the normalcy of city life.

It's important to take note here that many fine graduate schools are also located in these major population zones, and that may prove convenient when it comes time to move ahead in your strategic plan to enter graduate school.

What's It Like to Work in Consulting?

There is no "typical" day for a research associate or financial analyst in consulting or investment banking. However, while there may be no daily routines (and that in itself may be an attraction for you), the following activities and roles played are fairly constant over time.

Information Resourcing. These associate positions all require finding answers, usually under pressures of time and cost. To succeed, you need to be inventive, be good on the phone, and believe you can do it to succeed. In most consulting and investment decisions, information needs to be of high quality and recent. Providing that information will be a big part of your daily job. Your day will probably begin by scanning several newspapers, watching for business and market information that might prove helpful. Begin that newspaper reading practice now. It'll come in very handy.

Julie DeGalan, one of the creators of the *Great Jobs* series, is fond of saying that the answer to any question is only "two phone calls away." She has demonstrated this time and time again, sometimes quite dramatically, in delivering the needed information. The persistence and positive attitude that underlies a philosophy of only "two phone calls away" would serve the research associate or financial analyst well in their jobs.

Financial analyst positions at investment banks or in the investment department of larger banks monitor the performance of particular stocks and securities on the world's stock exchanges and stay well informed about the industries they track. Generally, you will focus on one or two industries in this kind of position.

Travel. Long-distance travel is more a function of the research associate in the consulting industry than the analyst in investment banking. Some entry-level consulting positions can involve a grueling amount of travel. Just as the problems are global, clients can be global as well. Consultants leave the States every day for China, Latin America, Eastern Europe. Many of our largest consulting firms and investment banking services have had a strong European presence for decades. This increasingly far-flung demand for consulting/analyst services gives an edge to the individual with language skill and/or cultural sensitivity. Both research and financial analyst positions can involve significant out-of-the-office time in meeting with and working on-site with clients. To succeed, you need to be flexible and willing to get up and go. When you are on-site with the client, there tend to be correspondingly long days, because your client knows you aren't going home, but to a hotel.

Analysis. Designing or running complicated computer models to evaluate corporations or monitor stock price movement or daily work with numerous databases to retrieve important information will consume much of your time. You will need to become familiar with all kinds of statistical digests, annual reports, Securities and Exchange Commission documents, spreadsheets, and financial market reports.

Whether you need to analyze the investment potential of a foreign firm, the comparable company activity pursuant to a merger, or the involved preparations prior to a public offering of stock, you will encounter data that need to be transformed into usable information by your analysis. This information will then become the basis for the consulting team's action plan for the client.

This manipulation and understanding of data will provide some of the most valuable experience you can bring to your future graduate program. It is perhaps one of the most crucial skills for graduate work; and your ability to transform "data" into "information" should help to make your progress through graduate school a smooth one. You will have an advantage over many of your peers, even those with business experience, because as a consulting associate or financial analyst, you are working for so many different clients on so many different projects that you will develop a broad understanding of resources and relevant techniques.

Presentation. In a consulting firm, for example, the work is underwritten by client fees. Though you may be working on several different projects simultaneously, all your work is client directed and available to the client for examination and review. Attractive presentation of materials is a skill you will begin to appreciate in consulting. The presentation may be a carefully prepared written document with charts and graphs (demanding mastery of software products), or it may be a public presentation with overheads, handouts, and your explanations of your material as well as responses to questions. Creativity, quality work with deadlines, and skills with a variety of presentation techniques are what you will take away from this experience.

Teamwork. As a research associate or analyst, all of your work supports more senior staff people who have the major responsibility for the success or failure of a client contract. Consequently, a team approach is important in everything you'll do. You'll learn to clearly communicate your activities to your team members in order to avoid overlaps, misunderstandings, and wasted effort on anyone's part. This team approach will stand you in good stead in graduate work.

TRAINING AND QUALIFICATIONS

Let's begin with a rather general statement on training for research assistants and financial analysts from the *Occupational Outlook Handbook* for 1996–97 published by the U.S. Department of Labor, Bureau of Labor Statistics.

> There are no universal educational requirements for entry-level jobs in this field. However, employers in private industry prefer to hire those with a master's degree in business administration or a discipline related to the firm's area of specialization. Those individuals hired straight out of school

with only a bachelor's degree are likely to work as research associates or junior consultants, rather than full-fledged management consultants. It is possible for research associates to advance up the career ladder if they demonstrate a strong aptitude for consulting, but, more often, they need to get an advanced degree to do so.

Employers of these positions will be looking for people with some very specific qualifications. A strong candidate will possess very strong quantitative, analytical, and communications skills. They will be able to work in fast-paced, demanding environments, and they will need to demonstrate achievements such as a high GPA, sophisticated academic and part-time work experiences, and extracurricular leadership positions.

Skills and Requirements

Financial analysis and research work is done in a wide variety of contexts by some of the most prestigious firms in the world. Generally what is looked for in applicants, both on their resumes and in personal interviews, is evidence of a facility in mathematics, the ability to digest, analyze, and interpret large amounts of material; an inquiring mind; and good communication skills. To your surprise perhaps, listening is a critical skill. In dealing with clients, if you don't understand their problem as they do, you're wasting your time in devising solutions! Consulting is about communication. Here's a quick checklist of skills and their level of importance:

Analytical skills: extremely high	Ability to synthesize: high
People skills: high	Creative ability: high
Sales skills: medium	Initiative: medium
Communication skills: high	Computer skills: medium

While your background may be in mathematics, you'll be joined by colleagues with degrees in economics, political science, business administration, finance, marketing, engineering, and law. Any of these degrees combined with an advanced degree in business administration is considered very attractive by hiring firms.

EARNINGS

Salaries in this path vary dramatically, sometimes almost astronomically, depending on the new employee's education, experience, and employer. Comparisons are futile, but we will suggest some boundaries. Median incomes for analysts are about $45,000. The middle 50 percent (according to the most recent edition of the *Occupational Outlook Handbook*) earned between $30,000 and $53,900. In your own search for analysts' salaries, you'll need to be watchful. Frequently on the Web, the term "analyst" will refer to data analyst positions, not the analyst positions we've described in this chapter.

The Association of Management Consulting weighs in with some additional information of note. Their most recent survey of firms indicates higher earnings, and this includes bonuses (very common in these jobs based on profitability) and profit sharing—research associates in member firms averaged $61,277 for entry-level analysts and consultants.

What you need to remember in reading these very generous salary figures is that these firms have their employees under tremendous scrutiny. If you don't perform, you'll be let go. This remains true even as you ascend the earnings ladder. Many of these firms have very specific expectations for when employees should be achieving certain levels of performance. When you see high earnings such as these, you shouldn't be surprised that the following are true: 1) getting hired will be correspondingly difficult and 2) you will work very hard indeed for that salary.

CAREER OUTLOOK

The volatile business environment in the nineties has challenged even smaller corporations with issues of global competition, dramatic technological advances, and an endless stream of new thinking and practices for organizational structure. Faced with this kind of dizzying environment, it's no wonder management cries, "Get us an analyst!"

Employment projections for analysts and consultants is for faster-than-average growth through the year 2005 as industry and government increasingly outsource these jobs to improve their performance. Companies today are more likely to "buy" from among this growing array of specific consulting services to solve problems, rather than hire permanent staff to accomplish the same things. It's cheaper and more efficient. As a result of this outsourcing practice, however, growth is expected to occur in large consulting firms, large financial services organizations, and the largest banks.

In today's competitive marketplace, consultants, banks, and financial service organizations offer many similar services to their clients. Someone may be in trouble over product development, staffing issues, profit and loss projections, or any of a host of complicated situations. Others are doing well and need assistance coping with rapid growth; still others need help increasing profitability or efficiency. Consulting can be utilized by any business for any aspect of a business's operation.

STRATEGY FOR FINDING THE JOBS

The career path to a possible master's degree we discuss in this chapter is structured around the strategy of first finding a position as an analyst. These analyst positions go by a variety of names including market and financial analyst, research analyst, and research associate. Though they are not all the same job, they share an interest in hiring the mathematics graduate. For these positions, your math education is as essential as it will be on your way to earning a master's degree in any of the quantitative disciplines. To find both the advertised and unadvertised analyst positions you should begin by identifying your particular skills, locate the jobs, identify the industries, prepare your tools, and begin the networking process.

Identify Your Skills

Locate the analyst positions that match your skills and experience. Let's look at the skills employers are seeking for these positions: an exceptionally strong mathematics background including a high GPA, presentation skills, good oral and written communications, teamwork, good telephone skills, an inquiring mind, research ability for business and market trends, a comfort level with the manipulation, analysis, and interpretation of large amounts of data, and the potential ability to analyze financial market reports. Look for positions that will value your undergraduate degree and positions that offer training or possible benefits for continuing your education.

Here are excerpts from two typical analyst position job postings:

> Candidates are required to have successfully completed an undergraduate degree with a distinguished record of leadership and academic achievement. Additional qualifications include excellent quantitative skills, the ability to communicate effectively, genuine dedication to team play, as well as high energy, personal integrity, initiative, and creativity.
>
> Candidates for this job should have a solid understanding of basic mathematical concepts, effective writing and communication skills, good computer programming skills, and an interest in applying these strengths to real-world problems. Other responsibilities include coordinating meetings, managing field work, and assisting with report and proposal writing.

Many of you reading this ad will not be surprised at the need for strong math skills. After all, that was your major. As career counselors, however, we find most math students are shocked at the emphasis on public presentations, excellence in writing, and client conferencing skills. If you're surprised as well, it's probably because none of your college math classes gave you an experience in these areas, nor did they indicate they would be important in your career. They are, however, very important and will be a strong theme throughout this chapter.

Locate the Jobs

As we mentioned earlier in this chapter, you should explore the concentration of employers which will be found in major metropolitan areas or the highway belts around such areas as Boston, Chicago, New York City, and San Francisco. The kinds of employers that use analysts frequently are concentrated in densely populated areas near transportation and major airports. Let's use Boston as an example and begin our search to locate the jobs, identify the industries, and explore some of the resources that list analyst positions.

Adams Publishing (*http://www.adamsonline.com*), publishers of *The Boston JobBank* and similarly named directories of employers for Atlanta, the Carolinas, Chicago, Dallas–Ft. Worth, Denver, Detroit, Florida, Houston, Los Angeles, Minneapolis–St. Paul, Missouri, Metropolitan New York, Ohio, Philadelphia, Phoenix, San Francisco Bay Area, Seattle, Tennessee, and Metropolitan Washington. Surrey Books (*http://surreybooks.com*) publishes another geographical guide, *How to Get a Job in Greater Boston*, and similar titles for Atlanta, Chicago, Dallas–Ft. Worth, Europe, Houston, the New York metropolitan area, the Pacific Rim, San Francisco Bay, Seattle/Portland, southern California, and Washington, D.C.

With these publications in mind, in our example, *The Boston JobBank* offers an overview of the Boston job market and the basic elements of a successful job search which states, "the direct contact method boasts twice the success rate of the others" when using techniques for a job search. The "direct contact" method centers on picking up the telephone and making calls to the hiring officials on your contact list. You can use a guide like this to begin formulating a list of contacts. In this guide, the employers are organized by industry with address, telephone numbers, a description of the company and the product or service it provides, and a contact name.

Identify the Possible Industries

As we continue our job search strategy using Boston as the geographic area, let's identify the possible employers. Here is a sample of the employers listed in *The Boston JobBank* that would be appropriate for our search for analyst positions in the Boston area:

Accounting	Education services
Advertising and public relations	Financial services
Banking/savings and loan	Government
Business services/non-scientific research	Health care: services, equipment, and supplies
Charities and social services	Insurance
Communications	Management consulting

Use the above list as your guide to find other industries in other similar publications that are also indexed by geographic area. Search for listings of marketing research firms. Companies turn to these firms for contracting out for services rather than supporting their own marketing department. Explore financial services, advertising, and those manufacturing firms producing consumer goods. Consulting firms, investment banking, and brokerage houses offer excellent employment prospects for analysts. A variety of government agencies provide the largest number of positions, but don't overlook economic consulting firms or financial institutions.

In *The Boston JobBank*, many of the employer listings offer a comprehensive list of possible positions under the phrase "common positions include." Look for market/financial analyst and research/business analysts in these sections. Just a quick check in this publication under the industry listing "Advertising, Marketing, and Public Relations" found the following listing (we've added the italics):

> XYZ Database Co., 50 Harvard Street, Burlington, MA 01803. Common positions include: Administrator; Computer Operator; Computer Programmer; Computer Systems Analyst; Customer Service Representative; Database Management Specialist; *Marketing Research Analyst; Marketing Specialist;* Secretary; Software Engineer; Statistician; Systems Analyst. Educational backgrounds include: Accounting; Business Administration; Computer Science; Economics; Marketing; *Mathematics.* Number of employees at this location: 750. Number of employees nationwide: 900.

Prepare the Job Search Tools

Design your resume to focus on the skills of the position description. Write a cover letter that targets the benefits of hiring you and describes your math education, skills, and experience in a way that draws parallels to the needs described in the position listing. If the hiring official finds a match between your skills and the employer's qualifications and needs, there is a good possibility they will ask to interview you. If an interview confirms the match between the skills and qualifications, then the final goal will likely be achieved—being hired!

Begin the Networking Process

Now that you have identified your skills, located the jobs and possible employment sites, and you have your job search tools ready to submit, you can begin to make telephone calls to your contacts and begin a network. In addition to your list of contacts, use your personal and professional contacts including your college math professors, students in your courses, colleagues from clubs on campus, and fellow members of organizations on and off campus. Let everyone know what positions you are searching for and in what geographic area. At the end of this chapter there is a section that lists professional associations that have job listings, so check on the website listed to see if they publish job postings in their newsletters or journals—or on-line.

Strategies for Market Analysts and Financial Analysts

As we learned earlier in this chapter, most analyst positions are found in metropolitan areas. Analysts work in large organizations whose success depends on a knowledge of the general business and financial climate. Major corporations, financial institutions, major teaching and research hospitals and HMOs, brokerage firms, investment companies, pharmaceutical concerns, and major transportation systems are but a few examples. No matter where the analysts work, their role is generally the same. Analysts (market, financial, or research) help to provide the expert advice that will help their employer or their employer's clients to invest wisely with the best return on their money or to anticipate or solve a business problem. The job titles for these positions include market analyst (MA) or financial analyst (FA) in many investment banks or investment banking departments of commercial banks, and research analyst or research associate (RA) in management consulting firms. Because these analyst positions have a variety of job titles, it's best to focus on the job description and not what the job is called. Here are actual postings for analysts found on the Internet:

> Marketing Analyst: Major Boston bank seeks marketing analyst to
> gather and manage data on consumer products and customer
>
> continued

continued

credit profiles. Perform custom segment analysis, profitability analysis, volume/trend forecasting, and budgeting. Provide recommendations to improve effectiveness of direct mail program. Requires SAS. Application of statistical methods, financial analysis, and experience with managing, and reporting, from large databases. Salary to $60K. Contact: Mable Kane at Common Analytic Recruiting, 22 East 42nd Street, New York, NY 10019; Fax (212-555-8849); E-mail:MKane@common.com (Word format preferred); Web:http://www.common.com.

Financial Analysts, Investment Banking. Description: Support of senior investment bankers' new business efforts through development of marketing material. Significant responsibility in executing all phases of transactions, including financial analysis, due diligence, marketing, pricing, and closing. Candidates are required to successfully complete an undergraduate degree with a distinguished record of leadership and academic achievement. Additional qualifications include excellent quantitative skills, the ability to communicate effectively, genuine dedication to team play, as well as high energy, personal integrity, initiative, and creativity. Contact: Julia LaBier, Associate Vice President; fax (212)555-3434 (preferred); phone: (212)555-3445. Website: http://www.finbank.com:fun/jobs/analyst.

Strategies for Research Analysts and Associates

Research analysts and associates help put together proposals, case studies, or analyses designed to help the consultant's client solve problems, determine future strategies, or implement programs. These jobs are often seen as opportunities to gain experience that leads to increased responsibility. Most research analyst and associate positions are designed to work either in a team or under collaborative supervision with a more senior team member. These positions appeal to graduates contemplating advanced education because the experience is applicable to their math background and turnover in these positions is normal and expected as job holders often move on to graduate school or more senior positions.

As you begin to review research analyst and associate positions, pay very close attention to the skills required. On-the-job training is very common in these positions, and you will want to devote some interview time to exploring how new analysts are trained in the firm you are speaking with. Here are two additional examples of positions that emphasize the skills of data analysis, running mathematical models, and proposal writing. Some of you will have some of the computer experience or software familiarity required, others will have only limited or partial skills in this area. Don't let that deter you from applying. If your computer skills are solid and you've had some exposure to statistical software and feel you have an ability to quickly learn other programs, express that in your cover letter or during an interview. Given the variety of software packages in use today, exposure to the specific brand is less important than familiarity with the type of software and an ability to read a user's manual and seek help for questions.

Research Analyst—XYZ is seeking applicants with technical B.A. or B.S. degrees and strong quantitative orientation for the position of research analyst. Candidates for this job should have a solid understanding of basic mathematical concepts, effective writing and communication skills, good computer programming skills, and an interest in applying these strengths to real-world problems. Research analysts at XYZ work on teams with other XYZ consultants on a variety of projects. Research analysts are primarily responsible for tasks such as data analysis, programming and running mathematical models, and programming computer-aided interviews. Other responsibilities include coordinating meetings, managing field work, and assisting with report and proposal writing. Contact: Jo Nolet, Employment Opportunities at XYZ Systems; jonetl@xyzsystems.com: http://xyzsystems.com.

Research Analyst—XYZ Investors, a Cambridge (Boston)–based quantitative investment management firm, is seeking an analyst to help develop equity strategies. The position entails gathering, maintaining, and analyzing data from a variety of electronic sources. The ideal candidate will have strong computer background with a demonstrated proficiency in UNIX, SAS, and Perl. Knowledge of financial data, databases, and vendors. Factset is highly desirable. Individuals should also possess an interest in domestic and international investing and strong interpersonal skills. B.A./B.S.-level degree is acceptable. CFA, advanced degrees, and/or quantitative research skills (statistics, applied mathematics) are a bonus. Immediate availability. Fax resume and cover letter in strict confidence to: Kim Smith at 617-555-4498 or jobs@investors.com.

Once again, we direct your attention to the importance of teams, collaboration, presentations, and writing in both these job postings. Using the job title "analyst" as our search discriminant on the Internet, the position listed below was found. As you can see, this position specifically speaks to the math major as an analyst:

Mathematician/Statistician—NY. Proprietary energy trading firm looking for an entry-level mathematician/statistician to develop and work on long-term/in-house projects; developing strategies. Simultaneously this person will be trained to trade derivatives and oil products. A B.S. in statistics or mathematics is required. The individual should have solid computer skills, a good work ethic, ability to show initiative, and be a team player. Please e-mail cover letters and resume to Sunsup@hotmail.com. No attachments—only text will be considered.

This mathematician/statistician position is interesting for more than just the use of your major in the job title. It's an analyst position with a job title that does not include the word analyst, yet the job description is similar to most market analyst roles; in this case, focusing on fuel oil energy markets. The employing firm is certainly committed to hiring a math graduate.

Here is an another job listing found on the Internet that describes the training process for a financial analyst position:

Financial Analysts—Multiple Locations. Location: Chicago, New York, Washington, D.C., and San Francisco. Financial analysts will experience an intensive training module approximately six weeks during the initial stage of the program. This phase focuses on corporate credit analysis and risk assessment, oral and written communications, accounting, and fundamental corporate finance skills. Concepts are explored through lectures as well as individual and group cases. Subsequent to the training module, each analyst will be assigned to a client team and will analyze clients' current operating performance, financial condition, and industry. In addition, analysts will participate in transactions, including the preparation of financial projections and client proposals. Successful candidates will be self-motivated and inquisitive, with strong analytical as well as oral and written

continued

---

continued

communication skills. A B.S./B.A. degree with a solid degree background in accounting or finance. Quantitative analysis skills required. Candidates must have permanent work authorization in the U.S. Fax resumes to Bank of Atlanta, Attn: Jacqueline Cadwell, 312-555-3849; Website: http://www.bankatlanta.com:4444/fun/jobs/analyst/analyst.html.

Jobs such as the ones listed above are highly desirable because of the quality of the training provided. After all, the results of this training will stay with you throughout your career. Firms spending this much time and money on your training have every reason to assist you in your career progress with their firm. They want you to succeed. On the other hand, you need to know that positions providing this much training are highly competitive, the selection process may be lengthy and rigorous, and your application and candidacy will come under close scrutiny.

POSSIBLE EMPLOYERS

Searching for possible employers is not an exact science. A good beginning is often the yellow pages of a telephone book for the area or city you are interested in. But your search can and will become more sophisticated. There are directories that do not focus on the geographic area in their titles but do offer a geographic index of metropolitan areas such as Boston which list employment contacts or job listings for math majors such as:

❑ Daniel Lauber's two publications, *Professional's Job Finder* and *Government Job Finder,* published by Planning Communications, *http://jobfindersonline.com*

❑ *Peterson's Job Opportunities for Business Majors*

❑ *The Book of Lists*, published by *Boston Business Journal*, *http://www.amcity.com/boston*

❑ *Finding a Job in the Nonprofit Sector,* published by The Taft Group, *http://www.taftgroup.com*

❑ *The Job Seeker's Guide to Socially Responsible Companies*, published by Visible Ink Press, *http://www.visibleink.com*

Here is a sample of some of the websites that were published in *Professional's Job Finder*:

J.P. Morgan and Company: job database for positions in banking, finance, management services, URL: *http://www.jpmorgan.com/corpinfo/careers/home_page.html*

Hoover's Online: homepages of over 2,500 companies that list job openings, URL: *http://www.hoovers.com*

Many of the associations listed at the end of this chapter provide job listings via a website. Other listings may be found through general job search sites such as:

http://www.careermosaic.com

http://www.usajobs.opm.gov. USA Jobs is a website operated by the Office of Personnel Management.

http://www.fedworld.gov/ or *ftp://ftp.fedworld.gov/pub/jobs/jobs.htm.* FedWorld is a database of 1,500 open federal job vacancies.

Hook Up, Get Hired!: The Internet Job Search Revolution and *Electronic Job Search Revolution* by Joyce Lain Kennedy are just two publications that give you a way to look for jobs and reach potential employers through the Internet. Another publication, the *Guide to Internet Job Searching* by Oserman, Riley, and Roehm and published by VGM Career Horizons, provides a good explanation of how to connect to the Internet and instructions for posting a resume electronically, as well as extensive listings of Internet sites with job ads and resume databases. It also has a directory of bulletin board services that offer job listings. There are sites on the Internet that can be searched by occupational title, such as analyst, research analyst, financial analyst, market analyst. The associations at the end of this chapter provide even more websites for your job search strategy.

The Harvard University Gazette lists several opportunities for analysts in an educational setting. Another resource for analyst positions: *Peterson's Job Opportunities for Business Majors*, which includes the categories Banking, Financial Analysis, Market Research.

An analyst by any other name is still an analyst! Look deeper into the job descriptions and not merely at the titles. Read the following job description and see if you can guess the title of this position.

Responsible for the research and preparation of confidential reports on potential donors and identification of new donors. Prepare concise, accurate, and thorough reports and briefings that analyze and evaluate individual institutional prospects for

continued

> continued
>
> solicitation. Work with fund-raising staff to identify new prospects in support of fund-raising goals, assist in matching priorities with donors.

The ad clearly outlines an analyst position as we have identified it. Yet, the job as listed in *The Harvard Gazette* is titled "Development Researcher"!

POSSIBLE JOB TITLES

Job titles will not be a reliable guide to analyst positions. Pay more attention to the job description than the position title. Some possible titles include:

Associate	Financial auditor
Associate consultant	Financial evaluator (trainee)
Associate to consultant	Investment manager
Business analyst	Market analyst
Chartered financial analyst	Research analyst
Financial analyst	Research associate
Financial assistant	

This is by no means a complete list, but should simply serve as a caution that you can't judge an analyst job by anything other than an understanding of the job duties and responsibilities.

RELATED OCCUPATIONS

Because the skills demanded of analyst positions are so valuable, it's no surprise to find the opportunities for transferring these skills to other occupations are excellent. Naming those related occupations, however, would be a challenge because they are so numerous and so diverse. In this chapter we have attempted to give the math major a good idea of the essential job skills needed as you look for analyst positions on your way to a master's degree. To then identify related occupations, you'd need to look to the specific skills required for any particular market or financial analyst or research analyst or associate and work from there. A brief list of the skills employers are seeking for these analyst positions include math skills, presentation skills, good communications, teamwork, good telephone skills, willingness to travel, an inquiring mind, ability to research business and market trends, ability to manipulate and understand data, and the skills to analyze financial market reports. So, as an example, if your particular employment involved client consulting skills, problem solving, data analysis, and constructing mathematical models, a change of careers could easily lead you to work in pension plan or retirement funding programs.

The *Occupational Outlook Handbook* listed some standard related occupations as actuaries, economists, financial managers, underwriters, credit analysts, loan officers, budget officers.

PROFESSIONAL ASSOCIATIONS

Here are some associations that relate to market and financial analysts, and research analysts and associates. Membership in one of these organizations might help in terms of job listings, networking opportunities, and employment search services. Some provide information at no charge. If you want to receive their publications that list job opportunities, you might need to join the organization. Check for student member rates.

Review the "Members/Purpose" section for each organization and decide whether the organization pertains to your interests. For additional information, use the *Encyclopedia of Associations* published by Gale Research Inc. Check the websites of these organizations for further career information or links to other sites that provide information related to market and financial analysts and research analysts and associates. See if these associations can assist you in your job search:

American Association of Professional Consultants
9140 Ward Parkway
Kansas City, MO 64114
Website: none
Members/Purpose: Professional consultants. Aids and guides members in the improvement of their professional abilities.
Journals/Publications: *The Consultant's Journal; The Consultant's Voice; Membership Directory*

Association of Managing Consultants
521 Fifth Avenue, 35th Floor
New York, NY 10175
Website: http://www.imcusa.org

Members/Purpose: Professional management consulting firms that serve all types of business and industry.
Journals/Publications: *Directory of Membership; Journal of Management Consulting;* Newsletter

Council of Consulting Organizations
521 Fifth Avenue, 35th Floor
New York, NY 10175
Website: http://www.imcusa.org
Members/Purpose: Is the umbrella organization that includes Institute of Managing Consultants and the Association of Management Consultants (http://www.amc.org). Individual management consultants who work privately or in consulting firms that meet the institutes' requirements.
Journals/Publications: *Directory of Members*

Council of American Survey Research Organizations
3 Upper Devon Belle Terre
Port Jefferson, NY 11777
Website: http://www.casro.org
Members/Purpose: Survey research companies in the United States. Provides a vehicle whereby survey research companies can interact with one another, sharing relevant information and addressing common problems; promotes the establishment, maintenance, and improvement of professional standards in survey research.
Journals/Publications: none

Institute of Management Consultants
521 Fifth Avenue, 35th Floor
New York, NY 10175
Website: http://www.imcusa.org
Members/Purpose: Professional management consulting firms who serve all types of business and industry.
Journals/Publications: *Directory of Membership; Journal of Management Consulting;* Newsletter

Marketing Research Association
2189 Silas Deane Highway, Suite 5
Rocky Hill, CT 06067
Website: http://www.mra-net.org
Members/Purpose: Companies and individuals involved in any area of marketing research such as data collection, research, or as an end user.
Journals/Publications: *Alert; Marketing Research Association Membership Roster; Blue Books Research Service Directory; Field Service Manual; Research Guidelines; Field Directors Manual; Interviewer Training Manual*

MBA/Business Executives: American Management Association
130 W. Fiftieth Street
New York, NY 10020
Website: http://www.amanet.org
Members/Purpose: Seeks to broaden members' management knowledge and skills.
Journals/Publications: *Compensation and Benefits Review; Compflash; Management Review; Organizational Dynamics; The President; Project Update; Supervisory Management; Management Solutions; Supervisory Sense; and Trainers Workshop*

Office of Personnel Management
Website: http://www.usajobs.opm.gov/

CHAPTER THIRTEEN

PATH 4: MATH IN THE MARKETPLACE: BUYER, SALES REPRESENTATIVE, AND PURCHASING AGENT

Jobs discussed in this chapter are jobs that use math as an important job skill and are directly related to the commercial marketplace and, therefore, tend to be dynamic environments characterized by high energy and lots of change. Because the marketplace is always seeking buyers and sellers, it's a field where decisions are often made quickly and often in an atmosphere highly charged with risk. Innovation, the ability to seize opportunity, intuitive knowledge of the marketplace and people, and a quick response mechanism are all phrases that might describe attributes for success in this environment. If those descriptions are appealing to your personality and your work style, you might consider exploring this career path.

There's no question you'll be needed and appreciated. In today's competitive marketplace, profit margins can be slim, costs must be carefully controlled, and business strategists are increasingly dependent on sophisticated mathematical models to anticipate possible outcomes with changes in variables such as the price of raw materials, advertising costs, competitive threats, the volatility of the stock market, packaging and shipping costs, and all the other host of variables that can affect the success of a business enterprise. The math graduate fits right into organizations that are working under these demands and pressures, and you might be that math major!

Every job brings its own environment and its own "package" of associated values. While everyone reading this book may be a math major, everyone reading this book is a different person with different needs. If you've read Chapter 1, "The Self-Assessment," and worked through some of those exercises, you may be beginning to build a mental picture of some of your particular personality dimensions, work attributes, and values. When you combine that growing self-awareness with your past work experience, you begin to understand that different jobs deliver different atmospheres, differing interactions with others, varying degrees of remuneration, and often dramatically different work experiences in terms of pace, location, energy, and so forth.

As career counselors, one of the most enjoyable aspects of working with math majors is letting them in on a well-kept secret—everybody wants to hire a math major! Career counselors listen to employers and recruiters complain frequently that math majors never interview with them. They wonder aloud, "Where do we find them? How can we get them to interview with us?" Even math department faculty can sometimes be guilty of hiding their majors from a larger world of employment because they themselves fail to realize where a math graduate can be employed.

One of the reasons career counselors are so enthusiastic about math majors is that they talk to employers all the time who need individuals with mathematical skills in the workplace. Many math majors are unaware of this demand and may even graduate and begin their own, often frustrating job search without any idea of the demand for their skills. It can then be easy to assign blame to your program or faculty, and that wouldn't be fair at all. The simple fact is that your math major is one of the most demanding scholastic majors offered in a college—so demanding, in fact, the small numbers of graduates are a good indication of your rarity and value in the marketplace! Mastering your college math curriculum requires many courses and credits and doesn't leave a lot of time for direct application by your faculty. It's common to be so involved in your program that it may have been hard to take time to explore career options. That's understandable. The reason for this book, and particularly for this chapter, is that it focuses on some areas you may not yet have encountered as career options.

So while this may all sound intriguing and attractive to you, you justifiably may be asking yourself, "What's the catch? What else do I need to know about working in the area of buying and selling?" What's behind these questions is the legitimate concern for what else the job may demand of you in addition to your math skill. You're correct in thinking that there will be other expectations beyond a facility with numbers. Some other attributes that will be helpful include, but are not limited to the following:

- ❑ An interest in and awareness of the commercial marketplace

- ❑ An appreciation for the competitiveness of the marketplace

- ❑ A willingness to assume management responsibilities, including staff supervision, budgets, hiring, and evaluation of employees

- ❑ Ultimately you will be asked to shed your technical abilities and take on increasingly conceptual responsibilities for strategic concerns, planning, and evaluation

This is a career path where you are hired for your math degree and something more, where you will use your math degree every day, but many other skills as well, and where you will be expected to assume the mantle of management responsibility in your preparation of professional staff work (business writing of reports, memoranda, and correspondence), in your staff supervision of employees and your ability to represent the organization you work for in a responsible manner. Let's look at some specific occupational areas in this career path.

DEFINITION OF THE CAREER PATH

Because this career path offers a number of exciting, but perhaps unfamiliar opportunities for the math major, let's begin by identifying some possible occupations in this area, acquaint you with some of the terminology, the job definitions, and typical career pathways in those fields. A caution is in order here: the jobs described below are just some solid examples and are not a finite (to use a math term) list by any means. Further on in this chapter we'll give you even more ideas of possible job titles and related occupations for this area. The jobs illustrated have been selected by the authors because

1) jobs in math are seeking math majors, 2) math majors are in demand in the marketplace, and 3) this path contains good general examples of career paths and job demands in the area of buying, selling, and marketing in the workplace.

In this final chapter, we'll look at series of sample jobs and job categories representative of those jobs that value your math education highly but demand other skills and interests in addition to your fluency with math. It may be decision making, it may be customer service, it may quite simply be your listening skills, but in this category math is but *one* of many important tools in your skill package that you'll need to do these jobs.

The positions we'll highlight in this chapter are

❑ Retail buyer and buyer/merchandising trainee

❑ Sales service representative

❑ Purchasing agent

What do they have in common? First, they are all part of the network of jobs that provide information and services to support the movement of goods and services from the manufacturer to the ultimate consumer. It's a huge part of our economy and an activity that can potentially use as many math majors as might apply for jobs in these kinds of activities. In fact, if you were to talk to your college alumni office or career office about surveys taken of former graduates of your institution, you'd discover a high proportion of math majors employed in the jobs listed above or in some of the related occupations listed further on in this chapter. Let's look at each of the four representative jobs listed above individually through the following categories.

Definition of the Career Path for Retail

Retailing is the sale of selected merchandise directly to the consumer. Though this definition of retailing might be satisfactory for an exam, in actuality retailing defies description! Retailing is an exciting career with enough change and excitement to keep you fascinated and on your toes for the life of your career. But retailing can also be a doorway, through which you can enter the worlds of statistics, purchasing, product management, or training and development. Many top managers in these fields began their careers in retail buying. Dramatic changes are taking place in the world of retailing. We'll look at a few examples of this marketing revolution to give you a sense of the range, scope, and decision-making potential for a math major looking for dynamic and fast-paced career opportunity:

❑ Viacom's MTV plans to develop a themed restaurant chain that will offer virtual reality technology and merchandise, in addition to food.

The preceding is a good example of how a career-minded retail professional must stay abreast of demographic trends and changing lifestyles and be ready to support high-risk decisions with facts. Retailing often is on the cutting edge of technology. Retail stores were the first to use videos on continuous loop in stores to stimulate customer awareness and interest in apparel products. Retailers are the first to sell in cyberspace and will be the first to use virtual reality to let shoppers "try on" clothes or experience home furnishings or outdoor equipment, and so on.

- Manufacturers, hoping to differentiate their brands from private-label brands, are increasingly opening their own retail outlets. Dr. Martins, Levi Strauss, Nike, and other large manufacturers are now increasingly appearing on streets and in malls as retailers.

- There is an increasing trend toward environmentally friendly "eco-stores." Recycling as a concern and reality is reflected in the merchandising of consumer goods. Analysts predict other retailers will adopt these concepts.

Retailing is no place for the amateur or for the faint of heart. It's a world that demands you take a risk—for only the strong survive. One reason why the math graduate is a welcome candidate for jobs in the retail sector is that the constant, unrelenting competition demands superb abilities to analyze quantitative data and then make solid decisions based on that data. In fact, the first thing that greets most retailing buying professionals each day is the printout of what has taken place in their store or stores the day before.

Why haven't you heard about retailing before this? There are three principal reasons why math students don't have the opportunity to seriously consider retail careers upon graduation. First and foremost is that the subject of retailing is a science unto itself. It is serious big business that incorporates healthy doses of psychology, human behavior, and intuition along with high tolerance for taking risks. The second obvious reason many students fail to consider retail is that retail puts no special premium on the attainment of a college degree. Of course, if you entered the executive suite of our largest retailers, everyone you'd meet would have a college degree. So would most of the preeminent retail managers, sales managers, and buyers. The third reason students don't take a more serious look at retailing as they graduate has to do with a misperception of retailing in the hierarchy of American jobs.

Let's take a look at a typical college job fair. Math majors are going to be attracted to the large corporations, and the prestige and esteem of classic "management" positions if not the more traditional statistics or actuarial positions. The retailers may also be at this job fair, but since math majors haven't had any in-depth exposure to retail careers in their major, all they're apt to see is store management and sales associate jobs. They don't consider the potential there.

The plain and simple reality is that almost any of the retailers present at that job fair will offer careers with more latitude, more fiscal responsibility, more decision-making authority, and more downright opportunities to take off (or crash and burn). Retailers will offer even more than any of the narrowly defined, computer-terminal-in-a-cubicle positions that exist beyond the impressive facades of the corporate management positions. Retailing is about giving talented people an opportunity to chart their own course, within the retailer's overall concept, for as long as any particular concept remains profitable. Retailing *listens* to employees' reasoning, and if it finds it sound, will support their decisions to add product lines, expand selling space, branch out into new markets, or redefine their image.

"Merchandising" is a term used to describe all the buying and selling activities within a store or chain. Merchandise managers decide what to buy based on what will sell. These are immensely complicated decisions. For example, if you are a buyer for men's shirts for a large chain, you must, months in advance of the selling season, choose from among hundreds of fabric possibilities (all cotton, nylon, silk, and blends) weaves (oxford, cambric, poplin, broadcloth, point-on-point, twill), collar styles (button down, tab, many varieties of spread collars, and collarless), cuff styles (French, buttoned) and, of course, price points at which all these various shirt models will be sold. A budget for shirts alone in a large branch department store could be hundreds and hundreds of thousands of dollars *a season*. If you are thinking spreadsheets, you're right on target!

People who succeed and rise to the top in retail are people who have the best sense of what their market will buy—and learn how to make the complex decisions (such as the example above) that will satisfy their particular market. They develop this strong sensitivity by mixing with the market "on the floor." A good merchandiser stays in touch with his or her customers by working the floor, selling merchandise, hearing complaints and praise about the products, and watching and noting the gender, age, and buying considerations of the public.

Retailing touches upon investment strategies, the costs of carrying inventory, pricing strategies, risk management, and many other planning tools that are highly sophisticated and require superb quantitative skills—in addition to decision-making ability and good communication skills, leadership, previous retail exposure, and the ability to juggle an ever-changing workload in a fast-paced environment. In retailing, what you can do and who you are counts more than degree attainment. The following ad for a major national retail chain store manager makes this point:

Who Says You Can't Have It All?

Store Management: An interesting career . . . a welcome challenge . . . *and* rewards. If you're ambitious and determined to make the most of your career, we want you to play an active role in our success and yours! As the nation's leading specialty retailer of imported home furnishings and related items, our store managers are involved in all aspects of our business. That's why we provide a comprehensive on-the-job manager development program to prepare you to take charge of a store, including P&L, visual merchandising, and people management.

We seek managers with strong retail experience, (*college degree a plus*), proven leadership abilities, a commitment to customer satisfaction, and the drive to handle a diverse workload in a challenging, fast-paced environment. Candidates must be willing to relocate. Investigate a career that offers it all, including competitive compensation and benefits, and stock purchase/401(k) plans.

Retailing is a field where you can jump right in and start a career *if* you are people-oriented, service-oriented, and willing to take advantage of opportunities. Retail personnel are in the front lines of getting the product to the consumer. They are the final marketing intermediaries. Customer contact and customer service is the key to unlocking the consumers' interest in purchasing your product. Customer contact provides the answers to ordering and pricing mysteries. Customer service is an art and a science, made up of both analytical and communications skills. It is these distinctions that keep your customers coming back.

Definition of the Career Path for Buyer/Merchandising Trainee

Buyers are those individuals whose job it is to choose merchandise. Most buyers actually spend only a small percentage of their working year in the buying process. And yes, for some shoes or leather articles, buying might take place in Italy, but more than likely, most buying will occur at a buying exposition for small leather goods in a convention hall in Atlanta or Dallas. Buyer jobs are hard work, and as you see from the ad listed below, they are also highly quantitative in their orientation:

Assistant Buyer: Reporting to the buyer, the assistant buyer's role is to assist in achieving sales, gross margin, inventory

continued

---

continued

turnover goals through proper merchandising management within company-defined guidelines. Focus in on the day-to-day operations of the department while learning long-range business strategy. Requirements: excellent PC, communications, organizational, and analytical skills are required—retail management training program a plus.

As a trainee buyer, you'll work under the supervision of a senior buyer. You'll need to learn to anticipate your customers' shopping needs several seasons before the merchandise is in the store. You will find yourself considering a variety of issues. Will men switch to a two-button suit? Will misses-size women tolerate a shorter skirt length? How many of each size children's shoe to order? And so on. There are mountains of paperwork and sometimes daily reports of sales to analyze. And, if you haven't bought right, your mistakes stare back at you from store shelves!

You'll learn to negotiate with vendors on costs, delivery dates, and shared advertising budgets. You'll work with store staff on merchandise displays, and as you gain experience, you will take on more responsibility in each of these areas. Before too long, you will be in charge while your senior buyer is away. Some organizations will require that your training include a stint in store management, so you may spend some time in a branch store. Promotion to buyer positions can take two to five years. Realize, however, that this movement to middle management is faster than in many other industries. Economic ordering models are critical for most retailers and absolutely essential for the biggest. The position listed below demonstrates an understanding that to get the best person for the job, they need someone with a math background:

Merchandising: Control Buyer. Seeking an individual to effectively manage the inventory of a category of goods so as to maintain an in-stock position on all key merchandise within planned inventory and sales levels. This highly visible individual will be a key liaison among Corporate Merchandising, Accounting, and vendors. Requirements: This position requires excellent verbal and written communications, analytical skills, and *strong math/figures aptitude.* PC knowledge required and forecasting/modeling experience a plus. Must be able to work well under pressure, be highly flexible, be detail-oriented, and have good organizational skills. College degree or related experience preferred.

Definition of the Career Path for Sales Service Representative

There's no question—sales is misunderstood as a career option. Sales certainly has had its share of image problems. The reality is far, far different for the college graduate. As practicing career counselors, we hear two sides to the question, "Is sales a career for me?" Students have one opinion of sales, generally not very positive. Employers have another view of sales, and that is not only positive, but exciting, challenging, and highly attractive. Well, since many of these employers were college students themselves not too long ago, you figure it out!

Teaching and counseling at a small public college, the authors are no longer surprised that few college graduates view a sales job as attractive. Many students have concerns about compensation, measures of performance, ethical issues surrounding product quality, and accuracy of sales information.

The authors have the opportunity to meet and talk with professional salespeople throughout the year. We meet them when they visit our campus to recruit, when we attend job fairs and professional conferences, and when we make site visits to employers. Some of these sales professionals are new college graduates themselves, others are mid-career veterans, and yet others are senior staff who have long years of experience. They represent a full spectrum of experience in the field. Without exception, they speak of the professional challenges of larger accounts, important presentations to management, exciting travel opportunities, superb professional development opportunities, and satisfying financial rewards. They speak most often of wonderful, interesting colleagues and business friends. Here's how they sum up sales:

Advantages: A ready hiring market that allows you access to employment immediately upon graduation. The opportunity to acquire specific product information and become an "expert" in your field. Countless opportunities to learn and improve interpersonal skills that will remain valuable assets throughout your working life.

Disadvantages: Not many. There is a strong emphasis on individual decision making, time-management skills, and self-direction. Increasingly, professional salespeople are required to be technically and quantitatively astute in order to manage a sophisticated use of technology needed in customer contact and service provision. They must meet a need to be more of a listener than a talker, a problem solver, not a solution dictator, and a consultant, not a high-pressured order taker.

Return on Investment: Significant! A sales career will transform even the most broad-based of business majors into a real specialist in business affairs. You'll understand marketplace economics, consumer behavior, and organizational systems in a way never possible in the classroom. You'll also gain immeasurably in your ability to interact with individuals and groups in every type of setting. Sales is a jump-start to a career in which recognition comes faster than in most any other employment sector.

Sales: The Insider's Surprising View. Most interesting is how they think of themselves. As a group, they are poised, professional, and comfortable in social situations. They would tell you, often as not, that a career in sales is the reason, not the other way around. Individually, they range from extroverted toastmasters to quieter, more scholarly types. Some are comfortable with large groups, others prefer one-on-one. Many think of their job as educational and informative, not persuasive and certainly not hard-sell. They are deeply respectful of the people who comprise their market and do not see them as easily manipulated.

Ask any successful salesperson, "What is the most important skill you have?" You might expect the answer would be "personal power," or "persuasiveness," maybe "the ability to overcome objections" or "product knowledge." While all these attributes of a salesperson have their place, the skill most successful salespeople say they value above all is the *ability to listen.*

Sales: Selling Through Problem Solving. Contrary to public opinion, the objective of sales—certainly sales as practiced by professionals with a college degree and working for a reputable firm—is not to *make* somebody buy your product. A computer salesperson describes it this way:

> I see myself as a problem-solver. I try to get inside and understand my customers' work, their needs, and their problems. I listen. After I've had an opportunity to think about it, I'll prescribe solutions to their problems. Those solutions will include my company's products, but sometimes, I will recommend a competitor's product if that is better suited to the job. I'm in this job for the long haul and my belief is, each time I sell only what the customers need, I build trust. The more trust I build, the less "selling" I have to do. If I continue to get good at what I do, I may never have to "sell" again.

Sales: The Job Specifications. There are as many different types of sales positions as there are individuals to fill them. Each job holds the potential for both personal and professional growth, to varying degrees. Each job also places different demands on the job holder in terms of work productivity, self-management, travel, professional relationships, and product knowledge. Of special interest to the math major, some sales jobs will place a greater premium on their math education.

Let's identify some of the activities engaged in by salespeople. How they do their job is highly individual. With top sales professionals, you'll often see a singular professional style that is not only highly idiosyncratic but also indulged and approved of by top management. Glancing over this list, you can immediately understand that this job is far more complex and sophisticated than popular myth would have it.

- Identifying and contacting prospective customers
- Assessing needs and maintaining good relations with existing customer base
- Designing and delivering sales presentations
- Keeping records/activity reports/sales performance records
- Tracking sales orders/delivery schedules and other details
- Handling complaints/returns when received
- Keeping an eye on the competition and reporting competitive activity
- Learning about new products and mastering marketing strategies

This short list of duties emphasizes communications, as you would expect, but there are many other skills and attributes that are suggested by this list.

Let's identify and examine some of these other important skills and attributes close up. Each is followed by a pertinent excerpt from a recently advertised sales job:

Promotability. In any organization that has a sales force, to begin work there is to understand the organization in a very concrete, specific way. In the sales force, you learn how the organization is perceived by the consumer. This is true whether you are an admissions representative for a college or selling industrial boilers. Customer contact and your understanding and appreciation of the demands of a sales job will be the foundation and source of your credibility and authority as you advance in your career. One of the surest paths to promotion is having graduated from a corporate training program. The training is usually exceptional, and it affords you an opportunity to meet lots of other people in the organization and gives you a broad overview of your employer. The following position we list obviously uses training as a direct grooming process to management:

Management Trainee. Program is a six-month to one-year assignment in which you learn every aspect of store operations. This program consists of both classroom and hands-on training. It is expected that those who successfully complete this assignment will begin a position of operations manager and will have the opportunity to progress to the position of general manager. Qualifications: Requires a bachelor's degree, retail experience desirable, leadership skills, ability to manage multiple priorities, team-oriented, and strong interpersonal skills.

Product Knowledge. You'll have to learn everything about whatever you're selling, whether it's corporate health plans, retirement systems, computer software, or large pieces of manufacturing equipment. Details, capabilities, costs, tolerances, competitive advantages, and a host of myriad details are crucial to being able to provide answers to questions. Product knowledge as a job demand can be confusing to those unfamiliar with retail. It doesn't mean an in-depth knowledge of what you prefer to buy, but an awareness of what different publics want in consumer purchases. Those publics may be classified by income level or by gender or age. Here's a very typically brief ad for retail sales that emphasizes product knowledge:

Retail Sales. For New England's leading specialty fitness retailer. Retail and/or fitness background preferred, but not required. Candidates must possess strong work ethic, and a desire to embrace increasing responsibilities with a rapidly expanding company.

Customer Knowledge and Contact. Sales is about meeting people—lots of people. Each of these persons has a different need and appreciation for your product. Most of the time you encounter your clients on-the-job. Since you have initiated the meeting, you will also encounter a variety of receptions from a warm welcome to a glacial stare. It's going to be up to you and your sales skills to make these moments work. One way you'll learn to do this is by appreciating exactly what each customer wants. Is it service? Perhaps it's product quality? It might be dependability. Sometimes it's the lowest price available. When customers are busy, you soon learn to judge each as an individual, find out what *they* need and get down to business! The ad below suggests a fast-paced retail environment where customer demand is high and salespeople and buyers must be creative and know both the stock and the customers:

> At XYZ Intimate Apparel, we pride ourselves on our culture of creativity, hard work, and high energy. It's a challenging atmosphere, our success relies on the contributions of our associates. We look for people who are smart, ambitious, outgoing, and interested in making a career with us. In return we offer a wide spectrum of opportunities. Our atmosphere is stimulating, cutting-edge, fast-paced, and exciting.

Communication Skills. No client believes you're interested in him or her if you're looking at your watch or tapping your foot while he or she speaks. Eye contact, your full attention, and the appropriate sounds and movements of affirmation and understanding convey the message "I'm listening to you!" Salespeople understand that communication is a complex business.

Sales is the art *and* science of communication. The communication is often about important issues such as product features, delivery dates, prices, conditions of sales, financing, and so on. A miscommunication can result in far more costly problems than just a lost sale. It's important that both parties understand each other. Professional salespersons become adept at ensuring that their message is correctly received and "decoded."

We've mentioned the importance of listening. Answering the client's concerns is also important. Ensuring that the client understands you can be accomplished through questioning, reframing and restating what you've said, and by writing things down. Who said salespeople were just great talkers? Salespeople need to be excellent writers, speakers, listeners, and nonverbal communicators!

> Sales/Service Representative, LA. XYZ Industries, world's leading manufacturer of interior furnishings, resilient flooring, installation products, ceiling systems, and comprehensive line of industrial specialty products. Duties include: training retail salespeople, display construction, inventory management assistance, sales to account management, retail promotion and merchandising. A four-year degree or five years related
>
> continued

> continued
>
> experience and excellent communication/organizational skills are required. Computer experience and ability to work independently toward team goals are assets. Some overnight travel expected.
>
> District Merchant. Provides service to our customers by providing the right merchandise. The DM proactively identifies opportunities to improve performance by reviewing/editing assortments and responding to the stores' requests concerning specific merchandise opportunities. The DM is aware of our competition's direction and communicates competitive data to our stores and store support. The DM uses store visits to coach store general managers and sales managers and reinforce training on presentation, business direction, assortment, and financial literacy. Depending on the market this position could travel up to three nights per week. A bachelor's degree, while not required, would be desirable.

Personal Attributes. Whenever we talk to people who are currently in sales or have enjoyed a sales job in their work history, they invariably speak of the "personal" skills that they gained from sales work. What are these personal gains, and why are they so important? We've identified some of the most critical skills below.

- *Poise.* Meeting new people, ease in all social situations, and the ability to chat and make friends with a variety of people all develop an unconscious poise and confidence in sales professionals. It stays with them throughout their career, no matter where that may be.

- *Ability to handle stress.* Sales situations—any situations involving people and negotiations—will involve stress as well. A sales career teaches the kinds of planning and strategies to anticipate and avoid stress and the social skills to define and minimize the tension of stress-producing situations.

- *Time management.* Most sales positions demand exceptional time management. Learning which clients to call on during which times, deciding when to do your paperwork, determining how to best use drive and fly time, and strategizing your week, your month, and your year for best effect all develop excellent time management skills. Many senior executives, when asked how they can be so productive, respond, "I began in sales and learned to use my time effectively."

❑ *Decision making.* Whether you're out on the road alone, in negotiations with a client, competing for a major account against a worthy adversary, or discovering new markets or sales opportunities, there will be a need to make decisions. Management knows you will frequently be called upon to think for yourself and the good of the firm. Your job in sales will continue to demand good decision-making skills, many times on the spot.

Definition of the Career Path for Purchasing Agent

Purchasing agents buy things for companies. But unlike the retail buyers discussed earlier in this chapter, they don't buy items for resale to the final consumer. They buy all the raw materials, products, and services their companies need to maintain operations. They buy forklifts, industrial cleaning services, paper towels, spark plugs, drill bits, pencils, and industrial boilers. For manufacturers, they'll buy maple syrup, raw lumber, industrial diamonds, or granite, whatever the manufacturers need to produce their product. The individual with the job below buys boxing equipment, balers, shrink wrap technology, graphic art designs, laminating equipment, and a host of other associated packaging requirements:

> Purchasing Agent, XYZ Major Clothing Retailer, CA: We are not afraid of change, and we depend on our employees to show us where it's needed. It's that involvement by bright, energetic people that makes our company one of the most recognized and respected names in fashion retailing around the world. Responsibilities include: manage the procurement, distribution, inventory, and financial accounting of point-of-purchase packaging for all divisions; responsible for an annual budget of $25.5 million; give cost-effective options to Marketing on new packaging designs; work on new packaging designs; work with Finance and Operations on annual packaging budget for all divisions. Minimum qualifications: two or three years purchasing experience; strong leadership experience; strong decision-making capabilities; excellent communication skills.

Often working under the direction of a materials manager, the purchasing agent's job is far more complex than simple buying. They establish the sources of supply for their firms. This often means visiting the vendor to ensure its operation is viable and it can do what its representatives say it will do. Because purchasing professionals buy so much product, they often can set prices and must be adept at the kind of calculations involved in adjusting quantities, discounts, and a host of other variables that affect pricing determination. In reading through this section, we hope you'll come to understand what an important job the purchasing agent has in an organization.

Purchasing agents are found not only in manufacturing, but in all kinds of employment settings: for example, schools, hospitals, and government offices. Wherever they are located, their job is essentially the same. They ensure the company has sufficient supplies of the materials needed to continue operating. *Sufficient* is the key word here. If the purchasing agents order too much, they have tied up operating capital that could have been used for other initiatives and may hurt overall profitability. Buying too much also subjects the stock to the risk of damage by deterioration, fire, theft, or simply being outdated by new and better products. Here's an ad for a purchasing agent in the natural foods area:

Purchasing Agent, Nutrition and Consumer Division, XYZ Company, CA. We focus on finding solutions to meet the growing global consumer demands for better food and nutrition. We're seeking a qualified individual who will be responsible for purchasing and production support for the development of policies and procedures in the area of purchasing production materials (reagents, chemicals, raw materials, ingredients, process aids) to include water-treatment chemicals, packaging materials, and transportation for the San Diego, CA, and Okmulgee, OK, plant sites. Responsibilities include purchasing materials at lower overall costs consistent with approved quality, performance, and delivery standards within the guidelines of the annual purchasing plan. We prefer a B.S./B.A. in purchasing/materials management, one to five years experience in transportation and logistics and/or raw material packaging is desired. Excellent communication, organizational, and problem-solving skills are essential to work in a detailed-oriented environment.

Because their role is so crucial, purchasing agents are part of the management team and are recognized for the important contribution they can make to the financial well-being of an organization. Not only do they have to know what to buy, but they have to make important decisions on the quality of the items they buy. Purchasing agents wouldn't be making a contribution by saving money on the purchase price of cheap items—poor-quality items wouldn't last very long and would have to be reordered frequently.

Ordering the right quantity and quality isn't the whole story, either. Purchasing agents make hundreds of decisions. For example, they must compute, not only the cost of the item they are buying, but how much it will cost to handle and transport the item. They must also ensure the vendor they are buying from can meet the promised delivery dates and quantity amounts, which can both be critical. If you can save your firm money by having needed parts and materials arrive *just* when you need them and not before, you can't do that without an enormous dependence on and trust in your vendor. Purchasing agents and vendors have very close relationships as their livelihoods are mutually dependent.

Part of this relationship means the purchasing agent must coordinate his or her firm's production schedules with vendor production schedules. In the summer before this book went to press, the United States experienced an unprecedented strike by the United Parcel Service's delivery drivers. This strike made a powerful impact, not just on everyday citizens who have come to depend upon UPS service, but many much larger organizations discovered they had become *too* dependent on one delivery service. Following resolution of the strike, there were many articles in business and trade publications analyzing the impact of the strike and indicating many purchasing agents had made significant changes in their use of delivery services for the future. Most of the changes involved distributing business between many delivery service vendors, including FedEx and the U.S. Postal Service, in order to weaken the effects of any future strikes on the cost of doing business.

It's the purchasing agent's job to anticipate problems such as that posed by the UPS strike and solve the problems that come with them. To do this, purchasing agents work closely with many other departments in their organization, including receiving, traffic, and supply departments. In small firms, one purchasing manager may do everything. However, in larger firms, a government arms contractor, for example, there may be over one hundred purchasing agents, each specializing in a certain class of material or machine.

Some purchasing agents begin as expediters and work their way up. Expediters handle much of the paperwork and other details involved in making purchases, arranging shipping, and settling claims. Their responsibility is to see that delivery commitments made by the vendor are kept, or if delays do occur, to figure out ways to speed things up. As an entry-level job in purchasing, it involves a lot of paperwork, although the job has expanded as firms seek to reduce the time between orders and delivery. It's a great way to learn the business. As an expediter, you'll have an opportunity to become familiar with most items purchased as well as who purchases them—that's the kind of information you'll need to move up in this field. Some entry-level positions are simply designated "trainees" within a purchasing department. Trainees learn on the job and may attend special classes. Often, this trainee period will include a rotation through other departments of the organization, as well.

WORKING CONDITIONS

Working Conditions for Retail Buyers and Buyer/Merchandising Trainees

Rapid Advancement. Talent is immediately recognizable in the fast-paced and highly responsive world of retailing. Ambitious people usually want positions that demonstrate their talent to advantage and then reward that talent with responsibilities and duties that will further stretch and develop their skill.

Action. Some people love to be busy, the busier the better. They cannot tolerate sitting at a desk all day, chatting around the water fountain, or catching up on business journals. The answer is retailing. Each day has a different outcome as each customer through the door presents a different collection of needs to be satisfied. Demands can be incessant. This is a business for the strong and energetic. If you're not happy, you'll see it as chaotic, frantic, and frustrating!

Contact with People. Sometimes job applicants make the mistake of telling the interviewer "I'm a people person." What does that really mean? In retailing, a "people person" must be comfortable with all kinds of people from all walks of life and, increasingly, from many different parts of the world. You will have to want to understand their needs and enjoy making an effort to fulfill those needs.

Mobility. Retailing careers offer unparalleled mobility. Retail opportunities exist worldwide and in every size and variety of emporium, so if you are anxious to live on the West Coast or in the Plains States, you can do it.

Entrepreneurship. This word has special meaning for retailers because, in a sense, every buyer is in business for himself or herself. Each department or operating unit in today's retail stores has its own printout of profit and loss. You will easily be able to demonstrate your entrepreneurial spirit.

Long Hours. Take a look around. Retailers are open holidays (even some of the most sacrosanct, such as Christmas), evenings, weekends, and late nights. Stores need to be staffed and maintained and managed. You'll be working many times when the rest of the world is out playing! Competition is intense in retail, and management often put in long hours on and off the floor to stay abreast of the competition.

No Glamour. Even when you obtain the coveted position of buyer you'll be shocked to find your office is a cubbyhole tucked behind the dressing rooms on the fifth floor. Store floor space is for merchandise. Employees take what's not usable or left over. Glamour is for the customers.

Working Conditions for Sales Service Representatives

Sales jobs are plentiful, but as this path indicates, they vary widely in quality, professionalism, training provided, use of your math background, opportunities to interact with colleagues, compensation, and growth potential. When you are a new grad out on the market for a sales job, there's a temptation to look at all the sales jobs available, rationalize away any concerns you might have, and take the first one offered you.

There are, however, three aspects of most sales jobs that are so dominant that they serve to define the nature of this employment experience, and you would be well advised to consider your suitability for a sales position against these criterion. Go back to the chapter on self-assessment and review what you learned about your personal traits, values, and skills. Measure what you've learned about yourself against the following three critical aspects of sales positions: the degree of sociability, nature of the client contact, and productivity/competitiveness.

Degree of Sociability. Most people remark on how easily sales professionals talk to just about anybody—the postal carrier, the cashier at a supermarket, the man or woman on the street. It's quite easy to explain. Despite the fact that their job emphasizes connecting with people, most sales professionals work alone and their contact with others is fairly brief and intermittent. They spend quite a bit of time alone with themselves and would tell you that you need to be comfortable with yourself to be good at sales.

Nature of the Client Contact. In most sales jobs, the actual "selling" of a product is not as challenging as connecting with the client. There are basically two ways to visit with a client: 1) an invitation through some sort of pre-screening or presales work that has the client requesting your visit, or 2) the "cold call" where you call upon a client who may not yet be aware of your product or service but whom you believe might be a good prospect for it.

Whether being invited or inviting yourself is more appealing or more challenging to you has much to do with your personality. Your tolerance of risk, your ability to handle new situations, and your ease in making acquaintances will be good barometers of which situation would be best for you over the course of a career.

Productivity/Competitiveness. Sales is often repetitive. It's not a career where you can sit home and rest on your laurels. For many in this profession, a success only motivates them to further achievement. This competitive drive may not be directed at others. It may simply be a competition with yourself. Because sales always involves seeking new markets and new clients for products and services, that competitive spirit is essential.

Working Conditions for Purchasing

Most of your time is spent in an office, although purchasing department employees will often visit plants or attend conferences. Though your workweek will probably be fairly standard in the early stages of your career, this is largely dependent upon your particular sector of employment. There are many industries that, due to intense seasonality of production, demand overtime beyond the standard workweek during periods of intense output. Purchasing managers will find they are called upon to solve problems, handle details, and coordinate many activities during such intense work periods.

TRAINING AND QUALIFICATIONS

Training and Qualifications for Retail Buyers and Buyer/Merchandising Trainees

The environment of retailing is less one of glamour, travel, and clothes than one of computer printouts and statements of profit and loss. Because computerized information can tell the retailer so much about what is required in terms of inventory, labor, and so on, students seriously considering retail careers need to consider mastering computer technology, including spreadsheet software and statistical packages, and have some exposure to database management. As our economy becomes increasingly technologically oriented, the candidate who can apply high-tech, information-based skills to a successful career in retailing has many advantages. In addition to these technical skills, there is a need for analytical skills. A course in marketing, general management, and/or economics might give you an even broader picture of the changing and very dynamic scope of retailing in our economy. The appearance of increasingly large merchandisers, whether they are department stores, warehouse showrooms, or grocery retailers, places demands on those candidates to understand the mechanics of big business.

Internships or, if your school has one, a co-op program, are ideal ways to help you ascertain your interest and suitability for the retail profession. Additionally, they help you to add valuable entries on your resume that will attract employers following graduation. Part-time employment in any area of the retail sector will give you immense credibility as a manager who can truthfully say to rank and file workers, "I've done that."

Training and Qualifications for Sales Service Representatives

Many are called, but few last. Success in sales positions often can't be determined well during the interview process. It may take several months of on-the-job work for an individual to assess whether he or she is right for sales. Some of the best sales organizations hope to improve the odds by having you interview with a large number of people to get a variety of impressions about you and your potential. Following selection, the very best sales firms have you undergo a lengthy (up to six weeks) training period which will involve role-playing, testing, and acquisition of needed product knowledge. These training programs are usually very professional, and you'll learn lessons that will stay with you throughout your entire working career. Some firms train you full time, others incorporate the training into part of the workday, and yet another option is to have you begin work and then have you return to train. The philosophy of this last option is that the worker who has experienced the job will understand the value of the training more easily.

Training and Qualifications for Purchasing Agents

Professional Qualifications. Entry into the field of purchasing is highly competitive, and college degrees are a must. In general, entry-level candidates with degrees in quantitative areas such as mathematics, computer science, and business degrees that focus on operations management are highly desirable qualifications.

A number of certification programs are available for purchasing professionals. In private industry, the hallmark of experience and professional competence is the Certified Purchasing Manager (CPM) that is awarded by the National Association of Purchasing Management, based on criterion involving years of experience and successful completion of a series of examinations. There is also a Certified Purchasing Professional (CPP) and a Certified Purchasing Executive (CPE) designation available through the professional development efforts of the American Purchasing Society. In governmental and public employment, there is the Certified Public Purchasing Officer (CPPO) that is awarded by the National Institute of Governmental Purchasing after meeting similar testing and experience requirements. It goes without saying that achieving this notable designation is enhancing to your career and your bank account.

These designations of excellence are a sign of how professionally the purchasing field handles itself. It should come as no surprise to you that continuing education is the norm and if you are located in a high-tech field, then continuing professional development will be imperative. Be certain to ask during your interview process what provisions are made for your training and continued professional growth by your employer. You'll be glad you did.

Personal Qualifications.

❑ High ethical standards

❑ Good analytical skills

❑ Strong communicator with good listening skills

If you've given this section on Purchasing Agents a close reading, it should come as no surprise to you when we suggest that high ethical standards are critical for the people who hold these influential positions in a firm. Imagine the responsibility that comes with such buying power and the ability to award contracts that represent huge sums of money. Purchasing agents are under incredible pressure from agents, salespeople, representatives, and vendor executives. There may be offers of kickbacks, special favors, and more frequently, just simple requests for you to overlook something. In keeping with the honesty with which we have tried to present the options available to math majors in this book, we want to issue a stern warning that if you decide to enter this field, you must make your ethical standards clear and out in the open to everyone, including your colleagues and representatives of vendor firms. The field is full of true stories of talented people who've lost their jobs because they thought they could bend the rules. Don't be one of them.

An analytical view is also a sought-after skill. Because purchasing professionals spend much time analyzing technical data in suppliers' proposals, making complicated buying decisions that cost large sums of money, they must be comfortable with complex data and have the ability to see that data from a number of perspectives. In many cases, analysis comes down to the ability to creatively employ a variety of perspectives on a problem in the anticipation that one of these viewpoints will suggest a solution.

Ethics and analytical skills are not the only important personal qualifications. Purchasing professionals are valued for their ability to communicate clearly and effectively. This is an area where "No" means "No" and where needs must be clearly articulated. Purchasing agents work closely with their vendors and develop strong business relationships. Consequently, language is critical and there can be no suggestion of promises when promises are not intended. So your ability to communicate well will be an important hiring criterion. You may want to polish your interview skills and refer to the opening chapters of this book.

Personal strength goes hand in hand with excellent communications and high ethics. Employers look for job candidates who know who they are, what they want, and how they best function effectively. A positive self-image and a preference for variety, challenge, and professional growth will be some of the characteristics being looked for in any interview situation for purchasing jobs.

EARNINGS

Earnings for Retail Buyers and Buyer/Merchandising Trainees

In 1997, buyers averaged $33,200 per year. To amplify that figure, the middle 50 percent of earners in this category earned between a low of $23,300 and a high of $45,900. The lowest 10 percent of earners were making less than $18,400 while those at the opposite end of the spectrum were earning more than $63,000.

If you are in a trainee role, your salary is apt to be somewhat less than a designated assistant buyer or assistant merchandise manager. Depending upon the employer's size (in terms of sales volume) and number of employees, you could expect a salary range of $21,000 to $24,000. Promotions out of the trainee role will bring a marked change in your pay. It's also important to note that benefits in these positions tend to be very competitive, and a benefits package can add up to one-third of your salary in value. You may not realize the importance of your benefit package until you visit an emergency room or have major dental work done, but if that should happen, you'll begin to discover the "hidden income" of your benefit package.

Earnings for Sales Representatives

Sales representatives' earnings offer the entry-level graduate the highest possible earnings available with a college degree, with a few exceptions (of even better salaries!) for some technical majors. High earnings are attractive to many students who graduate with some debt burden and a strong motivation to begin to live on their own and make a life for themselves.

A recent survey by the Dartnell Corporation reports that today's salesperson earns about $36,000 in an entry-level job. Intermediate level sales professionals average about $46,000, and senior sales positions can easily exceed $63,000. An additional 30 percent of those incomes is given out in benefits.

Positions in selling pay either a salary, a commission, or a combination of the two. As an entry-level salesperson, you will probably be more attracted to a salaried selling position. It seems less risky and seemingly puts less responsibility on you to produce than a commission system does. Straight salary plans work best for employers when it is difficult for management to determine which person on the staff actually made the sale or when the product involved has a broad, cyclical sales pattern, which would leave the sales staff with virtually no income during the slow periods if commissions were involved.

Sales professionals who have gained skills and confidence in their abilities are often more attracted to commission plans. Commission plans offer them unlimited income if they are successful. Straight commission gives the greatest incentive to salespeople while maintaining a predictable sales cost in relation to sales volume. Two factors working against straight commissions are 1) high turnover and burnout of sales staff and 2) a sales process tainted by the need of sales personnel to "move" product to pad the salesperson's paycheck regardless of a customer's true need for the product or service.

Consider compensation plans carefully, regardless of your financial needs. It can be very disheartening to leave a position because of a disagreement over the pay arrangements when a little forethought might have anticipated problems.

Combination plans exist with fixed salaries and incentive features added on. This builds continuity in the sales force, yet allows superior sales staff to shine, and it encourages everyone to develop more business.

The bouquet of roses of each pay scheme has its own thorns. A straight salary job cannot reward superior achievement, and that may grow to be a frustration if you are exceptionally successful in your position. If you expect to be the best you can be, shouldn't your paycheck reflect that? With a straight salary job, you and the poorest performer take home the same paycheck!

Commission rewards ability and performance, and that can be attractive to the confident sales pro. However, be sure you understand what the minimum performance levels are, how much you need to do to earn your commission, and how feasible those goals may be. What is the waiting period, following a successful sale, before you receive your compensation? Occasionally, when commission salespeople are "too" successful, an organization will redivide their territory and add sales staff. The philosophy behind that move is that if one individual can do so well, there may be even more opportunity if additional sales staff are employed. However, for the successful salesperson, this only means less territory and much harder work to realize the same income as before.

Commission is not as risky as most graduates think. If (and this "if" is important) the organization that hires you is spending money and time on your training, its managers do not want to see you fail and are taking steps to ensure you succeed. These compensation plans are based on experience born of what past salespeople have done and what incentives they needed to do it. There is no success if salespeople drop out because they can't make any money. The organization would suffer and, ultimately, fail.

Earnings for Purchasing Agents

This is a well-paid profession with median annual earnings averaging about $33,200 in 1996 as reported in the last edition of the *Occupational Outlook Handbook*. The average annual salary for purchasing agents and contract specialists in the federal government were $28,700 and $51,110 respectively. Because of the nature of the firms they work in (size, number of employees, and income production), these positions would, in almost every case, receive excellent benefits packages, including medical, dental, life, and health insurance, vacation and sick leave. It is not uncommon in the profession to also receive case bonuses based on firm performance.

CAREER OUTLOOK

Retail Buyers and Buyer/Merchandising Trainees

This employment group is expected to continue to grow as many job openings are created each year. At least for projections through the year 2006, additional openings will grow faster than all occupations because the growth in population overall creates retail demands. Additionally, there is significant turnover in these fields as people transfer to other occupations or use their skills to relocate.

The variety and scope of retailing today is obvious to us all. Disposable income is increasing among the middle and upper middle classes, and people are constantly seeking retail outlets that offer the mix of goods they want. As the largest segment of our population, the "baby boomers," reach their peak earning years, demographics suggest an increasing demand for retailing services and the management staff to direct those initiatives.

Career Outlook for Sales Service Representatives

The outlook for sales service representatives is excellent. This group will grow much faster than the average for all occupations, at least through the year 2006, in response to the growth of the businesses employing them. Note, however, that within this overall strong growth picture, much depends on the particular industry and its individual trends. For example, growth in office and factory automation will lead to increased jobs for technology and data processing sales representatives.

As with all the jobs in this path, turnover is high, and as individuals leave sales for other occupations, new openings occur. You'll find this turnover highest among those firms that offer the least training and whose products are the least sophisticated. There has not been much invested in the employee, nor has the employee invested much in the employer. As a result, leave-taking is easier.

People who hire for sales positions know best how difficult it is to predict who will do well in this profession. Hiring professionals know all this, as well. But they also know the demands of the marketplace and the sophistication and educational background of people you'll be meeting. They know the increasing demands of sales automation require an ability to master the computer and to manage one's own time and workflow. They have found a college degree to be the best training ground and math to be an excellent preparation for many of the demands of today's professional sales consultant.

Though you may have some natural ability for sales, you will need further training in sales skills. In addition, you will want to be provided with a structured opportunity to learn about the products and services you'll be selling. The best sales positions offer the greatest amounts of formal training. However, the training is not always provided before you begin selling. Some firms have their new sales recruits attend formal sales schools, complete with dormitories, exams, and classroom presentations before you meet the public. Other organizations have found training to be more worthwhile following a brief period of actual field sales, perhaps three to six months. The philosophy behind this decision is that some exposure to the demanding role of the sales professional will help you to appreciate the training and be more aggressive in your studies. Both philosophies have merit.

Be wary of those positions that ask you to fund yourself until you are paid, provide your own transportation, or offer no formal training. This kind of employment structure places no responsibility on the hiring organization. Consequently, rapid turnover (common in these jobs) is not very damaging since the organization has spent little money on each salesperson. A firm that invests in your training has invested in you and wants you to succeed.

Career Outlook for Purchasing Agents

The projected slower-than-average growth for jobs in purchasing as predicted in the *Occupational Outlook Handbook* is largely a result of the computer. Though economic activity is very high as this book goes to press, the demand for workers does not need to keep pace with this economic activity because the computer has significantly reduced the paperwork intensity of purchasing jobs, especially at the lower levels of the hiring hierarchy. As purchasers write longer-term contracts with larger organizations that can supply more products and services from one location, it dramatically reduces the time normally spent on negotiations and the personnel traditionally involved with that.

On the public purchasing front, new laws affect purchasing employees. In 1994, the federal government mandated electronic purchasing for all items under a specified dollar amount (the Federal Acquisition Streamlining Act) and that certainly has restricted demand for new hires.

This kind of minimum-paperwork buying occurs in more than just the government sector. Here on our college campus, we have purchasing agents whose functions correspond very closely with the job specifications we've listed in this chapter. But even here, on a college campus, the purchasing agent's role is changing. Up until just recently, everything we purchased was processed through our purchasing office. Now, with the issuance of purchasing credit cards (no different than the ones you might carry in your own wallet), we are able to make purchases while at conferences, conventions, shopping on our own, or over the Internet. Innovations such as this kind of "direct buying" have certainly affected the number of purchasing agents needed in the marketplace.

STRATEGY FOR FINDING THE JOBS

Strategies for Retail Buyers and Buyer/Merchandising Trainees

Retailing holds many exciting possibilities for the mathematics graduate. The jobs are creative, demanding, and well worth your investment in your math education. The future of retailing is full of surprises but is certain to include increased quantification, increased technology, and innovative new ways to both reach and satisfy the consumer market.

The earnings statistics cited demonstrate the possibility for strong earning potential if you have what it takes to grow with this profession. Additionally, the projections of growth for the retail sector should lead you to the conviction that if you really want to enter retailing as a career and have the personal characteristics the industry is seeking, there is a job waiting for you. These personal characteristics are the ability to formulate and solve practical problems in retail business. Remember as a mathematician in the retail environment you have a wonderful advantage in your ability to analyze relationships among variables, solve complex problems, develop models, and process large amounts of data.

Retailing is, however, an incredibly diverse field. Merchandise lines run the gamut from lingerie to lawnmowers, and there are big names in each field (Victoria's Secret/John Deere). Geographically, retailing is literally all over the map, and you can find retail employment throughout the United States and the world. So, in addition to product lines (merchandise) and location options, there is equally as much choice about job duties: buyer, merchandise manager, store or department manager, site development, advertising, finance . . . the list goes on and on.

With the following outline you can develop a successful strategy for finding the right job *for you* in the retail sector. If you 1) have enough time to do a thorough job search, 2) have access to all the options listed below, and 3) want to be sure you've covered all possibilities, then go through this plan step by step. Not only will you succeed in finding the jobs, but the process of implementing this search will also make you a better and more informed interview candidate and increase your chances of being selected because you will truly understand the world of retail. However, if time or your options are limited, then pick and choose from this list for what is most doable for you.

1. Shop Locally! If you're a mathematics major, your own school is apt to have plenty of ways for you to get your career search in high gear. Use them.

Marketing/Retail Clubs. Campus clubs that bring students together for common interests are wonderful sources of information about a possible career in retailing. Many schools offer a campus branch of the American Marketing Association, and that group would be delighted by a math major's interest in their field. Try to meet each guest speaker that comes to campus to speak to the club on business issues. Let them know of your career plans as a math major interested in retail and ask their advice. Serve on club speaker committees and special career-related projects. If your club has an opportunity to attend a national convention, try to be part of your school team and use that opportunity to meet guests, gather information, and network.

Cooperative Education. Your college may provide an opportunity for you to elect a work/study plan called co-op. If you can manage it (it may add anywhere from a semester to a full year to your degree), cooperative education is a proven way to access a career, learn the ropes, meet influential people in your degree path, and be exposed to the dimensions of your chosen field while you earn some money for tuition.

Internships. The single most effective way to improve your ability to move from graduation to a job is through an internship. Internships are generally nonpaid or low-paid training positions in your chosen field that give you broad exposure to a variety of tasks and management role models. They can last from a few weeks to a semester and sometimes longer. Internships can often be used for college credit toward your degree. Many successful interns have been offered positions at their internship sponsoring organization upon graduation. Many others credit their job success to their internships. *Internships 1998*, a Peterson's publication, lists some superb retail internship opportunities.

Alumni Career Connections. Either the career office or alumni office on your campus can put you in touch with former graduates of your college who are now working in the retail job market. These alumni connections can be very helpful, offering informational interviews, background on the firms that employ them, and general insights into the retail job market. Depending upon the sophistication of your school's alumni database, they may be able to actually isolate who's working as a buyer, a merchandiser, or store manager, including other former math majors. Remember, when contacting these individuals for career guidance, that you are representing your college *and* every other student who may someday want to use this valuable referral service. Be prepared with a list of questions for your alumni contact and use his or her time wisely. You'll make a good friend and have increased insight into your chosen career field. Many alumni will invite you (distances permitting) for a visit to their place of business and may offer to assist with your resume or job search strategy.

Campus Job Postings. The intranet computer listings (or actual three-ring binders) that contain some of the hundreds of job advertisements that come through the mail to your career office on campus can inform you of many excellent retail entry-level jobs. These may be duplications of the advertising copy that was placed into a newspaper classified want ad section, or they may be a special recruitment mailing to a local college for qualified applicants. These job postings are easy to scroll through and, because they change frequently (new ones arrive weekly), should make this kind of "catalog shopping" a weekly activity! Many colleges provide this service from off-site locations, utilizing a password or student identification number.

Internet Job Searching. Many of the professional associations listed at the end of each chapter provide job listings via the website. In addition to the campus career office website with its own job bank mentioned above, there may be resume databases for students that offer links to websites such as Jobtrak (*http://www.jobtrak.com*), a job database targeted to college students and alumni. These are job banks which allow you to search through a database of openings, resume databases where you can post your resume on-line, career information services which offer advice on resume writing and job search techniques, and virtual career centers, which offer you two or three of the services that were just mentioned. Check with your career center. They may have some tried and true sites that they have found that can speed up your search. Other listings may be found through websites such as:

The Riley Guide, developed by Internet job-search and recruiting consultant Margaret Riley, *www.dbm.com/jobguide*

Catapult, provided by the National Association of Colleges and Employers, *www.jobweb.org/catapultcatpult.htm*

USA Jobs is a website operated by the Office of Personnel Management, *http://usajobs.opm.gov*

FedWorld, a database of 1,500 open federal job vacancies, *http://www.fedworld.gov/* or *ftp://ftp.fedworld.gov/pub/jobs/jobs.htm*

In addition, *Hook Up, Get Hired!: The Internet Job Search Revolution* and *Electronic Job Search Revolution* by Joyce Lain Kennedy are just two publications that give the reader ways to search for jobs and reach potential employers through the Internet. Another publication, the *Guide to Internet Job Searching* by Osserman, Riley, and Roehm and published by VGM Career Horizons, provides a good explanation of how to connect to the Internet and instructions for posting a resume electronically, as well as extensive listings of Internet sites with job ads and resume databases. It also has a directory of bulletin board services that offer job listings. These sites on the Internet can be searched by occupational title, such as buyer, merchandise manager, purchasing agent, or sales representative. These sites can be searched geographically as well. *The Government Job Finder* lists a publication, *Purchasing Notes*, published by the National Institute of Governmental Purchasing, that posts job vacancy listings to its members at *http://www.nigp.org*. The professional associations at the end of this chapter provide additional web-sites for your job search strategy.

On-Campus Recruiting. The employers from the retail sector who visit your campus are giving you a strong indication of their interest in your school's students. Sign up for every recruitment interview with a retailer that you possibly can. On-campus interviewing can and does lead to actual job offers. It's excellent interview practice, as well. Most importantly, you will begin to develop a sense of what each employer is offering and start to make dis-tinctions about what you feel is the best "fit" for you in a retail career offer-ing. Unlike the job fairs, these are private interviews, one-on-one with a senior representative from the retail organization. Even better, it's held on campus in familiar surroundings which should prove helpful to you in con-trolling those interview jitters. Your campus career office probably maintains files on all the recruiting firms to allow you to be thoroughly prepared for your interview.

2. Shop Around!

Job Fairs. Job fairs are valuable job search tools for the student seeking a retail career opening. First, they are very efficient. How else would you be able to meet and talk with so many possible job contacts *in one day?* Second, retailers use them! Rosters of employers at past job fairs indicate retailers are traditionally very well represented. Retailers enjoy job fairs because it allows them to meet and see a number of highly qualified majors. Third, the job fair process of walking up to an employment representative, greeting him or her and giving a one-minute "infomercial" about who you are and what you might have to offer his or her organization is a perfect example of the spe-cific kind of people skills retailers seek out.

If a recruiter at a job fair is interested in you, he or she may ask you to submit a formal application or you may be invited to one of the employer's "open houses" or an actual interview. The recruiter may extend this invita-tion at the job fair or by telephone or letter at a later date. Strong student job candidates who take full advantage of job fair opportunities are consis-tently amazed at both the number of responses and how much later after the fair some of them arrive.

"Careers '99," the nation's number-one college recruitment conference, always offers a premier gathering of some of the country's top retailers at its annual job fairs for college seniors each spring in New York, Atlanta, Wash-ington, D.C., and Chicago. Your career office at college will have applica-tion forms for this prescreened job fair as well as a folder of forthcoming job fairs in your area that will be featuring jobs in retail. Some of these fairs are free, some have a modest fee. Take advantage of all of them for they vastly improve the efficiency of your job search.

3. Shop By Mail!

The Classic Cover Letter/Resume Campaign. Get to your nearest college library and dig out some of the excellent reference books listed in the "Additional Resources" section at the end of this book. Books like *The Corporate Address Book* and *The 100 Best Companies to Work for in America* or *The Encyclopedia of Business Information Sources* might be a good beginning, too. Start to list all of the retailers you might enjoy working for and send them your resume with an interesting, informative cover letter as suggested in Chapter 2 of this book. Be ready to follow up your letter with a phone call and see if you can arrange an interview. Don't be concerned if the retailer's headquarters is far away from your campus. They may have an executive attending a conference in a nearby city who could interview you or a senior buyer at a trade show might have time to meet and talk with you and report back to the home office on the impression you made.

4. No Obligation to Buy!

The Option of "Temping." A wonderful book, *Temp by Choice*, makes a strong case for the possible benefits of "temping." The benefits to the employer are well known; no benefits, no commitment, and the ability to expand or shrink the workforce according to demand without severance costs or legal problems.

For you, the advantages are a chance to look inside the kind of organization you might eventually call home. You'll be paid for your work, of course, but more importantly, you'll meet people, network, add a relevant job to your resume, and perhaps be able to access the organization's internal job posting system. A recent survey has indicated more college graduates were hired through temping than through on-campus recruiting.

Temping has changed. Once a source of clerical and light industrial workers, now temping provides any level of professional or managerial expertise needed.

Some Special Interview Tips for Talking with Retailers. Eventually you are going to be called upon to sit down and interview for your position. Chapters 5 and 6 of this book contain all the information you need in order to prepare a solid interview. Polish and performance will come with experience.

However, there are three special considerations you'll want to be aware of in talking to professionals in the world of retail:

1. Be prepared to talk trends! Each issue of *Fortune* magazine has a column entitled "Selling" devoted to tracking current trends in population, changing lifestyles, and buying patterns that form the seeds of any present and emerging strategies and technologies for selling in the retail sector. Here's a job ad for a control buyer for a major off-price women's dress store that mentions "trends" twice in this simple job description. It's all the clue you need to know that a discussion of women's fashion trends is going to surface in your interview.

> Control Buyer: Based on merchandise selected, as well as historic and current fashion trends, you will plan and buy a category for our stores. This will include monitoring merchandise levels and rebuying based on customer demands and trends. This challenging and visible position will also track and expedite vendor deliveries.

2. Understand consumer behavior. This one is apt to be a challenge for the math major, because college math curriculums seldom have much "ease" to take additional course work, especially outside of the major or minor requirements. So, while having a course in consumer behavior is certainly desirable, it may simply not have been possible. Just as important are courses in the liberal arts, such as psychology, sociology, anthropology, and philosophy. They help you as a potential retail employee to understand better, and consequently, interact more effectively with the consumer. If course work is not able to be documented, be ready to talk about your personal reading in this area through books, magazine articles, and business newspapers. This advertisement for a very upscale British retailer of clothing and small home furnishings is obviously concerned with their employees' ability to relate to and communicate effectively with their clientele:

> Shop Manager: In the retail industry, we are known for quality, superior English fashions, and home furnishings. We seek an enthusiastic, aggressive shop manager to join us. All candidates must have excellent customer service standards and be creative and poised problem solvers.

3. Are you ready to analyze? Good retailers have a strong grasp of mathematics, accounting, and business organization. Here's a job ad that centers around analysis but requires superb "people" skills as well. If you're both a math major and have strong interpersonal skills, you can see that you would be a candidate for this position:

Merchandise Analyst: You will be responsible for maximizing customer satisfaction and company profits by providing and replenishing each store with the proper quantity mix and presentation of merchandise. By reviewing store performance and analyzing store history, trends, and planned promotional activities, you will develop and adjust store ranks by class, category, and style. Maintaining close contact with merchants, stores, and logistics staff are also key responsibilities. Candidates should have strong analytical skills.

Strategies for Sales Service Representatives

Your Job Search Approach May Be Your Ticket to a Job! There's something interesting about the hiring of sales personnel that's different from the hiring of other kinds of professionals. With retail buyers, merchandisers, sales service representatives, analysts, purchasing agents, or administrative support, the employer looks for professionalism in the resume and cover letter, but that is not the focus. They will be more interested in finding out what the job candidate knows, what his or her experience has been, and whether he or she seems adequately prepared for the job under consideration.

In the sales personnel market, every aspect of the coming together of the candidate and potential employer provides a clue to the candidate's potential in a sales job. What better exercise in persuasiveness is there than the job search? Can you think of any other activity that puts as much emphasis on the kind and quality of one's communication as the job search and the interview itself? A job search is by and large a sales exercise, and if you wish to become a sales professional, an employer has every right to expect to see the beginnings of brilliance in how you go about seeking your job!

The Significance of the Resume and Cover Letter. All sales jobs involve some degree of written communication. In fact, it's probably a fair corollary that the more important or senior the sales position, the more it will involve written proposals, presentations, and projects. Early signs of a sales person's professionalism might be the resume and cover letter. Do they:

❑ Get to the point?

❑ Interest and excite the reader?

❑ Look attractive and distinctive?

❑ Display the hallmarks of attention to detail and accuracy?

It is no exaggeration to say that many resume/cover letter readers have every right to expect that if you cannot put together a perfect sales package for yourself, you won't be able to do it for them, either.

When executives have only a day to devote to interviewing (and when using your math skills to calculate the cost of that day lost from regular business, you realize how expensive job search activities can be for a firm), and they must reduce a pile of two hundred resumes and cover letters to eight to ten candidates, the first ones to go in the wastebasket are those that have typographical errors, the ones that look confusing or "tricky" with too many typefaces or overly fancy graphics. Even resumes where two lines of text have run too close together in a printer error are thrown out! "Gee, the candidate must not have proofed his or her work. Poor attention to detail. I wouldn't want something like that going out under our letterhead." Thus, another resume ends up discarded.

The Unique Importance of the Interview for Sales. For a sales position, the key to being hired is the interview. It is the most obvious early demonstration of your oral communication skills, your facility at presenting yourself, and your ability to make a winning case for your employment. Even acknowledging your newness at interviewing and the anxiety of most new college grads during interviews, most recruiters will still want and expect to see some nascent indications that you have what it takes. If you're shy and retiring or fail to demonstrate your skills, you'll disappoint your interviewer. If you are overly confident, a braggart, or loud and pushy, you'll turn the interviewer off.

Try to balance the interview as best you can. Give as much information as you receive, and answer questions as fully as you can. If the interviewer ends up doing all the talking, he or she will learn nothing about you. If you do all the talking, you miss a great opportunity to learn more about the organization.

Sales is about communication, but sometimes that communication is not just about the product or service you are selling. Interviewers will be interested in what you're reading, your opinion on current events, and your views on national legislative issues. Salespeople need to be well-read and have high levels of general information, for they will need to draw on that each day as they communicate with a diverse range of customers.

Chapter 5 of this book contains information on how to prepare for an interview. For the sales job candidate, there are additional considerations for both the telephone and person-to-person interview.

The Telephone Interview for Sales. When sales work involves the telephone or when a firm needs to screen a large number of applicants, the telephone interview as a first-stage interview technique is helpful and a low-cost option for employers. Some important tips for sales candidates in the phone interview include:

❑ Arrange to take the telephone call where you will not be disturbed and where background noise will be at a minimum. You don't want to miss any information, nor do you want the interviewer to be distracted by background noise.

❑ Have a large writing surface near the phone and try to note as much of the information being given as possible. It'll come in handy later. Don't be shy about asking to have important details repeated or to ensure you have a proper name correctly.

❑ Speak very clearly and distinctly into the mouthpiece. Don't let your responses go on and on. When you've finished a response, it should be clear to the listener.

❑ Most of all, try as best you can to let your voice express its natural warmth. Be yourself and be as natural and as relaxed as a job interview situation allows. Using your facial muscles to smile when thinking about a question or expressing pleasure is a technique many successful phone speakers employ to help convey emotions through the voice.

The Personal Interview for Sales. The key word here is "appearance." Your first impression is largely determined by how you look. Interviewers know the impression you make in an interview is basically the impression you'll be making on the organization's clients and potential customers. Many, many sales representatives are selected in large part for their personal appearance. It's called "referent power," and it is the ability of clients or customers to relate to the salesperson as someone of their standing, background, or education.

❑ *Make the most of what you've got!* We all can't look like models, but we can certainly arrive at the interview making the most of what we do have. When buying suits for the interview process, seek help to ensure clothes fit in a becoming way and that patterns and colors are appropriate for you and your body type. For women who choose to wear makeup, consult with makeup professionals in a major department store for appropriate colors and techniques for business wear. For both men and women, hairstyles in sales positions are often dramatically different from the styles you have been accustomed to in college. Check out business magazines or professional sales journals for cues as to how practicing professionals wear their hair. Then select a style that looks right for you!

❑ *Don't make a fashion statement.* Err on the side of conservatism in the early stages of the interview process. In sales, you want the customer's reactions to be focused on your product, not on your personal appearance. Think of dressing professionally, not in a distracting manner.

❑ *Now, forget how you look and focus on connecting!* If you've taken sufficient care with your appearance, you can focus on what are, ultimately, the important issues. The interview is a time to display your intelligence, perceptiveness, verbal dexterity, listening skills, and your warmth and sense of humor—whatever personal qualities make you the unique individual you are.

Strategies for Purchasing Agents

Much of the general job search information outlined for both the retail and merchandising positions and sales service representatives holds true for the purchasing agent job search. There are some qualitative differences, in the search, however. While a math degree is valued, but not essential for jobs in retail and sales, it is a far more important resume item for a purchasing job. Additionally, since there are at any one time fewer purchasing jobs than retail or sales positions (which number among the most populated jobs), your candidacy is going to be closely scrutinized because it will be more competitive.

As a math major, you will probably have had little, if any exposure to purchasing careers during college. That's okay. Most purchasing professionals learned their trade on the job. And while purchasing agents' jobs can be remarkably similar, with allowances for both the size of the firm and nature of the work that employs them, you may want to begin your search by focusing on one or two or three of these possible employment sectors. For example, you may decide that you want to work in a setting such as a hospital or educational facility or corporate hotel firm where in all these cases your buying would be of finished goods. Concentrating in these three sectors will help you to focus your interview skills, add specific vocabulary and concerns that recur in your interviews, and generally allow you to better target your search. But you could just as easily focus on the aircraft industry, defense contractors, or the automobile subcontractor sector. Most firms will have a preference for a bachelor's degree candidate with an emphasis in quantitative or business skills.

POSSIBLE EMPLOYERS

Possible Employers for Retail

Any retailer would be pleased to add to the company's employment ranks a freshly minted math graduate interested in a career in merchandising. That doesn't mean, however, you should necessarily be interested in that particular company! This book has made a strong case for using your employment to add portable skills to your resume—skills that are not industry specific but that you can move with you from job to job. One of the best ways to ensure you are adding those skills is by selecting those employment sites with high-quality management, a respect for your math degree, and possible training options.

Possible Employers for Sales Service Representatives

Sales Jobs Are Everywhere: How Do You Find the One for You? It's true! Sales jobs (of every type and description) seem to be everywhere. In fact, many other kinds of job seekers complain that sales jobs are all they ever see. Each sales job describes itself differently and each job description seems to focus on a different aspect of the position. For some, it's customer contact, for others it's product knowledge, and yet others emphasize productivity or profit margin. How do you judge what's best for you?

Make a list of what you want in a sales position. We all want different things, so list your requirements. Perhaps financial security is number one on your list. Then, you need to be on the lookout for those sales jobs that offer a salary and avoid commission status. Perhaps you want to further your education and want additional training. Seek out those sales positions advertising training programs or emphasizing high-quality professional development for the sales force. Other priorities might be travel, activity level, productivity, income production, calling on established clients, or making cold calls on prospective clients. Whatever it is, you need to draw up your own working list of elements you're seeking in a sales position so you can adequately judge and compare the market offerings.

Begin with the best and establish your own criteria. Start with a reference work such as *The 100 Best Companies to Sell For* and learn the particulars of the sales job from the crème de la crème of sales organizations. This book will give you valuable insight into

- Entry-level salaries for sales

- Senior-level salaries for sales

- Products and services offered by each company

- Benefits (including bonuses, perks, and so on)

- Corporate culture and style

- Training—which firms stress formal training programs and which emphasize on-the-job experience

- An in-depth discussion of the firm and the role of sales in the organization

- Criteria used in selecting sales candidates

Now that you have drawn up a list of your criteria and you have read about and understand the criteria of the best in the business, you want to begin the process of applying for the jobs that seem to meet your needs both as a mathematics major and a new entry into the job market.

Sales jobs are widely advertised and recruited because hiring firms often have to talk with and screen a number of candidates before they find one that fits their needs. You will have to do the same in your search. For that reason, the job search for sales is a busy one with lots of resume mailing, telephone interviewing, job lead follow-up and cold calling before you "connect" with that perfect job. Some of the best places to look are

- *Your career office.* Your college career office will not only contain numerous subscriptions to job posting newsletters offering entry-level sales jobs, but is also on the mailing list of many employers who look on college campuses to fill sales jobs, especially in the spring. Your career office can direct you to resources that you might otherwise never discover. For example, *Sports Market Place 1999* contains thousands of sales positions in sporting equipment and sports-related products and services. Visible Ink's *Marketing and Sales Career Directory* is another rich source of employers seeking sales candidates.

- *Large metropolitan newspapers.* An excellent source for sales jobs, especially the Sunday edition. Check them out every week.

❑ *Job Fairs.* Job fairs come in all varieties, specializing in many kinds of jobs. The sales job fair is one of the most common types. These provide a good way to distribute your resume, meet lots of employers, practice your stand-up interviewing skills, and check out the competition.

Alumni Networks. Informal or formal networks amongst your college alumni are a fine way to tap into the hidden job market. You'll need to be just as on-your-toes as you are in the job search, but alumni contacts can give you the inside track to unadvertised job openings.

Possible Employers for Purchasing Agents

Resources. Review the listings in the newspapers, watch for listings in your career office, make contact with the associations we list at the close of this chapter and try, through your career or alumni office, to meet and interview graduates of your college who are working in purchasing. At job fairs, purchasing jobs won't generally be what's being recruited, but ask the recruiters to put you in contact with purchasing agents at their firms. Working purchasing professionals will be a great source for information about the availability of purchasing trade shows, conferences, and meetings where there may be both networking and/or a job postings board.

Check the Internet for positions such as the government listings with the National Institute of Governmental Purchasing Inc. (*http://www.nigp.org*) or the National Association of Purchasing Management (*http://www.napm.org*) and other professional associations listed at the end of this chapter for purchasing agents. Some of these professional associations may require membership to have access to the job postings. These professional associations offer links from their homepages to other possibilities and career information for purchasing agents.

About 50 percent of the purchasing agents work in manufacturing industries. Interestingly, half of all purchasing agents report working in departments of five or less people. The following resources would be helpful to you in your job search strategy: *Great Jobs for Business Majors, The Corporate Address Book, The 100 Best Companies to Work for in America,* and *The Encyclopedia of Business Information Sources.* Other resources in your campus careers library that have job opportunities listed under the occupational area of purchasing include *Government Job Finder, Peterson's 1998 Job Opportunities for Business, Professional's Job Finder, The Job Hunter: The National Bi-Weekly Publication for Job Seekers.*

POSSIBLE JOB TITLES

Retail Buyers and Buyer/Merchandising Trainees

Assistant buyer   Merchandise manager

Buyer   Sales associate

Buyer trainee   Store manager

Department manager

Sales Service Representatives

The sales industry works very hard to improve the professional standing of its salespeople and move them out from under any stigmatizing labels or job titles that might inhibit their ability to do their job. So, you'll see several titles listed below that don't even contain the word "sales." Get used to that in seeking out sales positions. It may be your first signal that the hiring organization has paid particular attention to the role of its sales force.

Account executive   Product line manager

Account representative   Product manager

Area director   Regional manager

Area manager   Sales director

District manager   Sales manager

Major account representative   Sales person

Market representative   Sales representative

National sales manager   Sales specialist

Outside sales representative   Service representative

Purchasing Agents

Possible job titles for those beginning in the field as a purchasing agent include

Assistant buyer   Purchasing clerk

Expediter   Trainee

Junior buyer

Other possible job titles in government include

Agent	Manager of materials acquisitions
Buyer	Manager of purchasing
Commodity purchasing manager	Materials analyst
Contract specialist	Procurement team leader
Contract supply manager	Purchasing director
Director of contracts, pricing, and procurement	Purchasing engineer
Director of corporate materials	Strategic planner
Director of materials management	Traffic manager
Inventory manager	

RELATED OCCUPATIONS

Retail Buyers and Buyer/Merchandising Trainees

Comparison shopper	Retail sales worker
Insurance agent	Services sales representative
Manufacturer's representative	Traffic manager
Procurement services manager	Wholesale sales representative

Sales Service Representatives

The skills you've acquired in sales tend to be rather universally esteemed: listening, speaking, public presentation, decision making, analyzing, time management, product specification knowledge, and an ability to "connect" with people authentically and quickly. Sales professionals are easily transitioned to a wide variety of occupations. A sampling would have to include the following:

Advertising	Consulting
Career counseling	Manufacturer's representative
Communications	Marketing management

Product management

Promotions

Public relations

Real estate

Trade fair design

Training and development

Travel agent

U.S. chambers of commerce

Purchasing Agents

Insurance sales agent

Marketing and advertising manager

Materials manager

Procurement services manager

Retail sales worker

Sales manager

Services sales representative

Traffic manager

Wholesale sales representative

PROFESSIONAL ASSOCIATIONS

Listed below are some of the associations that relate to retail buyers, buyer/merchandising trainees, sales service representatives, and purchasing agents. For more information about these professional associations either check the website listed or use the *Encyclopedia of Associations* (annual) published by Gale Research Inc. Review the "Members/Purpose" section for each organization and decide whether the organization pertains to your interests. Memberships in one of these associations might help in terms of job listings, networking opportunities, and employment search services. Some associations provide information at no charge. If you want to receive their publications that list job opportunities, you may be required to join the association. Check for student member rates. Check the websites of these associations for further career information or links to other sites that provide other information related to this chapter's occupational paths. Investigate these associations to see how they might help you in your job search:

Retail Buyers and Buyer/Merchandising Trainees

American Marketing Association
250 S. Wacker Drive, Suite 200
Chicago, IL 60606

Website: http://www.ama.org/
Members/Purpose: Professional society of marketing and marketing research executives, sales and promotion managers, advertising specialists, and others interested in marketing.
Journals Publications: *American Marketing Association—Proceedings; International Membership Directory; Journal of Health Care Marketing*

ARMS—The Association of Retail Marketing Services
3 Caro Court
Red Bank, NJ 07701
Website: none
Members/Purpose: Devoted to the promotional needs of the retail industry. Recommends incentive promotion at the retail level.
Journals/Publications: *ARMS—Membership Directory; Directory of Top 50 Wholesale Grocers*

Institute of Store Planners
25 N. Broadway
Tarrytown, NY 10591
Website: http://www.ispo.org
Members/Purpose: Persons active in store planning and design, visual merchandisers, students and educators, contractors and suppliers to the industry. Dedicated to the professional growth of members while providing service to the public through improvement of the retail environment.
Journals/Publications: *Directory of Store Planners and Consultants; ISP International News,* Newsletter

National Retail Federation
325 Seventh Street NW, Suite 1000
Washington, DC 20004
Website: http://www.nrf.com
Members/Purpose: Retailers of men's and boys' clothing and furnishings. Maintains government liaison.
Journals/Publications: *Better Retail Salesmanship; Members Newsletter*

Museum Store Association
4100 E. Mississippi Avenue
Denver, CO 80222
Website: none
Members/Purpose: Sales departments in museums, including museums of fine arts, history, ethnology, and science. Encourages dialogue and assistance among members.
Journals/Publications: *Membership List; Museum Store; Product News*

United Buying Services
39 S. Milwaukee Avenue
Wheeling, IL 60090
Website: http://careports.com
Members/Purpose: Serves as clearinghouse for the exchange of
information and ideas relating to buying services. Acts as centralized
distribution source for promotion of national products.
Journals/Publications: None

National Association of Men's Sportswear Buyers
60 E. Forty-second Street, Suite 2430
New York, NY 10165
Website: none
Members/Purpose: Sponsors trade shows for buyers of clothes for
menswear stores. Conducts media interviews to discuss menswear and
educational programs.
Journals/Publications: *Newsletter*

National Retail Federation (NRF)
325 Seventh Street NW, Suite 100
Washington, DC 20004
Website: none
Members/Purpose: Department, chain, mass merchandise, and specialty
stores retailing men's, women's, and children's apparel and home furnishings.
Journals/Publications: *Retail Control; STORES Magazine*

Office Products Dealers Alliance
Business Products Industry Association
301 N. Fairfax Street
Alexandria, VA 22314
Website: http://www.bpia.org
Members/Purpose: Objectives are to serve as a resource for branch store
dealers, to help increase professionalism, and to develop ways to combat
competition. Seeks to explore areas of interest for retail dealers, including
merchandising and product representation, advertising, store financing,
personnel development and training, and strategic business planning.
Journals/Publications: *Dealer Operating Profile*

Retail Advertising and Marketing Association (RAMA)
333 N. Michigan Avenue, Suite 3000
Chicago, IL 60601
Website: http://www.ramarac.org
Members/Purpose: Persons in retail sales promotion and advertising and
persons serving retailers in promotional capacities.
Journals/Publications: *RAC Digest; Who's Who in Retail Advertising*

Sales Service Representatives

American Marketing Association
250 S. Wacker Drive, Suite 200
Chicago, IL 60606
Website: http://www.ama.org/
Member/Purpose: Professional society of marketing and marketing
research executives, sales and promotion managers, advertising specialists,
academics, and others interested in marketing.
Journals/Publications: *American Marketing Association—Proceedings;
International Membership Directory; Journal of Health Care Marketing*

Association of Incentive Marketing
1620 Route 22
Union, NJ 07083
Website: http://www.aim-online.org
Members/Purpose: Conducts education and information programs to
improve the effectiveness of incentive merchandising through the influence
of the professional incentive executive.
Journals/Publications: *Incentive Casebook: How Marketers Motivate;
Association of Incentive Marketing—Incentive Report; Association of Incentive
Marketing—Membership Directory*

Direct Selling Association
1666 K Street NW, Suite 1010
Washington, DC 20006
Website: http://www.dsa.org
Members/Purpose: Manufacturers and distributors selling consumer
products door-to-door, by appointment, and through home-party plans.
Journals/Publications: *Direct Selling World Directory; International
Bulletin; Membership Directory; News from Neil; Who's Who in Direct Selling*

Hospitality Sales and Marketing Association International
1300 L Street NW, Suite 800
Washington, DC 20005
Website: http://www.hsmai.org
Members/Purpose: An international organization devoted entirely to
education of executives employed by hotels, resorts, and motor inns.
Journals/Publications: *Directory* (annual); *Marketing Review* (quarterly);
Update (eight year)

National Association of Publishers Reps
P.O. Box 3139
New York, NY 10163
Website: http://www.naprassoc.org

Members/Purpose: Independent publisher's representatives selling advertising space for more than one publisher of consumer, industrial, and trade publications.
Journals/Publications: *Bulletin; Roster of Members*

National Society of Pharmaceutical Sales Trainers
5 Homestead Lane
Avon, CT 06001
Website: http://www.nspst.com
Members/Purpose: Seeks to improve professionalism within the field by raising standards of development and training programs; encourages members' self-development by facilitating information exchange.
Journals/Publications: *Newspost; Roster*

Promotion Marketing Association of America (PMAA)
322 Eighth Avenue, Suite 1201
New York, NY 10001
Website: http://www.pmalink.org
Members/Purpose: Promotion service companies, sales incentive organizations, and companies using promotion programs. Supplier members are manufacturers of premium merchandise, consultants, and advertising agencies.
Journals/Publications: *Outlook; PMAA Membership Directory; Promotion Marketing Abstract*

Radio Advertising Bureau (RAB)
261 Madison Avenue, Twenty-third Floor
New York, NY 10016
Website: http://www.rab.com
Members/Purpose: Membership includes radio stations, radio networks, station sales representatives, and allied industry services, such as producers, research firms, schools and consultants. Exhorts advertisers and agencies to promote the sale of radio time as an advertising medium.
Journals/Publications: *RAB Instant Background: Profiles of 50 Businesses*

Sales and Marketing Executives International (SMEI)
5500 Interstate N. Parkway
Atlanta, GA 30328
Website: http://www.smei.org
Members/Purpose: Seeks to make overseas markets more accessible by interchange of selling information and marketing techniques with executives in other countries.
Journals/Publications: *Marketing Times; SMEI Leadership Directory*

Society for Marketing and Professional Services
99 Canal Center Plaza, Suite 250
Alexandria, VA 22314
Website: http://www.smps.org
Members/Purpose: Employees of architectural, engineering, planning, interior design, landscape architectural, and construction management firms who are responsible for the new business development of their companies.
Journals/Publications: *Membership Roster; SMPS Marketer*

Women in Advertising and Marketing
4200 Wisconsin Avenue, NW, Suite 106–238
Washington, DC 20016
Website: none
Members/Purpose: Professional women in advertising and marketing. Serves as network to keep members abreast of developments in advertising and marketing.
Journals/Publications: *Membership Directory;* Newsletter

Women in Sales Association
8 Madison Avenue, Box M
Valhalla, NY 10595
Website: none
Members/Purpose: Promotes professional development of women in sales. Provides opportunity to establish business contacts and to share information and ideas.
Journals/Publications: *Membership Directory, Sales Leader*

Women's Direct Response Group—New York Chapter (WDRG)
224 Seventh Street
Garden City, NY 11530
Website: none
Members/Purpose: Seeks to advance the interests and influence of women in the direct response industry; provides for communication and career education; assists in the advancement of personal career objectives; and serves as a professional network to develop business contracts and foster mutual goals.
Journals/Publications: *Women's Direct Response Group—Membership Roster;* Newsletter: *Women's Direct Response Group*

Purchasing Agents

Federal Acquisition Institute (MVI)
Office of Acquisition Policy
General Services Administration

Eighteenth and F Streets NW, Room 4019
Washington, DC 20405
Website: http://www.gsa.gov/staff/v/homepages/history.htm
Members/Purpose: FAI is part of the U.S. General Services
Administration (GSA), which acts as the executive agent for the FAI. The
Office of Federal Procurement Policy, Office of Management and Budget,
is responsible for providing for and directing the activities of the FAI. The
FAI provides expertly managed space, supplies, services, and solutions to
enable the federal employees to accomplish their missions. Workspace,
security, furniture, equipment, supplies, tools, computers, and telephones
are also provided. The FAI is found on the GSA's website and offers on-line
training, educator's conference, on-line resources, federal acquisition
regulations, bulletin boards, forums, publications, associations, legislative
links, judicial links.
Journals/Publications: See website.

American Purchasing Society
430 W. Downer Place
Aurora, IL 60506
Website: http://www.american-purchasing.com
Members/Purpose: Seeks to certify qualified purchasing personnel.
Maintains speakers bureau, library, and placement service. Conducts
research programs; compiles statistics including salary surveys. Provides
consulting service for purchasing, material management, and marketing.
Journals/Publications: *Cost Cutter; Directory of Buyers and Purchasing
Executives;* Journal; *Professional Purchasing*

American Society for Hospital Materials Management
c/o American Hospital Association
1 N. Franklin
Chicago, IL 60606
Website: http://www.ashmm.org
Member/Purpose: Individuals active in the field of purchasing, inventory
and distribution, and materials management as performed in hospitals,
related patient care institutions, or government and voluntary health
organizations, and who are employed by an organization eligible for
institutional membership in the American Hospital Association; associate
members are individuals active in the areas of health care supply
manufacturing, distributing, and consulting. One of the related purposes
includes to help provide access to the latest ideas, methods, developments,
information, and techniques in the field of hospital purchasing and
materials management.

Journals/Publications: *Hospital Materials Management News; Resource Catalog; Collection of Fellowship Readings; American Society for Hospital Material Management—Perspectives; American Society for Hospital Material Management—Conference Proceedings*

National Association of Purchasing Management
Customer Service
2055 E. Centennial Circle
P.O. Box 22160
Tempe, AZ 85285
Website: http://www.napm.org
Members/Purpose: Purchasing and materials managers for industrial, commercial, and utility firms; educational institutions; and government agencies. Issues reports on market conditions and trends; disseminates information on procurement; works to develop more efficient purchasing methods; conducts programs for certification as a purchasing manager; operates placement service.
Publications/Journals: *International Journal of Purchasing and Materials Management; NAPM Insights; Report on Business*

National Association of State Purchasing Officials
c/o Council of State Governments
167 W. Main Street, Suite 600
Lexington, KY 40507
Website: http://www.naspo.org
Members/Purpose: Purchasing officials of the states and territories. Council of State Governments serves as staff agency. Operates "Marketing to State Governments" seminar.
Journals/Publications: *NASPO News; Contract Cookbook; State and Local Government Purchasing; How to Do Business with the States: A Guide for Vendors*

National Contract Management Association
1912 Woodford Road
Vienna, VA 22182
Website: http://www.ncmahq.org
Members/Purpose: Individuals concerned with administration, procurement, acquisition, negotiation, and management of government contracts and subcontracts. Works for the education, improvement, and professional development of members and nonmembers through national and chapter programs, symposia, and workshops; develops training materials to serve the procurement field. Offers certification in contract management (CPCM and CACM) designations.

Journals/Publications: *Contract Management; National Contract Management Journal*

National Institute of Governmental Purchasing, Inc.
11800 Sunrise Valley Drive, Suite 1050
Reston, VA 20191-5302
Website: http://www.nigp.org
Members/Purpose: Federal, state, provincial, county, and local government buying agencies; hospital, school, prison, and public utility purchasing agencies in the United States and Canada; develops simplified standards and specifications for governmental buying; promotes uniform purchasing laws and procedures; conducts specialized education and research programs; conducts certification program for Professional Public Buyer and Certified Public Purchasing Officer; offers consulting services and cost-saving programs and tools for governmental agencies, including purchasing software for desktop computers; maintains specifications library for public purchasing.
Publications/Journals: *National Institute of Governmental Purchasing— Letter Service Bulletin; NIGP Dictionary of Purchasing Terms; Technical Bulletin*

National Minority Supplier Development Council
15 W. Thirty-ninth Street, Ninth Floor
New York, NY 10018
Website: http://www.trainingforum.com/
Members/Purpose: Minority businesspersons, corporations, government agencies, and other organizations who are members of regional purchasing councils or who have agreed to participate in the program. Regional councils certify and match minority-owned businesses with member corporations that want to purchase goods and services. Conducts sales training programs for minority entrepreneurs, and buyer training program for corporate minority purchasing programs.
Journals/Publications: *Minority Supplier News; Minority Vendor Directory; National Minority Supplier Development Council—Annual Report*

Newspaper Purchasing Management Association
Orlando Sentinel
633 Orange Avenue
Orlando, FL 32801
Website/e-mail: none
Members/Purpose: Purchasing executives (purchasing agents, buyers, purchasing officers, and directors of purchasing) in the newspaper publishing industry; promotes the study, development, and application of

improved purchasing methods, practices, and techniques in the industry; encourages and cooperates in the institution of ethical standards in buying and selling; fosters and promotes interchange of ideas and cooperation among members.

Journals/Publications: *Newspaper Purchasing Management Association— Membership;* Newsletter: *Newspaper Purchasing Management Association*

ADDITIONAL RESOURCES

ABI/Inform on Disc
UMI-Data Courier, Inc.
620 S. Fifth Street
Louisville, KY 40202

American Association of University Professors
1012 Fourteenth Street, NW, Suite 500
Washington, DC 20005-3465

American Bank Directory
McFadden Business Publications
6195 Crooked Creek Road
Norcross, GA 30092

American Salaries and Wages Survey
Gale Research Inc.
P.O. Box 33477
Detroit, MI 48232

America's Corporate Families
Dun and Bradstreet Information Services
899 Eaton Avenue
Bethlehem, PA 18025

America's Federal Jobs
JIST Works, Inc.
720 N. Park Avenue
Indianapolis, IN 46202

America's Top Internships: 1999
by Mark Oldman and Samer Hamadeh
The Princeton Review Publishing Company, Inc.
2315 Broadway, Third Floor
New York, NY 10024-4332

ARTSearch
Theatre Communications Group, Inc.
355 Lexington Avenue
New York, NY 10036

The Banking Job Finder
Mainstream Access, Inc.
Prentice-Hall, Inc.
Englewood Cliffs, NJ 07632

The Best Towns in America
Houghton Mifflin Co.
222 Berkeley Street
Boston, MA 02116

Best's Insurance Reports
A.M. Best Co.
Oldwick, NJ 08858

Book of Lists
The Boston Business Journal
200 High Street
Boston, MA 02110

The Boston Globe
The Globe Newspaper Co.
135 Morrissey Boulevard
P.O. Box 2378
Boston, MA 02107

Braddock's Federal-State-Local Government
Braddock Communications
909 N. Washington Street, Suite 310
Alexandria, VA 22314

Business and Finance Career Directory
Visible Ink Press
A Division of Gale Research Inc.
835 Penobscot Building
Detroit, MI 48226-4094

Business Rankings Annual
Gale Research Inc.
P.O. Box 33477
Detroit, MI 48232

CAM Report: Career Movement and Management Facts
Priam Publications, Inc.
P.O. Box 1862
East Lansing, MI 48826

The Career Guide: Dun's Employment Opportunities Directory
Dun & Bradstreet Information Services
899 Eaton Avenue
Bethlehem, PA 18025

Career Information Center
Macmillan Publishing Group
866 Third Avenue
New York, NY 10022

Careers Encyclopedia
VGM Career Horizons
NTC/Contemporary Publishing Group, Inc.
4255 W. Touhy Avenue
Lincolnwood, IL 60646

Careers for Number Crunchers and Other Quantitative Types
by Rebecca Burnett
VGM Career Horizons
NTC/Contemporary Publishing Group, Inc.
4255 W. Touhy Avenue
Lincolnwood, IL 60646

Careers in Business
Careers in Communications
Career in Computers
Careers in Finance
Careers in Government
Careers in High Tech
VGM Career Horizons
NTC/Contemporary Publishing Group, Inc.
4255 W. Touhy Avenue
Lincolnwood, IL 60646

Careers in State and Local Government
Garrett Park Press
Garrett Park, MD 20896

The Chronicle of Higher Education
1255 Twenty-third Street, NW
Washington, DC 20037

College Placement Council Annuals
62 Highland Avenue
Bethlehem, PA 18017

College to Career: The Guide to Job Opportunities
by Joyce Mitchell
The College Board
Box 866
New York, NY 10101

**Community Jobs: The National Employment Newspaper for the
Non-Profit Sector**
ACCESS: Networking in the Public Interest
50 Beacon Street
Boston, MA 02108

Companies That Care
by Hal Morgan and Kerry Tucker
Simon & Schuster/Fireside
Simon & Schuster Building
Rockefeller Center
1230 Avenue of the Americas
New York, NY 10020

The Complete Guide to Public Employment
by Ronald Krannich and Caryl Krannich
Impact Publications
4580 Sunshine Court
Woodbridge, VA 22192

Consultants and Consulting Organizations Directory
Gale Research Inc.
P.O. Box 33477
Detroit, MI 48232

Consultants Directory
Dun and Bradstreet Information Services
899 Eaton Avenue
Bethlehem, PA 18025

Consultants News
Kennedy Publications
Templeton Road
Fitzwilliam, NH 03447

The Corporate Address Book
Michael Levine
G.P. Putnam's Sons
200 Madison Avenue
New York, NY 10016

County Executive Directory
Carroll Publishing
1058 Thomas Jefferson Street, NW
Washington, DC 20077

Current Jobs in Art
Current Jobs for Graduates
Current Jobs for Graduates in Education
Current Jobs in Writing, Educating and Communications
Plymouth Publishing, Inc.
P.O. Box 40550
5136 MacArthur Boulevard, NW
Washington, DC 20016

Dialing for Jobs: Using the Phone in the Job Search (video)
JIST Works, Inc.
720 N. Park Avenue
Indianapolis, IN 46202

Dictionary of Holland Occupational Codes
Consulting Psychologists Press, Inc.
577 College Avenue
Palo Alto, CA 94306

Dictionary of Occupational Titles
U.S. Department of Labor
Employment and Training Administration
Distributed by Associated Book Publishers, Inc.
P.O. Box 5657
Scottsdale, AZ 86261

Directory of American Firms Operating in Foreign Countries
World Trade Academy Press
50 E. Forty-second Street
New York, NY 10017

Directory of American Research and Technology
Reed Reference Publishing
121 Chanlon Road
New Providence, NJ 07974

Directory of Corporate Affiliations
National Register Publishing
121 Chanlon Road
New Providence, NJ 07974

Directory of Directories
Gale Research Inc.
P.O. Box 33477
Detroit, MI 48232

Directory of Management Consultants
Kennedy and Kennedy, Inc.
Consultants News
Templeton Road
Fitswilliam, NH 03447

Directory of Manufacturers
Dun and Bradstreet Information Services
899 Eaton Avenue
Bethlehem, PA 18025

DISCOVER
American College Testing
Educational Services Division
P.O. Box 168
Iowa City, IA 52244

Educational Testing Service
SIGI PLUS
P.O. Box 6403
Rosedale Road
Princeton, NJ 08541

Effective Answers to Interview Questions (video)
JIST Works, Inc.
720 N. Park Avenue
Indianapolis, IN 46202

Electronic Resume Revolution
by Joyce Lain Kennedy and Thomas J. Morrow
John Wiley and Sons, Inc.
Professional, Reference and Trade Group
605 Third Avenue
New York, NY 10158

Employer's Expectations (video)
JIST Works, Inc.
720 N. Park Avenue
Indianapolis, IN 46202

Encyclopedia of Associations
Encyclopedia of Business Information Sources
Gale Research Inc.
P.O. Box 33477
Detroit, MI 48232

Environmental Opportunities
Environmental Studies Department
Antioch/New England Graduate School
Keene, NH 03431

Equal Employment Opportunity Bimonthly
CRS Recruitment Publications/CASS Communications, Inc.
60 Revere Drive
Northbrook, IL 60062

Federal Career Opportunities
Gordon Press Publishers
P.O. Box 459
Bowling Green Station
New York, NY 10004

Federal Jobs Digest
Breakthrough Publications
P.O. Box 594
Millwood, NY 10546

Federal Times
6883 Commercial Drive
Springfield, VA 22159

***Fermat's Enigma: The Quest to Solve the World's Greatest
Mathematical Problem***
by Simon Singh
Walker & Co.
435 Hudson Street
New York, NY 10014

***Fermat's Last Theorem: Unlocking the Secret of an Ancient
Mathematical Problem***
by Amir D. Aczel
Delacorte Trade Paper
Division of Bantam Doubleday Dell
666 Fifth Avenue
New York, NY 10103

Finding a Job in the Nonprofit Sector
The Taft Group
123000 Twinbrook Parkway, Suite 450
Rockville, MD 20852

Government Job Finder
Planning/Communications
7215 Oak Avenue
River Forest, IL 60305

Graduate Management Admissions Test
Graduate Management Admission Council
P.O. Box 6108
Princeton, NJ 08541

Graduate Record Exam
Graduate Record Examinations Board
Educational Testing Service
P.O. Box 6000
Princeton, NJ 08541

Guide to Internet Job Searching
by Margaret Riley, Frances Roehm, Steve Oserman
VGM Career Horizons
NTC/Contemporary Publishing Group, Inc.
4255 W. Touhy Avenue
Lincolnwood, IL 60646

Handbook of Private Schools
Porter Sargent Publishers, Inc.
11 Beacon Street, Suite 1400
Boston, MA 02108

Handbook for Business and Management Careers
VGM Career Horizons
NTC/Contemporary Publishing Group, Inc.
4255 W. Touhy Avenue
Lincolnwood, IL 60646

Harrington-O'Shea Career Decision Making System
American Guidance Service
4201 Woodland Road
P.O. Box 99
Circle Pines, MN 55014

Harvard Business School Career Guide: Management Consulting
Harvard Business School Press
Cambridge, MA 02138

Harvard Gazette
Harvard Office of News and Public Affairs
Holyoke Center 1060
Cambridge, MA 02138

Hook Up, Get Hired! The Internet Job Search Revolution
by Joyce Lain Kennedy
John Wiley and Sons, Inc.
Professional, Reference and Trade Group
605 Third Avenue
New York, NY 10158

Hoover's Handbook of American Business
The Reference Press
6448 Highway 290 E, Suite E-104
Austin, TX 78723

How to Get a Job in Atlanta
How to Get a Job in Greater Boston
How to Get a Job in Chicago
How to Get a Job in Dallas/Fort Worth
How to Get a Job in Europe
How to Get a Job in Houston
How to Get a Job in the New York Metropolitan Area
How to Get a Job in the Pacific Rim
How to Get a Job in the San Francisco Bay Area
How to Get a Job in Seattle/Portland
How to Get a Job in Southern California
How to Get a Job in Washington, D.C.
Surrey Books, Inc.
230 E. Ohio Street, Suite 120
Chicago, IL 60611

How to Write a Winning Personal Statement for Graduate and
Professional School
by Richard Stelzer
Peterson's
P.O. Box 2123
Princeton, NJ 08543

Human Services Career Connection
372A Broadway
Cambridge, MA 02139

Index of Majors and Graduate Degrees
College Board Publications
Box 886
New York, NY 10101

Infotrac CD-ROM Business Index
Information Access Co.
362 Lakeside Drive
Foster City, CA 94404

InternAmerica
The Internship Newsletter and News Service
105 Chestnut Street, Suite 34
Needham, MA 02192

Internships '98
Peterson's Guides
P.O. Box 2123
Princeton, NJ 08543

JobBank series:
Atlanta JobBank
Boston JobBank
Chicago JobBank
Dallas–Ft. Worth JobBank
Denver JobBank
Detroit JobBank
Florida JobBank
Houston JobBank
Los Angeles JobBank
Minneapolis JobBank
New York JobBank
Northwest JobBank
Ohio JobBank
Philadelphia JobBank
St. Louis JobBank
San Francisco JobBank
Seattle JobBank
Washington, D.C. JobBank
Bob Adams, Inc.
260 Center Street
Holbrook, MA 02343

Job Hotlines USA
Career Communications, Inc.
P.O. Box 169
Harleyville, PA 19438

The Job Hunter: The National Bi-Weekly Publication for Job Seekers
Career Planning and Placement Center
University of Missouri–Columbia
100 Noyes Building
Columbia, MO 65211

Job Opportunities in Business
Peterson's
P.O. Box 2123
Princeton, NJ 08543

Job Seekers Guide to Private and Public Companies
Gale Research Inc.
P.O. Box 33477
Detroit, MI 48232

The Job Seekers Guide to Socially Responsible Companies
by Katherine Jankowski
Visible Ink Press
Division of Gale Research Inc.
835 Penobscot Building
Detroit, MI 48226-4094

Kennedy's Career Strategist
1150 Wilmette Avenue
Wilmette, IL 60091

Manufacturing Directories
Tower International
588 Saco Road
Standish, ME 04084

Marketing and Sales Career Directory
The Career Press Inc.
P.O. Box 34
Hawthorne, NJ 07507

Million Dollar Directory: America's Leading Public and Private Companies
Dun and Bradstreet Information Services
899 Eaton Avenue
Bethlehem, PA 18025

Moody's Manuals
Moody's Investors Service
99 Church Street
New York, NY 10007

Myers-Briggs Type Indicator
Consulting Psychologists Press, Inc.
3803 E. Bayshore Road
Palo Alto, CA 94303

National Ad Search
National Ad Search, Inc.
P.O. Box 2083
Milwaukee, WI 53201

National Association of Colleges and Employers (NACE)
62 Highland Avenue
Bethlehem, PA 18017

National Business Employment Weekly
Dow Jones and Co., Inc.
P.O. Box 300
Princeton, NJ 08543

National Center for Education Statistics
America's Teachers: Profile of a Profession
U.S. Department of Education
Office of Educational Research and Improvement
Washington, DC 20208

National Directory of Internships
National Society for Internships and Experiential Education
3509 Haworth Drive, Suite 207
Raleigh, NC 27609

National Directory of State Agencies
Cambridge Information Group Directories, Inc,
7200 Wisconsin Avenue
Bethesda, MD 20814

National Education Association
1201 Sixteenth Street, NW
Washington, DC 20036

National JobBank
Bob Adams, Inc.
260 Center Street
Holbrook, MA 02343

National Trade and Professional Associations of the United States
Columbia Books Inc.
1212 New York Avenue, NW, Suite 330
Washington, DC 20005

Nelson's Directory of Investment Research
Nelson Publications
1 Gateway Plaza
P.O. Box 591
Port Chester, NY 10573

NewsLinks
International Schools Services
15 Roszel Road, P.O. Box 5910
Princeton, NJ 08543

The Number Sense: How the Mind Creates Mathematics
by Stanislas Dehaene
Oxford University Press
198 Madison Avenue
New York, NY 10016

NYNEX Business to Business Directory
1-800-44-NYNEX

Occupational Outlook Handbook
Occupational Outlook Quarterly
U.S. Department of Labor
Bureau of Labor Statistics
Washington, DC 20212

Occupational Thesaurus
Lehigh University
Bethlehem, PA 18015

The 100 Best Companies to Sell For
by Michael Harkavy and The Philip Lief Group
John Wiley and Sons
605 Third Avenue
New York, NY 10158

The 100 Best Companies for Gay Men and Lesbians
by Ed Mickens
Pocket Books
Simon and Schuster, Inc.
1230 Avenue of the Americas
New York, NY 10020

The 100 Best Companies to Work for in America
by Robert Levering and Milton Moskowitz
Bantam Doubleday Dell Publishing Group, Inc.
666 Fifth Avenue
New York, NY 10103

101 Challenging Government Jobs for College Graduates
Prentice Hall Press
New York, NY 10023
(out of print but can be found in many career libraries)

Opportunities in Banking
Opportunities in Federal Government
Opportunities in Health and Medical
Opportunities in Insurance
Opportunities in Marketing
Opportunities in Nonprofit Organizations
Opportunities in State and Local Government
VGM Career Horizons
NTC/Contemporary Publishing Group, Inc.
4255 W. Touhy Avenue
Lincolnwood, IL 60646

Patterson's American Education
Patterson's Elementary Education
Educational Directories Inc.
P.O. Box 199
Mount Prospect, IL 60056

Peterson's Grants for Graduate Students
Peterson's Guide to Independent Secondary Schools
Peterson's Guide to Two-Year Colleges
Peterson's Guide to Four-Year Colleges
Peterson's Guide to Graduate Study
Peterson's Internships
Peterson's Job Opportunities for Business Majors
Peterson's Job Opportunities for Engineering and Computer Science
    Majors
Peterson's Job Opportunities for Health and Science Majors
Peterson's
P.O. Box 2123
Princeton, NJ 08543

Places Rated Almanac
Prentice Hall General Reference and Travel
15 Columbus Circle
New York, NY 10023

Professional Careers Sourcebook
Gale Research Inc.
P.O. Box 33477
Detroit, MI 48232

Professional's Job Finder
by Daniel Lauber
Planning/Communications
7215 Oak Avenue
River Forest, IL 60305

Recruiting Trends Survey
Michigan State University
Collegiate Research Institute
113 Student Services Building
East Lansing, MI 48824

Regional, State, and Local Organizations
Gale Research Inc.
P.O. Box 33477
Detroit, MI 48232

Research Centers Career Directory
Gale Research Inc.
P.O. Box 33477
Detroit, MI 48232

Security Dealers of North America
Standard and Poor's Corp.
25 Broadway
New York, NY 10004

The Skills Search (video)
JIST Works, Inc.
720 N. Park Avenue
Indianapolis, IN 46202

Social and Behavioral Sciences Job Handbook
Prospect Press
Box 3069 Diamond Farms Branch
Gaithersburg, MD 20878
(out of print but can be found in many career libraries)

Sports Market Place
Sportsguide
P.O. Box 1417
Princeton, NJ 08542

Standard and Poor's Register of Corporations
Standard and Poor's Corp.
25 Broadway
New York, NY 10004

State Executive Directory
Carroll Publishing Co.
1058 Thomas Jefferson Street, NW
Washington, DC 20077

State Government Research Directory
Gale Research Inc.
P.O. Box 33477
Detroit, MI 48232

Strong Interest Inventory
Consulting Psychologists Press, Inc.
3803 E. Bayshore Road
Palo Alto, CA 94303

Temp by Choice
by Diane Thrailkill
Career Press
180 Fifth Avenue
P.O. Box 34
Hawthorne, NJ 07507

The Tough New Labor Market of the 1990s (video)
JIST Works
720 N. Park Avenue
Indianapolis, IN 46202

U.S. Industrial Outlook
Superintendent of Documents
P.O. Box 371954
Pittsburgh, PA 15250

U.S. News and World Report
2400 N Street
Washington, DC 20037

The Upper Valley Teacher Training Institute
106 Hanover Street, Suite 202
Lebanon, NH 03766

The Video Register and Teleconferencing Resources Directory
Knowledge Industries Publications
701 Westchester Avenue
White Plains, NY 10604

Ward's Business Directory of Corporate Affiliations
Gale Research Inc.
P.O. Box 33477
Detroit, MI 48232

What Can I Do With a Major In . . . ?
by Lawrence Malnig with Anita Malnig
Abbott Press
P.O. Box 433
Ridgefield, NJ 07657

***Where the Jobs Are: A Comprehensive Directory of 1,200 Journals
Listing Career Opportunities***
by S. Norman Feingold and Glenda Hansard-Winkler
Garrett Park Press
P.O. Box 190
Garrett Park, MD 20896

World Chamber of Commerce Directory
P.O. Box 1029
Loveland, CO 80539

Y National Vacancy List
YMCA of the USA
101 N. Wacker Drive
Chicago, IL 60606

INDEX

ABOUT THE AUTHORS

Stephen E. Lambert is Director of Career Services at Plymouth State College where, in addition to counseling students and developing year-round career workshops, he directs experiential education programs for a number of departments. Mr. Lambert's degrees include an M.B.A. in Marketing, a Master of Education in Counseling, and a Certificate of Advanced Graduate Studies (CAGS). He is currently pursuing doctoral studies at the University of Sarasota, Florida.

Ruth J. DeCotis serves as Director of Recruitment Services at Plymouth State College. She holds a master's degree in counseling and an undergraduate degree in administrative management and communications. She is a strong proponent of the mind-body connection and takes a holistic approach to counseling her clients.